THE SHAAR PRESS

THE JUDAICA IMPRINT
FOR THOUGHTFUL PEOPLE

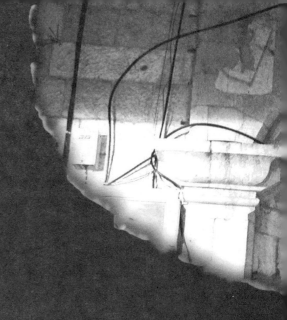

holy

A
SHAAR
PRESS
PUBLICATION

Woman

The road to greatness of
Rebbetzin Chaya Sara Kramer

SARA YOHEVED RIGLER

This book is dedicated to two great women:

In memory of my mother

Leah Lintz Levinsky

לאה בת ישראל ע"ה

*Who launched my writing career before I could write,
by typing out the mental compositions of a five-year-
old poetess. Her unconditional love never waned.
Rebbetzin Chaya Sara called her a "tzaddikah,"
and indeed she was.*

And

In honor of my mother-in-law

Evelyn Gilbert Rigler

חוה בת אסתר תחי'

*An expert in loving, giving, and caring.
Her inner flexibility and willingness
to grow and learn at any age are an example
I can only hope to follow.*

Table of Contents

Acknowledgments

M y heart overflows with gratitude to:

HaKadosh Baruch Hu, Who blessed me with a myriad of gifts to enable me to write this book, the greatest of which is that He directed the path of my life to intersect with the royal highway of the great *tzaddekes* Rebbetzin Chaya Sara Kramer.

The Rebbe of Amshinov, shlita, without whose guidance I would be a lost child wandering helplessly in search of the road.

Rebbetzin Chaya Milakovsky of Amshinov, who not only gives me encouragement and guidance at every step, but who also translated from Yiddish — tapes, written material, and live interviews.

Rebbetzin Tzipporah Heller, who accompanied me on interviews to Rebbetzin Kramer, answered my *hashkafah* questions, checked references, read and made suggestions about the manuscript, and taught me half of all the Torah I know through 20 years of inspired, insightful, and interesting teaching. Blessed is the student who drinks of the sweet water of Rebbetzin Heller's Torah.

Rabbi Leib Kelemen, who made invaluable suggestions and corrections in the manuscript and who taught me Torah and Mussar in a way that has transformed my life.

Rabbi Meir Fund, Rabbi Yosef Pollak, and *Rabbi Dovid Din, a"h,* who got me started on the wondrous path of Torah.

Rabbi Yitzchak Berkowitz, who answered my *shmiras halashon* questions and instructed me what to delete so that this book would be worthy of the *tzaddekes* it is written about.

Rabbi Nechemia Coopersmith, my editor at aish.com, who spurred on my writing career and who taught me to write in ways that the reader can hear.

Rabbi Berel Wein, who provided historical background and who answered a stranger's phone call with graciousness.

Dr. Tzvi Hirsh (Herb) Caskey, whose faith in me and in this book enabled me to start researching it six years ago, when I could still run to the Rebbetzin and ask her my questions. Without his help, this book would not be what it is.

Naomi Bohbot, my research assistant, for setting up interviews, conducting interviews, translating from Hebrew, and always exerting herself to find the answer to "just one more question." I could not have written this book without her help.

Elisheva Chana Buxbaum, who introduced me to Rebbetzin Kramer and who read the manuscript and made suggestions.

Rebbetzin Chana Kelemen, who read the manuscript and made detailed, vital corrections and improvements.

Avigdor Galandauer for providing letters from the Kramers, photographs, tapes of the memorial services, stories, and many contacts. His enthusiasm for this book almost surpassed my own.

Hasya Batya Heller, whose idea it was to write this book, and, to prove how badly it was needed, bought me the only two books about *tzidkanios* then in print.

Uriela Sagiv, the best editor in the Jewish world, who read each chapter and showered on me praise and drizzled on me constructive criticism.

Pamela and Aba Claman, who allowed me to begin and finish this book in the holy atmosphere of their mitzvah-house.

Evelyn Rigler, my beloved mother-in-law, who not only gave me love and encouragement, but also wrangled up the laptop that enabled me to write in every quiet place I found.

Lloyd Rigler, a"h, my uncle, who gave me a computer and printer to write this book.

Ruth Shlossman, who lovingly offered her expertise to organize my speaking tour.

Penny Saracik, whose selfless giving transformed my life.

Miriam Israeli, Rochel Succot, and Ronit Humberstone for translating.

Sherry Natkow, my oldest friend, who gave me my first computer, and thus launched my writing career.

Chaya Rochel Benedikt for taking time to find Rebbetzin Kramer's letters and to translate them from Yiddish.

Etty Tajjer for telling me about the documentary that provided background about the Sephardi immigration.

Rebbetzin Baila Berger for sharing her office space with me.

Mrs. Chana Shenberger, my nonagenarian landlady, for providing a quiet space for writing.

The ArtScroll team: Shmuel Blitz, who recognized the potential of this book and helped to bring it into reality, *Avrohom Biderman,* who handled the final editing with patience and scrupulous care for truth. *Devorah Rhine,* who did the copy-editing with a light hand. *Eli Kroen* for the exquisite book design and cover. *Mrs. Judi Dick* for the final editing. *Shevy Grossman* for the beautiful graphics. She really proved herself. *Sara Rivka Spira* for typing the edited manuscript. *Mrs. Faygie Weinbaum* for her expert proofreading. *Mendy Herzberg* for coordinating the project. All of them turned the manuscript into a book that can help many.

My father, Irving Levinsky (Yisrael ben Yosef Yehudah, ז"ל), who taught me to aim high, to reach beyond my strength to help others, and to never be satisfied with yesterday's achievements.

Leib Yaacov Rigler, my husband, whose love and encouragement are the wind beneath my wings, and who graciously put up with an absentee wife during the final weeks of writing this book. S.Y.R., the author, owes him much. S.Y.R., the woman, owes him everything.

Pliyah Esther and Yisrael Rohn Rigler, my precious children, who give me the joy to attempt great feats.

My profound gratitude to each of the people who gave their time and energy to be interviewed for this book:

Rivki Adler
Chanah Simmi Beer
Esther Ben Chaim
Chaya Rochel Benedikt
Naim Benino
Baila Berger
Sara Berkowitz Danziger
Toiba Blender
Avraham and Naomi Bohbot
Mattisyahu Bohbot
Chana Bortz
Rav Chaim Breish
Zissie Brody
Rav Avraham Cohen

Chaim and Tamar Cohen
Chaya Cohen
Shimon and Kreindy
    Dankowitz
Rav Yaakov Deutsch
Rav Shia Ehrenreich
Ruthie Feldman
Rav Asher and Miriam
    Gabbai
Avigdor Galandauer
Eliezer and Naomi Gevirtz
Baruch Goredetsky, *a"h*
Rav Yaakov Sholomo
    Gross, *a"h*

Yenta Rivka Gross
Shmulik and Simcha
   Heizler
Rivka Rochel Hess
Rav Yaakov Hillel
Reizl Hus, *a"h*
Rav Naftali Hertz Kahana
Anni Kalfe
Aliza Kevisa
Margalit Kramer
Shlomo Kramer, *a"h*
Pnina Kubitchek
Leah Landau
Sheindy Leiber
Golda Lerner
Moshe and Shani Lisser

Rav Menachem Mendelsohn
Rav Yitzchak Mendelsohn
Miriam Michaely
Esti Munk
Miriam Berkowitz
   Neumann
Sara Dina and Dr. Reuven
   Pachler
Miriam Stern
Sharona Shtiglitz
Tzviki Shtiglitz
Yossi Shtiglitz
Zev Shtiglitz
Esther Schutz
Chaya Winkler
Moshe and Yaffa Yunion

May the improvements readers make in their *avodas Hashem* from reading this book be for the *aliyas neshama* of Elisheva Chana bas Avrohom, who first directed me to Rebbetzin Chaya Sara. It all started with Elisheva Chana, *a"h*.

Author's Note

This book is a historical account. All of the facts are true, to the extent that I have been able to verify them. To avoid *lashon hara*, however, whenever a story has a negative connotation, I have changed the names of those involved.

Any reader who has additional anecdotes or photos of the Kramers is requested to please send them to me at: 2 Ararat Street, Jewish Quarter, Jerusalem, Israel or srigler@netvision.net.il

Introduction

Slovakia: 1932

What began as a childish altercation ended in Ivan's death. The villagers of Rapide called it murder. They said that the Jewish girl, 8-year-old Chaya Sara Weiser, had murdered the Christian 15-year-old with her curse.

Mendel Yosef Weiser was on his way home from work at his shoe store in nearby Chenegiev when he heard the church bells ringing. The church bells rang on a weekday only to announce a funeral.

"Who died?" Mendel Yosef asked a Christian neighbor. He was not aware that anyone in their village had been sick.

"The Chelnov boy. Ivan," came the terse reply. "Your daughter killed him."

Mendel Yosef paled. Was this some kind of blood libel? Anti-Semitism was rampant in Europe in 1932, and occasionally pogroms flared. The chassidic Weiser family would be an easy target. Mendel Yosef hurried home, his long red *peyos* bobbing as he ran.

At home, little Chaya Sara, blustering with righteous indignation, was only too happy to tell her father what had happened. She had gone to the communal chestnut grove on the outskirts of the village to collect the chestnuts that had fallen from their three trees. Each family in the village, including the seven Jewish families, had been allocated three trees. She took great care to gather only the chestnuts under the trees belonging to her family.

Without warning Ivan had accosted her and accused her of stealing chestnuts that belonged to the Christian families. "You Jews are always taking what belongs to us!" Ivan had charged.

Spunky Chaya Sara was not one to be cowed. "These chestnuts belong to my family," she retorted, as she continued to deposit the chestnuts into her basket.

"You dirty Jew!" Ivan scoffed. He pushed her down. The village children watching the scene laughed.

Chaya Sara's face flushed with anger. "You should die today," she cried. "Today! You should die today and they should bury your body in the ground where the worms will eat it!" Then she raced home, before he could strike her again.

Her sister, 17-year-old Raizel, continued the story as she had heard it from the neighbors. Later that afternoon Ivan's parents drove their wagon into town, leaving Ivan home with his younger brother. The boys began playing with their father's gun, which they did not realize was loaded. Somehow his brother shot Ivan. The older boy collapsed and lay motionless in a pool of blood. His brother ran for help, but by the time they returned Ivan was dead. The village children who had witnessed the fight in the chestnut grove blamed Chaya Sara's curse.

Silently Mendel Yosef gazed at his youngest daughter. Finally he spoke: "If you have the power to curse, you have the power to bless."

Israel: 1985

I was in Israel, hot on the trail of a relatively unknown holy woman. I had only an address and a name — Rebbetzin Chaya Sara Kramer. Her husband, R' Yaakov Moshe Kramer, was considered by several of Israel's greatest rabbis to be one of the *lamed-vav tzaddikim,* one of 36 undivulged holy men whose merit sustains the world. "Rebbetzin Chaya Sara is as great as he is," my source, Elisheva Chanah, had told me.

As the bus pulled out of Jerusalem's Central Bus Station, I settled in for a long ride, grateful for the time to think. I had been in Israel for barely two months, learning about my Jewish background. Having spent years living in an Indian ashram, I had many unresolved issues with Judaism.

My major obstacle, which I called "Issue Number One," was accepting the emphasis on having children. For many years I had invested myself in a celibate path, having been taught by my guru that marriage would dissipate spiritual energy, and that children were little noisemakers who made it impossible to meditate. I believed that children and spiritual practices were mutually exclusive, and that if I pursued the path of Judaism, all my spirituality would end up in the diaper pail.

My "Issue Number Two" was a sense of spiritual alienation from most of the other Jews I met in Israel. I could not see how I, a modern American woman and a feminist, could ever adopt the lifestyle of the long-sleeved, hair-covered, religious women I met in Israel.

When I finally arrived at Rebbetzin Chaya Sara's small rural community, I made my way to the home of Naomi Bohbot, who had arranged the meeting.

Naomi filled me in on Rebbetzin Chaya Sara's life. Born in the Carpathian Mountains, she had been taken to Auschwitz at the age of 20. Her parents and sisters were murdered there, but young Chaya Sara had been allowed to live in order to be experimented upon by the notorious "Angel of Death," Dr. Joseph Mengele.

After the war, she made her way to Palestine, where she married Yaakov Moshe Kramer, likewise a Holocaust survivor. The couple never had children of their own, although they raised many brain-impaired children who had been left on their doorstep, including one who, 35 years later, was still living with them. They lived in abject poverty, eking out a meager income by raising poultry and a few dairy cows.

"Through it all," Naomi concluded, shaking her head in wonder, "Rebbetzin Chaya Sara is always smiling. I see her almost every day, and she is never without a smile. I still can't figure out what she has to smile about."

The following morning, Shabbos, I went to the community's simple synagogue. Except for two young girls who ran in and out several times, I was the only one in the women's section, a gallery overlooking the unadorned sanctuary below. Suddenly the door swung open, and a stout woman wearing a quilted kerchief and two housedresses, one over the other, walked toward me, smiling broadly, her arms outstretched. She greeted me with a bear hug, like a long-lost daughter. I instinctively knew that this was Rebbetzin Chaya Sara.

As I stared at her, she took my new *siddur* from my hand. She leafed through it to find *Pirkei Avos,* Ethics of the Fathers, aphorisms of the sages of two millennia ago. Handing the *siddur* back to me, she pointed to a passage, and asked, "Have you ever seen this one?"

As I read the words she was pointing to, I broke out in goose bumps. Here was a rejoinder to Issue Number One: "Rabbi Shimon ben Yehudah says ... Beauty, strength, wealth, honor, wisdom ... and children — these befit the righteous and befit the world ..."

As I stood there dumbfounded, she took my *siddur* again and turned a few pages. Handing it back to me, she pointed to another passage and asked, "And have you ever read this one?"

Staring at me were the words: "Hillel says: Do not separate yourself from the community." Issue Number Two in stark rebuttal.

I looked up in consternation. The holy woman laughed, then turned and left.

Later that afternoon, I followed Naomi's directions to Rebbetzin Chaya Sara's home, which looked like a shack from the old world. I came upon Rebbetzin Chaya Sara as she was setting out a dish of food for the cats. She greeted me with a beaming, gap-toothed smile and invited me in.

The interior of her shack was even more rundown than the outside. The rough concrete floor was not covered with flooring — not even *ballatot*, the de rigueur inexpensive stone tiles found in nearly every Israeli dwelling. The walls were bare of plaster or paint. The front room had a corrugated tin roof. Its only furniture was a rickety wooden table and several unmatched chairs.

Soon we were engrossed in conversation. We spoke Hebrew, a language that I barely knew, but somehow I understood everything she said.

She asked me about my background. I told her about the ashram. Then I asked her about her experiences during the Holocaust, a subject with which I have always been obsessed. She described how, on that first night in Auschwitz, a long-term inmate had pointed to the smoke issuing from the chimney of the crematoria and told her, "That's your parents."

Nevertheless, she asserted, "Auschwitz was not a bad place."

What? I must have misunderstood. I asked her to repeat her statement.

"Auschwitz was not a bad place," she repeated clearly. "There was a group of religious girls there. We stuck together. And all the *mitzvos* [commandments] that we could keep, we did keep. For example, one girl kept track of the days, so we always knew when it was Shabbos, and whenever possible, we avoided doing any forbidden work. We recited *berachos* (blessings) over our food, meager as it was. And every morning, when the guards weren't looking, we *davened Shacharis.*"

The holy woman fixed me with her pale blue eyes. "A bad place is a place where Jews can observe the *mitzvos*, but don't do them. For you, the ashram was a bad place."

She had just turned my whole reality upside down. A bad place had nothing to do with bad things happening *to* you. No matter that the Nazis had murdered her whole family. No matter that Dr. Mengele had used her for his nefarious experiments. All that really matters is what issues *from* you.

In a flash I realized how my mind was so busy evaluating the content surging through the intake pipe into my life that I paid scant attention to the output pipe — the thoughts, words, and actions that flowed from me. The holy woman, on the other hand, evaluated her life only according to the output pipe.

No wonder she was always smiling, despite her barrenness, despite her poverty, despite the grueling hardship of her daily life. She was performing *mitzvos*. She was bonding with G-d. She was projecting her own light, both now and before, in the darkness of hell.

I had spent years traveling through three continents searching for holiness and spirituality. I had met religious figures venerated by millions. But sitting in that bare room with its tin roof, eating cucumbers and farmer's cheese across a rickety table from Rebbetzin Chaya Sara, I felt like I had just emerged from a whole lifetime spent through the looking glass. I had been seeing everything in reverse. Now here I was at the top of the rabbit hole, awakened from the dream, my eyes squinting at the brightness of a world of total spiritual clarity.

I looked long and hard at Rebbetzin Chaya Sara. She gazed back at me, and laughed.

The problem inherent in biographies of great spiritual people can be illustrated by a story: A tourist got lost in the hinterlands of Maine. He saw a farmer pitching hay in a field, drove up close to the fence, got out of the car, and called, "Can you please help me? How do I get to Craigsville?"

The farmer leaned against his pitchfork, pondered the question for a few long minutes as he chewed his tobacco, and then replied: "You can't get there from here."

Too often when we read biographies of spiritual luminaries, we are left with a sense of, "You can't get there from here." The level of altruism, dedication, kindness, joy, and humility that these great souls achieved seems so far beyond our grasp that we are left admiring them with no hope of emulating them.

The Rambam states that every person is capable of becoming a *tzaddik*, like Moshe Rabbeinu [Moses, our Teacher]. This does not mean that every person can become the leader of the Jewish people, but rather that every person can attain his or her maximum spiritual potential. In other words, Judaism equates greatness with fulfilling one's unique potentials, and this greatness is available to all.

The purpose of this biography, about an astounding contemporary *tzaddekes* [righteous woman], is to inspire the reader to follow her up the ladder of spiritual attainment. Everyone reading this book can be as great as Rebbetzin Chaya Sara Kramer. Everyone reading this book, by starting on the rung on which he or she presently stands, can ascend as many rungs of the spiritual ladder as Rebbetzin Chaya Sara scaled.

This book is intended as a road map. A good map clearly defines where the highway one is traveling on intersects with a different highway, and which direction to turn in order to reach the designated destination.

Rebbetzin Chaya Sara's journey was replete with intersections, where she was required to choose her course. Looking back at a life so exquisitely lived, we might be fooled into thinking that her road was a single, unbranching line from childhood powers to mature greatness. *No such life exists.* Every soul faces challenges, temptations, and the fatigue of the journey. While we cannot presume to know the inner workings of Rebbetzin Chaya Sara's conflicts and struggles, we can be sure she repeatedly had difficult choices to make. Therefore, at every point in the narrative where she made a choice, the road-map logo appears. By becoming aware of the different routes open to Rebbetzin Chaya Sara at every crucial junction, the reader will recognize when similar crossroads appear in his or her own life.

For example, every human being regularly encounters a fork in the road where the choice must be made between being a taker and being a giver. A thief may have to choose whether or not to take someone else's money. A *tzaddekes* like Rebbetzin Chaya Sara may have to choose whether or not to be happy when she gives a total stranger the entire sum she had saved for a hot-water heater. Those somewhere between these two extremes, people like you and me, may have to choose whether to give to a worthy charity the amount we can afford or a little less or a little more. Although the level of the test is different in each case, the difficulty of the test is the same. It is as hard for a Rebbetzin Chaya Sara to be joyous as she gives away her only chance for running hot water as it is for a thief to walk away from the cash he notices lying in an open drawer. The purpose of this book is to show the reader, through dozens of inspiring true stories about her life, that just as Chaya Sara Kramer passed her tests, so can we. Not that we can pass *her* tests, rather that we can pass *our own* tests.

A guide on a nighttime hike carries a light — a lantern or, in our days, a flashlight — to illuminate the path for those following behind. Rebbetzin Chaya Sara was not a guide; she rarely told people which way to proceed. Rather, she herself *was* a light. (Even physically, her face looked as if a 500-watt halogen bulb was turned on beneath her skin.) By following her glow, may we all succeed in reaching our own highest potential.

CHAPTER ONE

Awesome Powers

NTIL THE AGE OF 8, CHAYA SARA WEISER seemed no different than the average child. Spunkier than most, to be sure, and, of course, she had her father's volatile temper. The few chassidic girls in the predominantly Christian village of Rapide stood out in their long sleeves and thick black stockings, even in summer. By and large, however, she was an ordinary child.

Then, the villagers muttered, Chaya Sara murdered Ivan Chelnov with her curse. A pogrom could have erupted in Rapide, but the Czech police who administered the village would not tolerate such violence from the predominantly Ukrainian populace. And — this is a historical truism — pogroms never occurred without the collusion of the local authorities.

Even Ivan's family, with all their grief, anger, and Jew-hatred, did not take revenge on the Weisers. Perhaps they were afraid of antagonizing this child whose very tongue possessed the power of death.

After that, strange things began to occur. A Jewish woman who had been married for 11 years without bearing children gave birth to a healthy baby. Rumor had it that she had received a blessing from the Weiser girl. Then the ailing father of another Jewish family in the village suddenly was seen working his farm, as hale and hearty as he used to be. His children claimed that Chaya Sara had blessed him.

Word slowly spread that Chaya Sara Weiser possessed miraculous powers.

People from the surrounding villages — both Jews and Christians — would come to her to ask for blessings. The barren came to ask for children; the sick came to ask for cures. By the time she was 12 years old, Chaya Sara was known throughout the region as a miracle worker.

Decades later, Chaya Sara described the process: "A woman who had no children would ask me for a blessing. I would bless her to have children. Then G-d would give her children. Not me. G-d would give her children."

Power corrupts. Spiritual power, just like political or financial power, can inflate the ego to grotesque proportions. Many people who are claimed to have special powers become megalomaniacs or use them for their own prestige or profit. Perhaps the greatest miracle of Chaya Sara's life is that she succeeded in retaining an awesome humility, which is a prerequisite to true holiness. In her later years, when someone would mention her greatness, she would shake her head, laugh in amusement, and reply, "I am nothing. I am less than a garlic peel."

Chaya Sara made the choice to recognize her miraculous powers as coming through her, but not from her. Everything came from "HaKadosh Baruch Hu — the Holy One, Blessed is He," as Chaya Sara always referred to G-d.

To not become smug and conceited by our gifts and talents, to recognize our abilities but attribute them to G-d, is an almost daily challenge for all of us.

Chaya Sara Weiser was born on 20 Iyar, 5684 (May 24, 1924), in the village of Rapide, near Munkacs, in the Carpathian Mountains. Every few decades the region underwent a change in sovereignty and was renamed. Until 1914, it was part of Slovakia in the Austro-Hungarian Empire. After World War I, it was awarded to Czechoslovakia. In 1939, when Chaya Sara was 14 years old, Hitler granted the area to Hungary. Today it is part of the Ukraine. Thus, while most of the residents of Rapide were Ukrainians, Chaya Sara attended a Czech school and learned to speak Hungarian.

Her parents, Mendel Yosef and Malka Weiser, had both grown up in Rapide. For many generations their families had lived in that area of the Carpathians. After their marriage, the young couple, too indigent to buy their own house, lived with Malka's parents in Munkacs, an hour's walk from Rapide. Due to the severe restrictions as to how a Jew was permitted to earn his livelihood, Mendel Yosef's father sold tobacco on the black market. When he passed away, his son Mendel Yosef inherited the four-room brick house in Rapide.

The Weisers were chassidim of the Munkacser Rebbe, Rabbi Chaim Elazar Shapiro, author of *Minchas Elazar*, who was known throughout the Jewish world as a towering, albeit controversial, figure. Rabbi Shapiro had inherited the mantle of leadership from his father in 1914. In a Europe where traditional Judaism was buffeted by the maelstrom of a rapidly changing world, the Munkacser Rebbe was an unyielding fortress of meticulous Torah observance. Known for his zealotry, Rabbi Shapiro was the mentor of the Satmar Rebbe, Rabbi Yoel Teitelbaum. The Satmar Rebbe would later figure prominently in Chaya Sara's story.

Munkacs, during the iron reign of the Munkacser Rebbe, was an island of staunch Torah observance amid a European sea of defection and assimilation.[1] Although there were few secular Jews in Munkacs, the observant Jewish population was fiercely divided between chassidim and those with Zionist leanings.

The Munkacser Rebbe was an ardent opponent of Zionism. He believed, based on Talmudic sources, that the return to Zion could take place only upon the advent of *Mashiach*. To launch a premature return, he thundered, would be catastrophic.

Despite such condemnations, many of Eastern Europe's religious Jews felt that a return to Zion was the only solution to the pervasive anti-Semitism of Europe. This religious Zionist faction drew together under the banner known as "Mizrachi." Munkacs boasted a large Mizrachi high school, to which Chaya Sara's parents would not dream of sending their daughters.

The Munkacser Rebbe was the staunchest opponent of the Zionists — both religious and secular — in the Europe of his time. The friction between the two camps formed the backdrop of Chaya Sara's youth and pursued her even after she settled in Palestine.

Chaya Sara remembers one Yom Kippur eve when her family, as always on the High Holy Days, attended the great synagogue of the Munkacser Rebbe. The Rebbe delivered a scathing sermon against Zionism. As the Rebbe left the synagogue, Zionists waiting outside pelted the Rebbe with stones.

---

1. Judaism, as defined by the Written and Oral Torah, regulated mainstream Jewish life throughout the world until the rise of Reform in Germany in the middle of the 18th century. The next 200 years in Europe saw a tidal wave of antireligious forces among Jews, principally the Enlightenment, Communism, and secular Zionism, all of which targeted traditional Judaism as outmoded and, even worse, as the cause of anti-Semitism. Urbanization and the destruction of thousands of *shtetl* communities by the upheavals of World War I also decimated the religious lifestyle of European Jewry, which was dependent on stable community institutions such as the synagogue, the *mikveh,* and the ritual slaughterer.

No less zealous than his Rebbe, Mendel Yosef, with a fearsome visage, chased the offenders away.

Throughout her life, Chaya Sara remained loyal to the ideology of the Munkacser Rebbe. She opposed the secular Zionist state and, although she lived in the Holy Land from 1946, she never became a citizen and never accepted any financial benefits whatsoever from the State. In 1967, the Israeli army recaptured the Western Wall, Judaism's most sacred site. Chaya Sara never again prayed at the Wall, lest she be hypocritical by accepting a benefit from an entity she did not support.

Most of us who are strongly allied with a particular ideology feel antipathy toward those who espouse the opposite view. Chaya Sara, by contrast, succeeded in vociferously opposing certain ideas, but not the people who espoused them. Her love was all embracing, and included those from every point along the political and religious spectrum.

In Munkacs, all the Jewish-owned stores were closed on Shabbos. Like the sounding of the siren in modern Jerusalem, a shofar was blown every Friday before sundown when it was time to light Shabbos candles. A shofar blast 10 minutes earlier served to remind those who tarried that Shabbos was nearly at hand.

The hegemony of religion in Munkacs between the world wars is portrayed by an eye-witness account of what happened to one errant shopkeeper. Hershel Ostreicher, who was a 17-year-old yeshivah student at the time, recounts how one Friday at sundown a chassid ran to tell the Munkacser Rebbe that "one of the *Yiddishe* stores was open after the shofar blast." The Rebbe, aghast, sent his *gabbai* to close the store.

A throng of chassidim descended on the store and began dancing in front. When a policeman summoned by the store-keeper arrived, the chassidim grabbed hold of him, drew him into their circle, and started dancing around him. They placed a *shtriemel* on the head of the hapless officer and kept him trapped within the circle. When the policeman was finally released, he fled. "After the policeman left, the *bachurim* pulled down the shutters in front of the store and locked the storekeeper in until Shabbos was over. This was Munkacs!"[2]

Mendel Yosef and Malka Weiser had nine children, only three of whom lived to adulthood. Only one of them, their youngest, Chaya Sara, survived the Holocaust. Their oldest daughter, Leah, was born in 1909, Reizel six years later, and Chaya Sara in 1924, after an interval of nine years.

Of the six children born in between, several died in infancy, others lived to the age of 4 or 6. Little Chaya Sara never knew the cause of their demise, only that whenever her father mentioned the deceased children, he wept. Her mother told him that it was forbidden to speak of them because remembering them bred only sadness, and sadness bred dissatisfaction with the way the Holy One, Blessed is He, ran His world. "Everything *HaKadosh Baruch Hu* does is good," Malka would remind her husband.

From her mother Chaya Sara learned that it was possible to control her emotions by controlling her thoughts. The Weisers were devout chassidim. A tenet of Chassidism is the belief that G-d can be served only with joy. Joy was not the *result* of a felicitous life situation, but rather the *cause*, the sine qua non of a well-lived life. To elicit joy, one had to

2. Rabbi Yitzchak Kasnett, *The World That Was: Hungary/Romania* (New York: Mesorah Publ., 1999), p. 94.

focus on the bounty the Creator bestowed on every single creature. The enemy of joy was focusing on what one lacked … or had lost. Thus, the deaths of six of her offspring was a tape Malka Weiser chose not to play, a dirge that would have drowned out all of the other melodies she sought to hear, an indulgence that would have undermined her service of Hashem.

Chaya Sara learned this lesson well. Although her post-Holocaust life was fraught with hardships, especially her failure to have children, Chaya Sara was always happy. Her broad smile became her trademark. When I once asked her how she had maintained such an elevated level of joy, despite her not having the children she so craved, she replied indignantly: "What! I should have been both barren and sad?!"

Happiness is a choice, not the result of getting everything — or anything — one wants in life. Like kindness and patience, joy is a quality that one must actively cultivate. Rebbe Nachman of Breslov used to say, "It is a great mitzvah to always be happy." We will subsequently delve into what Rebbetzin Chaya Sara would tell herself in order to effect a joyous state. Her first step toward this accomplishment was her decision to regard happiness as a choice.

The worldview that enabled the Weisers to come to terms with the deaths of their six children included a basic belief in reincarnation, or what Judaism calls *gilgul neshamos* (literally, "recycling of souls").

The underlying concept of reincarnation in Judaism is that souls come into this world to do *tikkun* [rectification], and often the mistakes of one lifetime must be rectified in the next. The Baal Shem Tov, the founder of the chassidic movement, told many tales of infants who were reincarnations of great souls, and who died as soon as they had accomplished the one action they came into this world to repair.[3] Thus, the Weisers were no doubt consoled that the children who had not survived were great souls who evidently had accomplished their *tikkun* in their brief time in this world.

A salient episode of Chaya Sara's childhood occurred when she was 6. On her way home one day, she was accosted by a gypsy woman, who tried to entice the pretty, blond child to come with her. When Chaya Sara refused, the gypsy woman grabbed her and tried to abduct her. Little Chaya Sara kicked, screamed, and bit the gypsy until the woman released her hold and fled.

In her later years, Chaya Sara would refer to this incident as an example of Hashem's great kindness to her, how He had saved her from a terrible fate. A moment's deliberation, however, reveals that Chaya Sara chose to frame the incident in this way, rightfully giving Hashem all the credit. She could just as well have taken the credit for herself. After all, had the spunky child not vociferously fought the gypsy woman, the abduction might have succeeded.

A hallmark of the Jewish concept of G-d is His hiddenness. "Olam," the Hebrew word for "world," is related to the root word meaning "hidden." Every human being has a choice of whether to see the obvious reality on the

---

3. According to kabbalah, a soul that undergoes the traumatic descent into this world and survives in the womb at least forty days has accomplished a *tikkun*. One Baal Shem Tov story tells of a Polish prince who converted to Judaism, thus incurring the wrath of his father. This righteous convert lived a pious life in hiding, until the minions of his father finally located him and offered him the choice to repudiate Judaism or die. The convert chose a martyr's death. He was subsequently reincarnated as a Jewish baby to fulfill his one desire: to undergo a proper circumcision on the eighth day, as the Torah mandates. Immediately after his circumcision, his soul returned to the higher worlds, leaving his parents bereft, until the Baal Shem Tov revealed to them the spiritual background relating to their son's life and death.

surface or to look deeper and notice the hand of G-d hidden behind the visible.

To the superficial viewer, there were only two actors in this drama: the gypsy woman and the child. In Chaya Sara's own perception of the incident, however, Hashem was not only a participant, but the hero.

In a letter she wrote 62 years later, summing up G-d's largesse in her life, Chaya Sara wrote: "Hashem Yisbarach always did great kindnesses for me from the moment of my birth. Someone tried to kidnap me when I was 6 years old, and Hashem saved me." How simple it would have been for a person of any age to take pride in her heroic resistance in fighting off the kidnapper. To remove the medal from her own chest and hand it over to Hashem was a choice young Chaya Sara made.

Human beings are free to make moral choices, but whether or not the gypsy succeeds is in Hashem's hands. Acknowledging G-d's involvement in the outcome is a choice open to all of us at all times.

Young Chaya Sara kept all the *mitzvos* incumbent on religious girls and women. The Torah directs a Jew's actions from the moment he/she awakens until the moment of falling asleep. To be an Orthodox Jew meant to embark on an all-encompassing spiritual path. For the deeply committed Weisers, the performance of the *mitzvos*, prayer, and *chesed* [acts of kindness] framed and filled every day. Neither the maelstrom of geopolitical events unraveling in Europe during those years nor the daily burden of chores to maintain the farm distracted the family from their focused commitment to their spiritual existence.

Young Chaya Sara, following her mother's example, *davened Shacharis* every morning and recited *Tehillim* [Psalms] every afternoon. In addition to the village school, which Chaya Sara attended through the eighth grade, a *melamed* [teacher of holy writ] was brought in to teach the girls to read Hebrew and Yiddish. Chaya Sara prayed from a Hebrew *siddur* with a Yiddish commentary. She also assiduously studied *Tzenah U'renah,* a Yiddish commentary on the weekly Torah portion.

Acts of kindness were a basic component of Malka Weiser's life. She would bake cakes and cookies and distribute them to the neighbors, both Jews and gentiles. She also served a full dinner to a group of seven orphans who came from a nearby village once a week.

Once Malka was on her way to deliver food to a sick neighbor when she happened upon little Chaya Sara hitting a village child with a stick. Her mother admonished her to stop right away. Chaya Sara replied defiantly that the child had hit her first, "and anyone who hits me once, I hit him three times!"

Her gentle mother rebuked her, insisting that she not hit back, that she simply walk away from a fight. Chaya Sara responded with realpolitik: "They're Ukrainians. If I walk away, they'll always hit me."

Only later in her life, when she lived among Jews, did Chaya Sara relinquish her zest to retaliate.

Young Chaya Sara's spiritual life did not consist of a conscious decision to adopt practices aimed at her self-improvement. To the end of her life, questions about how she achieved this or that quality always drew a blank expression. Rather, her spiritual practice conformed more to a model that contemporary readers may recognize as "inner game theory."

In the 1970's, a popular book called *The Inner Game of Tennis* proposed that the best way to learn any skill, such as playing tennis, is not to learn the specific steps necessary, such as holding the racket this way or swinging one's arm like this, but rather to watch an expert player in action. Some subconscious mechanism in the brain internalizes the coordinated movement of the expert and reproduces it.

An appreciation of this method underlies the Jewish ideal of spending time with a *tzaddik*. As one famous chassidic aphorism puts it: "I did not go to my Rebbe to learn Torah from him, but rather to watch the way he ties his shoelaces."

(In fact, an appreciation of this method underlies the writing of this book. The concept behind *Holy Woman* is that by observing Rebbetzin Chaya Sara living her life, the reader will, to one extent or another, assimilate her virtues.)

Some people's spiritual path is a mirror into which they glance every few minutes, adjusting this behavior, putting that wisp of stray consciousness into place. Chaya Sara's spiritual path was a window. She gazed at her mother and emulated her movements: her kindness, her piety, her loving manner, her yielding nature, her adamantine faith. Gradually, unselfconsciously, she molded herself into the vision she cherished. (Later in life, she did this by emulating her husband.)

In truth, both in nature and appearance, Chaya Sara was a duplicate of her father. Except for her blond hair (his was red), Chaya Sara looked exactly like her father. She also resembled him in temperament: volatile, forceful, and quick tempered. Mendel Yosef often yelled at this boisterous child of his. When she was particularly naughty, like the time she overturned the cans filled with the milk from the family's cows, he spanked her.

Her mother, on the other hand, was quiet, even tempered, always ready to give in for the sake of peace. "They lived like two doves," Chaya Sara would reminisce, "because it takes two sticks to make fire." Malka would never retort to her husband's outbursts. She cultivated the character trait called *vatranus* — the quality of yielding, waiving one's precious ego-rights for the lofty goal of peace. In Jewish teachings, every person should practice *vatranus*, which is neither weakness nor repression, but a sacrifice of one's own egotistical desires and status on the Divine altar.

The driving force of Chaya Sara's inner struggle was that she was innately endowed with the character traits of her father, but aspired to the traits of her mother.

According to Rabbi Yisrael Salanter, the founder of the Mussar Movement, it is easier to learn the entire Talmud than to change a single character trait. Nevertheless, human beings come into this world to rectify their character traits. The feeling that one's inherent personality traits are as immutable as one's skin undermines spiritual growth, which is a process of perfecting oneself. Rabbi Yisrael Salanter taught that all base traits can be redirected and refined, although it takes tremendous energy and commitment to succeed in this endeavor.

The most fundamental choice a human being can make is the choice to change. Chaya Sara chose to transform her own nature, to acquire the traits she so admired in her mother. Her quest to tame her fiery disposition to submit to the Divine will succeeded in producing a person in control of her temper, stripped of the urge to retaliate, as sweet as she was spicy, a true "vatranis."

Mendel Yosef and Malka were farmers. They raised cows and chickens, and cultivated a small plot of corn and other vegetables. To supplement their income, Mendel Yosef opened a shoe store in the neighboring commercial village of Chenegiev, importing shoes made in the Czech Republic.

Chaya Sara was 5 years old when the Great Depression ravaged the world's economy. Her memories of her youth were of poverty. While there was always enough to eat, due to the farm's yield, there was little money for anything else

— including that most important of all expenses, a dowry needed for the girls to marry.

Leah, the oldest, was wed before the Depression. She had four children. Although it was customary for Chassidic girls to marry young (between the age of 16 and 18), dowryless Reizel was still unmarried when, at the age of 28, she was transported to Auschwitz. Chaya Sara passed her 19th birthday, with no prospect of marriage, when the Nazis invaded Rapide.

Virtually alone among the Central European countries, the government of Czechoslovakia, under the enlightened leadership of Tomáš Masaryk and Edvard Beneš, treated the Jews as equal citizens. Thus, Chaya Sara's early years were spared the scourge of state-facilitated anti-Semitism that was devastating the Jews of Poland, Germany, the Soviet Union, and other countries during the 1930's. In the course of that decade, Jews throughout Central and Eastern Europe were excluded from most economic activities, barred from practicing the professions or attending university, and subjected to pogroms and pillaging. The Jews under Czech sovereignty, however, were protected by their government, and the inveterate anti-Semitism of Rapide's Ukrainian population was held in check by the Czech police.

All this changed on March 15, 1939, when Germany invaded Czechoslovakia from the west. Germany's ally Hungary, with Hitler's blessing, took control of the Munkacs region. Yeshivah student Hershel Ostreicher described the entry of the Hungarians into Munkacs:

> They entered with a big parade, with dancing and singing. It was very festive .... I rose at 5 a.m. the next morning to go to the yeshivah ... .As I walked along the sidewalk, I passed two Hungarian soldiers on the street. They suddenly attacked me, trying to cut off my peyos. Screaming, I ran through the yard of the shul with the soldiers running after me, following me

*right up the stairs of the shul itself. The men learning inside
quickly locked the doors after I dashed in.*[4]

Hungarian anti-Semitism had been exacerbated in the wake
of a Communist coup in 1919 led by Bela Kun, a Jew, with a
coterie of revolutionaries, many of whom were also Jews.
Kun's Communist regime lasted barely five months, but the
conservative backlash unleashed the "White Terror," a series
of pogroms that resulted in the murder of 3,000 Jews.

Soon after taking over the Munkacs region in 1939, the
Hungarian government passed anti-Jewish legislation. The
first blow was the revocation of government licenses allowing
Jews to operate businesses.

Even before this regulation went into effect, non-Jewish cus-
tomers would enter Mendel Yosef's shoe store, try on the shoes
they liked, and take them without payment, knowing that the
Hungarian police, unlike the Czech police, would not lift a
finger to protect a Jew. Within days, Mendel Yosef's stock was
virtually decimated, and he was forced to close his store.

Between 1938 and 1941, the Hungarian government passed
the First, Second, and Third "Jewish Laws," which reduced
the percentage of Jews in the economic sphere to 5 percent
and ultimately duplicated the Nuremberg Laws of Germany.
However, the Hungarian Regent Nicholas Horthy and Prime
Minister Miklós Kallay resisted Hitler's demand that Jews
be compelled to wear the yellow badge. They also refused to
initiate the deportation of Jews to the East.

Thus, Jews in Hungary, including those in the newly
annexed territories, lived a precarious existence rife with
abject poverty, the drafting of men into slave labor battalions, and the deportation of Jews with Polish citizenship.
This included the new Munkacser Rebbe, Rabbi Baruch
Rabinowitz, who had been elevated to the position upon the

---

4. Kasnett, op. cit., p. 120.

demise of his father-in-law in 1936. Chaya Sara's brother-in-law, Leah's husband, was among the young men drafted for the labor battalions, never to be seen again.

The Weiser family responded to the encroaching doom with the same faith they had always evinced. They believed absolutely that everything comes from G-d, and that G-d, Who is all good, bestows on human beings as much good as is good for them.

For example, once during Chaya Sara's childhood her father, in an attempt to improve his economic fortunes, purchased a forest. Forestry was a common Jewish livelihood in Eastern Europe, usually a lucrative one. It would, of course, take several years for the trees to grow to marketable maturity, but Mendel Yosef considered his venture the investment of a lifetime. Two years after he purchased the property, a fire destroyed the entire forest. He was left with nothing. Mendel Yosef's response was to assert that the fire, like everything else in the world, came from the one G-d (because Jewish monotheism means that there is no other power except G-d), and that whatever *HaKadosh Baruch Hu* does is completely right and good.

All human beings live with certain philosophical premises that constitute the lenses through which they perceive reality. For some, the inalienable rights of the individual are axiomatic. For some, democracy and its attendant values are the ultimate truth. For Jews who subscribe to the teachings of the Torah, the greatness and goodness of G-d is the given. The forest fire, like the deaths of their six children, was a devastating blow to the Weisers. However, these episodes affected their faith in G-d as little as a raging hurricane affects the bedrock of the earth.

This faith was, in fact, Malka and Mendel Yosef's greatest legacy to their daughter. It prepared Chaya Sara for the challenges and hardships that would constitute the rest of her life.

When she was liberated from Auschwitz, Chaya Sara carried with her into her future not a single keepsake from her parents' home — no Shabbos candlesticks, no heirloom rings, no photographs, no dog-eared letters, but only the faith in G-d's absolute goodness that her parents had exemplified.

It was sufficient.

CHAPTER TWO

With G-d in Auschwitz

*O*NE NIGHT CHAYA SARA DREAMED OF ELIYAHU HaNavi [Elijah the Prophet]. The atmosphere of the dream was dark and ominous. Eliyahu HaNavi showed her row after row of long, low wooden barracks. Frightened, young Chaya Sara woke up and ran to her father. "Something is going to happen," she cried. "Something terrible is going to happen."

The Weisers, of course, had heard rumors — bizarre tales about the Germans rounding up Jews and deporting them, not to resettlement in the East but to ghoulish death factories, where men, women, and children — even babies — were murdered in showers that sprayed poison. Obviously, the Weisers knew, such stories could not possibly be true. After all, this was not the Middle Ages, but the 20th century. And the Nazis were not Cossacks,[1] but Germans, the most highly

---

1. In 1648 and 1649, the Cossacks of the Ukraine, under the leadership of Bogdan Chmielnicki, brutally murdered approximately 100,000 Jews and wiped out some

educated and cultured people in the gentile world. No, Malka and Mendel Yosef concluded, the Ukrainians might descend to such savagery, even the Poles, but not the Germans.

By early 1944, the Jewish community of greater Hungary — 750,000 strong — was the only one in Europe (except for the small Jewish communities of neutral Switzerland and the Iberian peninsula[2]) not decimated by the Holocaust. Hungarian Prime Minister Kallay, supported by Regent Horthy, stubbornly refused to obey the repeated orders from Berlin to deport the Jews.

On March 19, 1944, Hitler lost patience with his erstwhile Hungarian ally and launched Operation Margaret. Nazi troops occupied Hungary, and Adolf Eichmann arrived in Budapest to implement the "Final Solution of the Jewish Problem." All Jews were immediately required to wear the yellow star.

The Jews of Munkacs were quickly disabused of their notion that education correlates with morality. On a Shabbos morning shortly after the German invasion, the Nazis brought all the leading rabbis of Munkacs into the great study hall and forced them to translate verses from the Bible that they felt degraded the gentiles. With each verse, the Germans savagely beat the rabbis — mostly elderly men. In the surrounding homes and synagogues, the Jews, trembling, could hear the horrifying howls emanating from the hall of study. Finally there was silence. The rabbis, bloody and limp, were brought out on stretchers and taken to the house of the Munkacser

---

300 Jewish communities with a savagery unparalleled until the Nazis. According to one account [Nassan Nota Hanover, *Y'vein Metzulah* (reprinted in Tel Aviv: 1945)]: "Some were skinned alive and their flesh was thrown to the dogs; some had their limbs and hands chopped off and their bodies thrown on the road to be crushed by wagons and horses; . . . Children were pierced with spears, roasted on open fires and brought to their mothers to be eaten." Since 1649, the name "Cossacks" has been synonymous with unbounded brutality and cruelty in the minds of Jews versed in Jewish history.

2. Approximately 20,000 Jews lived in Switzerland and a mere 7,000 in Spain and Portugal.

Rebbe, which had been commandeered to become a makeshift "hospital," most of whose "patients" would die for lack of food and water.

The Nazis had cast their net around Hungary, but had not yet drawn it in. The Weisers discussed the possibility of escape. A Christian family in the village had offered to hide them, for payment. Malka rejected this option. She did not trust gentiles. Once the other Jewish families had been removed from Rapide, their family would certainly be betrayed and shot, and then there would be no other Jews to bury them in the old Jewish cemetery. No, she insisted, it was better to die among Jews than to have their bodies left at the mercy of the local Ukrainians. Besides, she was sure, the fate that awaited those who disobeyed the Nazi orders would be worse than whatever fate awaited those who obeyed.

In this Malka Weiser was proved right. A Jewish woman in Rapide who attempted to hide was discovered. She was tied to a horse and dragged through the village until she died a prolonged and gruesome death.

Another option was to run away to Budapest and try to pass as gentiles. For Malka, Reizel, and Leah and her children, all with jet-black hair and dark eyes, this would never work. Red-headed Mendel Yosef rejected the idea out of hand. All eyes fell on 19-year-old Chaya Sara, with her blond hair and blue eyes. She shook her head. She could never pass, not the way she spoke Hungarian with a thick Yiddish accent. She would be caught the first time she uttered a word. Besides, as she would later recount, "I wanted to be a Jew till the end."

As a septuagenarian, Chaya Sara would remember her years in her parents' home — despite the poverty and her deflated dreams of marriage — as the happiest period of her life. It all ended abruptly on a Friday in March, when the Germans arrived in Rapide. They told all the Jews to assemble in a local school. Mendel Yosef gave the SS men his meager cache of money and gold so that they wouldn't beat his family. Then, in wagons commandeered from the local Christians, they took the Jews to a ghetto in the town of Shayavitz.

The Weisers remained in the ghetto for two months. According to Chaya Sara, the ghetto was worse than Auschwitz. The Hungarian Nazis, known as the Arrow Cross, beat Jews to death on the streets. The Jews avoided going out of doors, but when it was time to collect food rations, they were forced to venture out. That's when the Arrow Cross would set upon them with iron pipes, murdering them amid jeers and laughter. Chaya Sara would look out the window of the small room they shared with several other families, and recoil in horror.

On May 15, 1944, nine days before Chaya Sara's 20th birthday, transports of Hungarian Jews began being sent off to Auschwitz. The Weiser family — Mendel Yosef, Malka, Leah and her four young children, Reizel, and Chaya Sara — were crammed together with over 100 other Jews into one cattle car. They traveled like that for three days, in sweltering heat, with no place to sit down or to relieve themselves. Water and food ran out quickly. Leah's children cried piteously, but there was nothing their mother, grandparents, or aunts could do for them. Many of the Jews died on the way, their dead bodies propped upright by the crush of the crowd.

When they finally arrived at Auschwitz, the Gestapo met the train with fierce, barking dogs, all the while yelling at them to evacuate the car. They were ordered to line up. There at the end of the train platform stood a man with a white baton — Dr. Josef Mengele — assigning each person to the left or to the right. When the Weisers' turn came, Dr. Mengele motioned Mendel Yosef, Malka, Leah, and her four children to the left. Reizel and Chaya Sara were sent to the right.

The separation happened so quickly that the two girls had no time to say goodbye to their parents. Hours later, on their way to their barracks, a veteran inmate pointed to the smoke issuing from the crematoria and told them, "There are your parents."

Chaya Sara and Reizel, after being tattooed with numbers on their left arms, were assigned to a special unit: Dr. Mengele's clinic for scientific experimentation. These innocent, sheltered young chassidic women were forced to submit to an examination by Dr. Mengele himself. Then they were given medication to take daily along with good food. After a while, Dr. Mengele examined them again. Then he dismissed them to the Birkenau section of the camp.

Amid scruples at the pain I was causing her with my questions, I managed to prod out of Rebbetzin Chaya Sara these bare details. Clearly, it was the only time she ever spoke of her experience in Dr. Mengele's clinic. Her brief time there, however, was sufficiently traumatic that for the rest of her life she bore a pathological aversion to doctors and hospitals, even when her life was in danger.

In Birkenau, Chaya Sara recognized the rows of long, low wooden barracks as those she had been shown by Eliyahu HaNavi in her dream. She had stumbled into her nightmare.

Reizel and Chaya Sara were asked if they had any skills. They replied that they knew how to work the land. Accordingly, they were assigned to plant a garden around the house of one of the Nazi commanders. The garden was to include an elaborate artificial waterfall constructed from rocks that the two young women were ordered to fetch in a wheelbarrow.

One day, as they were carrying the rocks from the wheelbarrow to the artificial waterfall, Reizel, weak from hunger and exhaustion, dropped a rock.

She dropped a rock.

The Nazi guard lifted his gun to Reizel's head and fired point-blank.

Reizel fell dead, blood spurting from her head.

Chaya Sara did not cry out. She did not fall to her knees beside her sister and scream, "Reizel! Reizel!"

There was nothing she could do for Reizel, dead because she had dropped a rock. There was nothing she could do to express her own tempestuous emotions that would not have cost her her life.

She kept on working. She kept on living.

Now she was the only one left.

In most ways, Chaya Sara's experience in Auschwitz was typical of the tens of thousands of Jews whose death sentences were postponed as long as they could still work — or until the whim of their Nazi guards decided otherwise. They subsisted on starvation rations; they were made to stand for roll call for hours every day in rain or snow, wearing only one layer of clothing; they slept on wooden tiers so crowded that if one inmate wanted to turn over, all the bedmates had to turn in unison; they worked as slaves, often performing arduous physical labor; and they were subject to frequent selections where the weak and sick were weeded out and sent to the gas chambers.

In only two areas did Chaya Sara's experience differ from most of the inmates of Auschwitz-Birkenau. The first was that she survived.

Years later she would contend that every Jew who survived the Kingdom of Evil experienced a miracle. She herself experienced four miracles.

Chaya Sara had a personality quirk: She was ultra fastidious about germs. In her parents' home, she refused to eat from food that any other family member had left over. While her mother, objecting to the sin of wastefulness, would eat others' leftovers, in this Chaya Sara refused to imitate her. She would rather go without than eat from someone else's plate, even her own sister's.

During one period in Birkenau, the Nazis would serve the women inmates their meals while they stood for roll call in the *appelplatz*. Perhaps for lack of sufficient plates, perhaps as a sadistic game to make the women fight among themselves, the thin stew was served on one plate for every five inmates. Each woman was supposed to eat her share, then pass the plate along.

On those days when Chaya Sara happened to receive the plate first, she ate her share. On those days when another woman ate from the plate first, squeamish Chaya Sara declined to eat at all, no matter how hungry she was.

One morning, the plate of food was handed to another inmate first. Chaya Sara's qualms got the better of her hunger, and when the plate was handed to her, she passed it along untouched. Roll call that morning took a long time. After a while, all the women standing around her started to hold their stomachs and groan. One by one, they collapsed, writhing, on the ground, and died.

The food had been poisoned.

Another time, Chaya Sara's group was sent to the gas chambers. Stripped of their clothes, hysterical with fear, the young women entered the "showers." Chaya Sara, standing in the corner, was calm and composed. She told her friends: "I'm afraid only of *HaKadosh Baruch Hu*. A human being can kill a person only once. *HaKadosh Baruch Hu* can kill many times, because we have different incarnations."

They waited expectantly, but neither gas nor water emerged from the showerheads. Something must have gone wrong with the gas, because, after what seemed like an eternity, the doors opened and the guards barked at them to leave and get dressed. This was Chaya Sara's second miracle.

The gas chambers of Auschwitz stopped their murderous operations at the end of October 1944. The German Final Solution to the Jewish Problem, however, had many innovative alternative methods of murder.

During one period, the women in her unit were assigned

to dig trenches and battle stations for the German army. They had to walk to work, 14 kilometers each way, a grueling two-hour march. The SS guards used whips and dogs to punish any Jews who walked too slowly.

On the way to work, they had to cross a temporary canvas suspension bridge that spanned a river flowing many meters below. One day, as Chaya Sara was about to step onto the bridge, a Nazi guard stopped her. Somehow the flow of Jewish slaves crossing the bridge had stopped at the other end, so that the bridge was filled to capacity. Chaya Sara, anxious not to be caught dawdling, begged the guard to let her move forward. He whipped her, but would not let her onto the bridge.

Suddenly, the bridge was cut at the other end, sending all the Jews on it plunging to their deaths in the river below. Chaya Sara, bleeding from her whipping, thanked G-d that she had been spared a third time.

Some time later, Chaya Sara's unit was assigned to work in a factory outside the camp. Their job was to tear rubber into elastic strings. Whoever did not fill the daily quota was killed.

One day an SS commander came into the factory and announced that something — she does not remember what — failed to meet the German standard. The Nazis started beating all the women so furiously that many of them died. Chaya Sara survived the beating. She considered it her fourth life-saving miracle.

Pay close attention to the four miracles that Chaya Sara recounted. Her congenital aversion to eating others' food, the malfunctioning of the gas chambers, and not being allowed onto the doomed suspension bridge can clearly be seen as acts of Divine intervention to save her life. But the beating? She survived where many of her co-workers died, but where was the Divine intervention?

The answer reveals the key to the whole way she viewed the world: Everything is Divine intervention. Every breath is a miracle.

Most people would have remembered the severe beating on their list of "Horrors suffered in Auschwitz." Chaya Sara listed it among her "Miracles bestowed in Auschwitz." She survived. She survived bleeding and bruised, but she survived. And life is a blessing beyond reckoning.

Most of us, consciously or unconsciously, categorize our experiences as "blessings" or "bummers." Whatever is painful, bothersome, or disappointing we assign to the latter list. Chaya Sara, even in Auschwitz, chose to keep only one list. For an experience to be assigned to her "blessings" list, it needed only one requirement: it left her alive. Because life itself is a blessing beyond reckoning.

Of the more than 1,500,000 Jews who passed through the notorious gates emblazoned with the words, "ARBEIT MACHT FREI," only 7,650 Jews survived to greet the liberating Red Army. Chaya Sara Weiser was one of them.

The second way that Chaya Sara's experience differed from most of the inmates of Auschwitz-Birkenau was the spiritual perspective with which she perceived the nightmare unfolding around her.

Chaya Sara lived in a universe ruled by an all-good, all-powerful G-d. Even Auschwitz was in the precincts of that universe. The Sages of the Talmud had declared: "Everything is in the hands of Heaven except fear of Heaven." This means that nothing happens, including the death of the righteous, without the imprimatur of the Divine Will. At the same time, human beings have free will at every moment to choose between good and evil.

In terms of the Holocaust, this meant that the Germans had complete freedom to opt for the evil they chose. Therefore, they were totally accountable for everything they did, and would definitely suffer the painful consequences in the Next World — the world where reward and punishment are meted out.

This also meant that, other than moral choice, everything in the universe, from the growth of a blade of grass to the movement of Dr. Mengele's baton, is empowered by the sole force that exists: the One G-d. Judaism's insistence on G-d's oneness means more than that He will not brook competition from a host of pagan deities. Rather, G-d's oneness means, as the liturgy asserts: "There is nothing besides Him." Pure Monism, absolute Oneness, was the creed in which Chaya Sara had been raised.

For Chaya Sara, the implications of her faith were clear: G-d willed the Holocaust.

"How could a good G-d have willed the Holocaust?" I asked her incredulously a half-century later.

"If we had acted right, there would not have been a Holocaust. It came because of our sins," Rebbetzin Chaya Sara answered sadly.

"But G-d is supposed to be our compassionate Father," I objected.

"The Holy One, Blessed is He, is compassionate," she asserted firmly, "but He allows human beings to do what they want. He allows a person to go on the path of good or the path of evil. Because many chose the path of evil, the Germans then succeeded in their path of evil."

"But many children and righteous Jews were killed in the Holocaust, including your virtuous parents," I rejoined.

Her eyes took on a faraway look. She had jumped the chasm of time and was back on the train platform of Auschwitz. "If we, as a people, had been good, if we had done G-d's will, this trouble wouldn't have befallen us."

"But why didn't G-d save Reizel?" I persisted.

Rebbetzin Chaya Sara shook her head. I was asking the wrong questions. "We have to ask *ourselves* why the trouble comes."

Many observant Jews, pointing to the horrifying Divine retribution promised to the Israelites who would forsake the Torah [*Deuteronomy* 28:15-68], believe that the Holocaust was Divine punishment for the wholesale abandonment of Torah that took place among European Jewry from the rise of Reform, which issued from Germany (note: *Germany*) in the 18th century, right through the first four decades of the 20th century. Even in Poland, the most Torah-observant country in Europe, by 1940, over 40 percent of the Jewish population no longer kept Shabbos. According to this view, the law of spiritual cause-and-effect demanded that the same Divine providence that had improbably kept the Jews alive through two millennia of exile (also promised in *Deuteronomy*) would now forsake them.

What is noteworthy about Chaya Sara's approach is that she spoke not in the third person, but in the first person. She did not point the finger for her suffering at *them*, the Reform Jews, the Communist Jews, the secular Yiddishists and Zionists, the Bundists who purposely held their annual banquets on Yom Kippur. "It came because of our sins."

"You are saying all this now, 50 years later," I prodded, "but how did you feel at the time? You were 20 years old and your whole family had been murdered. What did you think of G-d's goodness *at the time*?"

"I thought: Whatever *HaKadosh Baruch Hu* does, that's the way it has to be."

"Were you never angry at G-d in Auschwitz?" I asked with disbelief.

"About *HaKadosh Baruch Hu* I didn't think anything except good," Rebbetzin Chaya Sara replied, as astonished by my worldview as I was by hers. "He created man and He sustains him. How can anyone doubt His goodness?"

Raised in a world where even for nominal believers tragedy evokes anger at G-d, or at least doubt, I felt like I had tripped into an antigravity chamber. Rebbetzin Chaya Sara's concepts did not behave according to the natural laws on my mental planet.

I should have stopped the interview, since by forcing her to relive her time in Auschwitz I was obviously causing her pain. But I felt like I was standing face-to-face with some fabled creature. I had to pinch it to make sure it was real.

"What about the first night, when someone pointed to the smoke issuing from the chimneys of the crematoria and said, 'That's your parents'? Where was G-d that night?" I probed.

She looked at me compassionately, as she must have looked at one of her mentally impaired wards after she had repeated the first letters of the Hebrew alphabet one hundred times, and he still didn't get it. Finally she summed up her stance: "You can't ask that question. Human beings may not be good, but G-d is always good."

Can fish rail against the water in which they're swimming? Can human beings be angry at the oxygen that fills their lungs? Chaya Sara's G-d-consciousness, even in the hell of Auschwitz, was such that she regarded anger at G-d not as a philosophical conundrum but as a lapse of clear perception. Who is animating the fist a bitter person shakes against Heaven anyway? No one but the good G-d Himself.

Chaya Sara banded together with a small group of Hungarian chassidic girls who, like her, were committed to keeping whatever *mitzvos* they possibly could in Auschwitz. They kept track of the days, and on Shabbos they tried to avoid doing forbidden work whenever possible. On Tishah B'Av and Yom Kippur they fasted. They recited their prayers, by heart and under their breath, whenever the Nazis weren't looking.

Even though Chaya Sara did not have the power to save her loved ones, by keeping up her religious practices to the extent possible, she exercised the only power she believed any human possessed: the power to choose good. In this sense, incredibly, she considered Auschwitz no worse than any other scene in the theater of this world. The choice is always between good and evil, and the ability to choose exists as long as the person does. From Chaya Sara's perspective, a person reclining in the luxury spa of a five-star hotel who insults the waitress who brings her a glass of iced tea is in a far worse place than a girl keeping Shabbos in Auschwitz. <u>The only thing that matters is the choice we make.</u>

Everything else — torture or comfort, poverty or wealth, illness or health — constitutes the challenge, the setup for our response, the cue for the line that we ourselves must compose and deliver. The cue itself cannot be evaluated as good or bad, but our chosen response has eternal significance.

One contemporary rabbi has asserted that the heresy of today is not rejection of belief in G-d, but rejection of belief in free choice. By hanging our moral failures on the hook of heredity and environment, we relinquish our uniquely human gift and the possibility of fulfilling our mission in this world: the mandate to choose good.

Chaya Sara's greatest choice in Auschwitz was to retain her faith in free choice. She did not allow the horror of her situation to rob her of her power to utter a blessing before partaking of her meager ration of stale bread. She understood that she had no power over her fate, but she had ultimate power over her conduct. And this was as true in the appelplatz of Auschwitz as it would have been in the mansions of Munkacs.

History tends to group together the bleeding remnant of European Jewry, the Holocaust survivors, as stereotypic,

scarred, taciturn persons plagued by nightmares and neu-
roses. In fact, every survivor responded to the Holocaust
in a unique way, ranging from dysfunctional persons and
abusers on one end of the spectrum to great humanitar-
ians, philanthropists, and tzaddikim on the other.

The lesson for our generation is clear: There is no envi-
ronment too hideous to produce great human beings.

On January 17, 1945, with the Red Army advancing toward
Auschwitz, the SS instructed 60,000 inmates to evacuate
the extermination camp and start marching west. Forced to
march for weeks over frozen, snow-covered roads, with scant
food and torn shoes, most of the Jews on this "Death March"
perished on the way, their corpses left to beasts of prey.

Chaya Sara decided not to go. She did not trust the Germans,
"because they were murderers," and somehow managed to
avoid the frantic orders of "*Aus, aus!*" that emptied the camp.

Ten days later, the Soviet army liberated Auschwitz. It was
a supreme anticlimax. Only 7,650 living skeletons remained
to greet their liberators. The Russians took over the camp and
announced to the prisoners that they were free to leave. "That
was all," recalled Chaya Sara many years later. "They didn't
give us food or help us in any way."

Ironically, the apathy of the Red Army toward the starved
inmates saved more lives than the compassion of the American
and British armies in other liberated camps. In Bergen-Belsen,
for example, the British troops who liberated the camp on
April 15 found 60,000 inmates. By October, 31,000 of them
died, most from eating the food that their kind liberators had
provided but their devastated gastrointestinal systems simply could not handle.

What did Chaya Sara think on the day of liberation? "That
HaKadosh Baruch Hu performed a miracle. I thought that
HaKadosh Baruch Hu does everything. He directs His world. Not

me and not another, only He. The person He decides will survive, that one survives. *HaKadosh Baruch Hu* saved me, although I was no better than anyone else."

Chaya Sara survived both the war and the liberation. She was 20 years old, alone, emaciated, and the Russians said she was free to go, in the dead of winter in a Europe still at war.

Still wearing her concentration-camp dress with its telltale wide stripes, she left immediately for ... Where else but home? After many weeks of perilous travel, she was among the first Jewish survivors to return to Munkacs. She trod the familiar road to Rapide, and walked up to the entrance of the brick house that had always been her home.

She was filled with apprehension. Would she find a Ukrainian family squatting there, sitting around the big wooden table, wearing her parents' clothes? She knocked on the door. No answer. To her surprise, the door was unlocked. She entered, and found the house exactly as they had left it eleven months — eons? — ago. Later she would find out that the Germans, no lovers of the Ukrainians, had issued strict orders against taking over or looting any Jewish property, which, according to them, belonged to the Third Reich. The Ukrainian villagers, who had witnessed ample evidence of German wrath, meekly complied.

Many of Europe's Jewish remnant returned to their homes and waited for the arrival of any of their relatives who might have survived. For Chaya Sara, however, there was neither uncertainty nor hope. She had seen her parents, her sister Leah, and her nieces and nephews consigned to the left, to the gas chambers. She had seen Reizel murdered before her eyes. The house in Rapide was as ghoulish as a corpse — the body intact, but the soul absent.

The family valuables had been sold during the years of poverty; the final cache her father had handed over to the Nazi soldiers in a futile attempt to buy his family's safety.

Chaya Sara grabbed two of her old dresses and a small valise. Then she fled, as from a graveyard on a dark, stormy night.

She had been in the house for less than half an hour.

She returned to Munkacs, and departed that same day. Alone, she made her way to Ungvar, another city in the Carpathians that had been noted for its vibrant Jewish life. There, too, she was unable to wake up from her bad dream, unable to find the borders of her nightmare. The next day, restless as a ghost, she returned to Munkacs.

Gradually, over 100 Jews returned to Munkacs. A kosher restaurant even opened to serve them. But whispers were circulating that the Russians were going to close the border. Afraid of being trapped, Chaya Sara fled, this time in the direction of Romania.

At every railroad depot along the way, she accepted whatever aid was being distributed to the masses of refugees, but feared ever again putting her name on a list. As she would later testify, "I made sure that wherever I went, my name was never registered."

Finally she reached Bucharest. There all the discussion among survivors centered on how to get out of blood-soaked Europe. Although Latin America, Canada, Australia, and South Africa would each eventually offer refuge to several thousand Holocaust survivors, the two major destinations for Jewish refugees was Palestine and the United States.

Emigration to either was fraught with difficulty. The United States, which would eventually accept 40,000 refugees, required visas and months or years of bureaucratic wrangling. The British, who had governed Palestine since 1917, had enacted a White Paper in 1939 that severely restricted Jewish emigration to the Holy Land. In November 1945, with the ashes of the crematoria barely cold, the British Foreign Minister Ernest Bevin renewed the White Paper policy, effectively barring the masses of Jewish refugees from the Jewish homeland.

The answer of the Zionists in Palestine was massive illegal immigration. The *Mossad L'Aliyah Bet* organized a vast, clandestine network, in which Jews from all over Europe converged on Italian ports, from where they were taken in vessels ranging from small boats to large ships to the shores of Palestine.

Faced with the choice between the United States and Palestine, Chaya Sara opted for Palestine. She was, after all, a country girl. What would she do in the big cities of America? In Palestine, Jews were working the land. There, she figured, she could make a life for herself.

She joined a group of survivors heading for Palestine via Italy. From Milan they would be clandestinely directed to one of eight Italian ports. As soon as they arrived in Milan, however, the Italian police arrested them, and turned them over to the British authorities, who interned them in a detention camp back in Romania.

Chaya Sara remained in that camp until the spring of 1946. Then the Haganah, the underground Jewish defense force that would become the Israeli army, spread word in the camp offering an escape plan for those willing to risk the journey to Palestine. Chaya Sara volunteered. The Haganah sneaked the group out of the camp, ushered them over the border to Yugoslavia, and from there to the coast. By cover of night, they were directed to board a ramshackle boat.

Even in the dark, Chaya Sara could see that the boat did not look seaworthy. In fact, of the 64 vessels that the *Mossad* employed to spirit Jewish refugees out of Europe during the years 1945-48, several sank in the Mediterranean along with their human cargo. To add to the danger, as of January of that year, the passengers on all boats intercepted by the British were arrested as illegal immigrants and interned in yet another detention camp, at Atlit, near Haifa.

Chaya Sara, undeterred, boarded the boat. Although, on its next voyage, the boat would indeed sink, this time it succeeded in ferrying the refugees to the shores of Palestine. On Saturday, May 18, 1946, undetected by the British Navy, their boat cast anchor off the shore south of Haifa.

It was Shabbos. While most of the refugees jubilantly descended into lifeboats to carry them to the beach, Chaya Sara and 20 other religious passengers refused to disembark. This was not a matter of life and death, which would have superseded the laws of Shabbos. If delaying until after nightfall would result in their arrest by the British and internment in Atlit, so be it. This was not Auschwitz. Here a Jew was free to keep Shabbos.

The British Navy did not discover the boat. Early the next morning, the religious refugees took their turn descending into the lifeboats. They rowed into shallow waters, and then waded to the shores of the Promised Land. There, on the beach, a *Mossad* bus was waiting for them. It carried them to Haifa, where they were quartered in a large building converted into a dormitory.

That day was Lag B'Omer, a minor festival in the Jewish calendar that marks the date, 2,000 years earlier, when the 24,000 disciples of the famed Rabbi Akiva stopping dying from a devastating plague. For 22-year-old Chaya Sara Weiser, that Lag B'Omer also marked the end of her season of death. In her wildest dreams, she could not have imagined the extraordinary life that awaited her in the Land of Israel.

CHAPTER THREE

Holy Land, Holy Husband

O N THE FIRST MORNING OF CHAYA SARA'S NEW
life in Palestine, a thin chassid with a long dark
beard walked up and down the corridors of her
dormitory, calling softly in Yiddish to any religious refugees
who might have arrived on the latest boatful of survivors. To
the 20 or so young men and women who responded to his
call, the chassid issued an invitation from the Satmar Rebbe.
The Rebbe, who was temporarily living in Jerusalem, offered
to bring them to Jerusalem, put them up in a small hotel in
Meah Shearim (the city's most religious neighborhood), and
take care of them until they were on their feet.

The alternative was to stay where they were, where the food
served was not kosher, until the Jewish Agency assigned them
quarters, probably on a secular kibbutz. The absorption process to which hundreds of thousands of Jewish immigrants[1]
would be subjected over the next six years included a deliber-

---

1. Some 83,000 survivors eventually emigrated to Palestine/Israel. More

ate agenda of "modernization." This translated into an attempt to strip the immigrants of their "old-fashioned" religious customs. This endeavor, in which young boys were shorn of their *peyos* and given shorts to wear, and teenagers were sent to secular kibbutzim where they were served bread on Passover, succeeded in secularizing an entire generation of immigrants.

Chaya Sara Weiser, who had kept her faith in Auschwitz, was not about to lose it in the Promised Land. She eagerly accepted the Satmar Rebbe's invitation. It took her only a few minutes to gather up her meager belongings. These consisted of a toothbrush, a comb and brush, one extra pair of shoes, and three dresses, all donated by American Jewish charities while she was in the camp in Romania.

The thin chassid was waiting patiently in the corridor. As Chaya Sara watched the way he related to the other survivors, with such kindness and gentleness, she thought to herself: "Would that I had a husband like that!"

The small group took a public bus to Jerusalem. There they settled into the hotel in Meah Shearim. Every Shabbos of the next few weeks, the thin chassid showed up and circulated among them, inquiring after their needs with a sensitivity that deeply impressed Chaya Sara.

On Shabbos, Chaya Sara and the others were invited to eat at the home of the Satmar Rebbe. The Satmar Rebbe was Rabbi Yoel Teitelbaum (1887-1979). He was the scion of a chassidic dynasty that had its roots in Ujhely, Hungary, with his illustrious great-great-grandfather, known as the Yismach Moshe (1759-1840). Rabbi Yoel Teitelbaum moved the dynasty to Satmar (Satu Mare) in Transylvania. After escaping from Europe during the Holocaust, he was living in Jerusalem for a brief period. The following year, 1947, the Satmar Rebbe

than 500,000 immigrants would come from the eastern countries of Yemen, North Africa, and the Arab countries of the Middle East, thus doubling the population of Israel in the first three years following its independence.

would emigrate to the United States, where he would reestablish a flourishing movement in the Williamsburg section of Brooklyn.

One Shabbos while Chaya Sara was at the Rebbe's house in Jerusalem, he approached her and asked her if she was interested in a *shidduch*.[2] Without hesitation, Chaya Sara replied, "Yes, but I want a good man."

The Satmar Rebbe replied: "A better man than this one does not exist."

The *shidduch* he had in mind was none other than the thin chassid. His name was Yaakov Moshe Kramer.

Yaakov Moshe was born in May 1910, in the village of Soka, Transylvania, to a well-to-do family who owned farmland, a distillery, and a produce store. Yaakov Moshe was the fifth of fourteen children.

His parents, Shmuel Zanvill and Chaya Kramer, were devout Jews, although not chassidim. Since only three Jewish

Chaya Kramer   *R' Shmuel Zanvill Kramer*

2. Among chassidim, the *shidduch* process traditionally worked like this: A third party would approach the parents of the prospective groom and the parents of the

families[3] lived in their village of 3,000 gentiles, there was no Jewish school to educate the Kramer children in the holy writ. Shmuel Zanvill hired a *melamed,* or private tutor, to teach his nine sons and, separately, his five daughters the Hebrew texts that every good Jew should know. When Jews from the neighboring villages asked Shmuel Zanvill if they could send their children to attend the Torah lessons and pay their share, Shmuel Zanvill agreed, but refused the payment.

The Kramers were farmers. Once the boys finished their schooling, they joined their father working in the fields. The family spoke Hungarian during the week, but on the holy Shabbos they spoke only Yiddish, the mother tongue of Europe's Jews. Hebrew, of course, was reserved for prayer.

When Yaakov Moshe was only 9 years old, he told his father that he had outgrown the *melamed,* and he wanted to go to learn Torah at the yeshivah of the Satmar Rebbe in Satu Mere, 50 kilometers distant. Although it was common practice in Europe for boys after the age of bar mitzvah to leave home and travel to distant yeshivahs to learn Torah until they married, it was virtually unheard of for a 9-year-old to do so. Nevertheless, Shmuel Zanvill, recognizing the unusual aptitude of this son, agreed to take him to Satu Mere.

The Satmar Rebbe took one look at the precocious Yaakov Moshe and told his father, "Leave him here with me." Yaakov Moshe remained in Satu Mere with the Rebbe for the next 23

---

prospective bride. If the parents, after thorough investigation, agreed that their children were well matched, the young man would come to the home of the young woman. The couple would meet, perhaps sit and speak in privacy for an hour, with the door to the room left ajar to avoid the prohibition of *yichud* (a man and a woman being alone in an enclosed space together). Then they would each inform the parents if the proposed match was agreeable. If so, the couple would not see each other again until the wedding ceremony. If not, the parents would continue their search for an appropriate match.

3. For the Kramers, as for the Weisers, a *minyan* (quorum of ten men for prayer) could be formed only with the help of Jews gathering from several adjacent villages.

years, until, during World War II, the Rebbe sent him away to Budapest to save his life. On Yaakov Moshe's tombstone would be engraved the words: *"Talmid muvhak of the Satmar Rebbe"* —a primary disciple of the Satmar Rebbe.

Three weeks after the 9-year-old boy was left with the Satmar Rebbe, Yaakov Moshe returned home for a visit, accompanied by an older *bachur*. They arrived on a Friday afternoon, just a few hours before Shabbos, when all the Shabbos food had already been cooked. Yaakov Moshe quietly approached his mother and told her that he couldn't eat any of her food because she cooked with the fat of geese that, because of the way they were treated, did not meet the high *kashrus* standards he had learned about in yeshivah in Satu Mere. His mother responded, "Fine. I'll boil some vegetables for you for Shabbos. And next time you come home, you'll have food made with *glatt*-kosher fat from poultry that are fine for you."

Chaya Kramer bought a new set of pots and henceforth cooked for her yeshivah *bachur* son separately, duplicating exactly what she made for the rest of the family. When she served Yaakov Moshe, she put a towel on the table beneath his place setting. Yaakov Moshe humbly asked his mother's forgiveness for causing her this extra trouble. She replied, "I have nothing to forgive you for. If, at the age of 9, you have the discriminating mind to ask to go to a yeshivah, you don't have to request forgiveness for anything."

His younger brother Shlomo would later recall how the whole family waited in eager anticipation for Yaakov Moshe's visits home every two or three months. Although he was more stringent in his observance than the rest of the family, wearing his *tzitzis* out (the only one in their village to do so) and, when he grew older, never cutting his beard, his entire family admired and adored him.

Those who have experienced a family member becoming more religiously observant, with all the demands that it imposes on the whole family's modus vivendi, will appreciate the sensitivity and gentleness with which Yaakov Moshe must have interacted with his family in order to elicit a response of admiration rather than resentment. "We all knew that he was very special," Shlomo testified five decades later, his esteem for his brother never diminishing with the years.

At the age of 17, Yaakov Moshe completed learning *Shas* for the first time.

During one visit, when Yaakov Moshe was 25 years old, he mentioned that the Rebbetzin of Satmar had found a bride for him. His parents knew nothing about the girl or her family, but they accepted that if the Rebbetzin of Satmar said she was suitable for their son, then she certainly must be.

Several months later, without ever seeing each other during their engagement, Yaakov Moshe and Leah were wed. They were married for six years, but never had children. Then, in 1941, Germany requested that its Hungarian ally send soldiers to assist the fighting on the eastern front. More than 200,000 Hungarian men were drafted. Although Jewish men were deemed unworthy to fight, some 60,000 Jewish men were drafted into slave-labor battalions. Considered totally expendable, they were sent to the battlefronts to place antitank mines in the fields, clear away Russian-laid mines, and perform other dangerous tasks, which claimed the lives of most of them. Yaakov Moshe, 31 years old, was of draftable age. The Satmar Rebbe advised him to escape to Budapest to avoid being seized.

In the early stages of the Holocaust, the Jews believed that only the men were in danger. The men, after all, were useful to the German war effort as slave laborers. What use did the Nazis have with women and children? the Jews asked rhetorically. Jewish men throughout Europe fled from their homes, facing the dangers of a fugitive life, never imagining that their wives and children, left "safely" behind, would face an even worse fate than the labor battalions. Accordingly, Yaakov Moshe left Leah in the family homestead in Soka, never to see her again.

Three of Yaakov Moshe's brothers (Peretz, Chaim, and Efraim) were drafted into the labor battalions. One winter Shabbos night after candle-lighting, the Hungarian police came to the Kramers' sprawling homestead and rounded up the remaining 36 members of the family, including daughters-in-law and grandchildren. The family were confined for eight days in open train cars, exposed to the winter elements; by the time they arrived in Auschwitz, of the 2700 Jews on the train, only 700 were still alive.

At the first selection on the train platform, Leah offered to help one of her sisters-in-law by carrying an exhausted child. This act of kindness cost her her life. Mistaking Leah for a mother of children, Dr. Mengele sent her to the left, along with Yaakov Moshe's elderly parents and all his sisters and nieces and nephews. At the end of the war, only two of the 36 would return from Auschwitz — Shlomo Kramer and one sister-in-law.

Meanwhile, in Budapest, Yaakov Moshe presented his recommendation from the Satmar Rebbe to the head of the Jewish community. He was given a job working in the Jewish cemetery, where he spent most of the war. When the job could no longer protect him, he grew a handlebar mustache and passed as a gentile, all the while cleverly concealing but not cutting off his *peyos*. And there was never a day during the war that he didn't put on *tefillin*.

Eventually he was discovered and sent to a labor camp in Yugoslavia. There he not only did backbreaking labor, but also helped other Jews too weak to complete their own assigned tasks.

After two months, he escaped with a group of 80 Jews. They joined a large band of partisans in the forest. From there he made his way to Romania, where he joined 20 other Jewish men who were determined to flee to Palestine. They reached the coast of the Black Sea, and succeeded in acquiring a boat to sail to Palestine. Something, however, was wrong with the navigational system of the boat. Instead of sailing south toward Palestine, for two weeks they sailed north toward Russia. They landed on the Russian coast, managed to repair the boat, and finally arrived in Palestine early in 1945.

Yaakov Moshe found a place to stay in the Haifa apartment of Avraham Yehudah and Tehilla Berkowitz, a devout couple dedicated to acts of *chesed*. The Berkowitz household included their own five children plus five war orphans, all crammed into a two-room apartment. Six decades later, Miriam Berkowitz Neuman would recall her childhood impressions of Yaakov Moshe Kramer: "He was out of the ordinary. He loved people, was always happy, and loved to do good."

Avraham Yehudah Berkowitz kindly granted his refugee guest the use of a small storage shed in a corner of their courtyard. It was barely big enough for one narrow cot. Yaakov Moshe turned it into a makeshift refugee center. When he would meet other survivors — broken in body and spirit — on the street, he would bring them home to his shed and take care of them. This implausible venture — the war refugee with no home of his own making a home for other refugees — foreshadowed the rest of Yaakov Moshe's life: the irrepressible giver never limited by his own lack.

Eventually the racket of too many "boarders" in the courtyard shed caused the neighbors to complain to the Berkowitzes' landlady. She came and irately informed Yaakov Moshe that, while he could stay, his charges would have to go. In soft, gentle tones, Yaakov Moshe explained to the landlady what these tortured souls had endured. This, too, was vintage Yaakov Moshe Kramer — battling his opponent not with darts of indignation nor with a cutlass of counterattacks (How could she be so callous!) but with a lever that pried open her heart. She relented; the survivors could stay.

Yaakov Moshe took a job working as a carpenter for the giant construction company, Solel Boneh. His co-worker R' Machloof Tanzee later testified that R' Yaakov Moshe refused to converse while they worked, lest he be guilty of stealing from the company. At one point they were assigned building work at a secular kibbutz. R' Yaakov Moshe, who was never particular about whom he gave to, but was scrupulous about not receiving benefit from those he disapproved of, would not so much as drink the kibbutz's water. He brought his own bottle of water with him.

Only after the war was over did Yaakov Moshe learn that his parents, wife, and most of his siblings had perished. His older brother Peretz made it to Palestine in 1946. For the next six years, every time Yaakov Moshe heard that a shipload of survivors had reached the shores of Haifa, he went to meet the boat and scour the faces in hopes of finding another of his siblings. In 1951, his search paid off. Among the 3,000 refugees who arrived at Haifa port one day, Yaakov Moshe found his brother Shlomo. Two other brothers, Chaim and Efraim, also survived and were reunited in the Holy Land.

Paradoxically, the true identity of Yaakov Moshe Kramer was both hidden and obvious. His long years in the yeshivah had produced an accomplished Torah scholar. However, since religious Jewish society confers status according to Torah scholarship, Yaakov Moshe's humility led him to conceal his Torah knowledge. Once, in the 1960's, when one of the handicapped children they took care of needed to be hospitalized, Yaakov Moshe sat by her bed all night reciting

Tehillim. A nurse noticed that this was no ordinary man. She asked him, "Are you a rabbi?"

"No," Yaakov Moshe replied. "I'm a farmer."

Whenever people seeking the *tzaddik* came to the Kramers' home and asked for "the Rabbi," Yaakov Moshe would naively send them to the house of the official village rabbi.

According to Chaim Cohen, a resident of their village, Yaakov Moshe always insisted that he didn't know Talmud. Once Chaim and his study partner were learning Talmud in the synagogue when they came to a particularly difficult passage. They worked on it for a long time, but could not untangle its complexity. The compassionate Yaakov Moshe, overhearing their struggle and frustration as he passed by, stopped and explained the passage to them. It was the only time in the 20 years of their acquaintance that Yaakov Moshe ever divulged his erudition.

Tzviki Shtiglitz, a young boy who used to frequent the Kramers' home, recounted how once, as he was approaching their house, he saw from a distance through the open window that R' Yaakov Moshe was sitting at the table learning from the distinctive oversized tome of the Talmud. Tzviki turned toward the door, losing sight of the window. As he approached, his footsteps made noise on the gravel walk. By the time Chaya Sara opened the door to him a minute later, Yaakov Moshe was holding a *Tehillim*, as if he were a simple Jew. The volume of Talmud was nowhere to be seen.

The irony of Yaakov Moshe Kramer's life is that despite his prodigious efforts to hide his scholarship, his holiness was so apparent on his face that even total strangers grasped his greatness. A chassidic woman in Brooklyn told how she and her husband were asked to host a "charity collector" from Israel. She knew nothing about her guest, but when she opened the door to his knock, she felt like she was standing "face-to-face with an angel."

Naim Benino described the first time he ever met Yaakov Moshe Kramer: "I was shopping in a store in Afula, which at that time was a completely secular town. My young son was waiting for me outside on the sidewalk. R' Yaakov Moshe passed by. He was surprised to see a boy with a *kippah* and long *peyos* in Afula. He greeted my son warmly and asked him where his father was. The boy pointed toward the store. R' Yaakov Moshe entered, embraced me warmly, and kissed me on my shoulders."

"A total stranger hugging and kissing you?" I asked. "Didn't you think he was weird?"

"Weird?" he raised his eyebrows. "How could I think he was weird with all that light streaming from his face? I thought he was Eliyahu HaNavi!"

Once, in the 1950's, Shlomo Kramer was driving his revered older brother to an appointment in Jerusalem. It was Shlomo's first trip to Jerusalem and, unfamiliar with the roads, he made an illegal turn. They were immediately stopped by a young Yemenite policewoman. She approached the car, asked to see Shlomo's license, then glimpsed Yaakov Moshe sitting in the passenger seat.

"For what you've done, you should have your license revoked," the policewoman sternly told Shlomo. "But I can't penalize you, because you have a very great *tzaddik* in your car." She then asked Shlomo where they were heading. When he gave her the address, which was in the opposite direction, the policewoman stopped all four lanes of traffic going in both directions, so that Shlomo could make a U-turn. Then she got into the back seat of the car and guided them to their destination.

The *shidduch* the Satmar Rebbe offered young Chaya Sara could not have been more ideal: the child miracle-worker matched to a person whom Rav Shach would one day call "a perfect *tzaddik*." Years later the Satmar Rebbe would say that he had come to Palestine just to make this *shidduch*.

Did Chaya Sara realize from the beginning, I asked her, how well matched were they?

"We were similar," she agreed with characteristic understatement. "We both came from farming families. We both wanted to work the land."

Chaya Sara immediately agreed to the *shidduch*. Two weeks later, they were married.

Although in chassidic circles it is customary for the bride and groom not to see each other between the engagement and the wedding, Yaakov Moshe visited Chaya Sara three times during that period. "You have no parents," he explained to his astonished bride. "If I don't look out for you, who will?"

Yaakov Moshe gave his betrothed money and food. In keeping with chassidic custom, he bought her a gold bracelet and a watch. Not in keeping with chassidic custom, he bought her a wedding dress.

They were married in a small synagogue in the village of Kfar Ata. Rabbi Binyomin Mendelsohn, then the rabbi of Kfar Ata, but later famous as the rabbi of Kommemiut, presided. The pale, blond bride, dressed in her white dress, circled the black-haired, dark-skinned groom seven times. For the wedding meal, Yaakov Moshe bought a kilo of fish that someone prepared and served.

It was not the wedding of which the young bride had dreamed. No relatives were present, except the souls of her deceased parents, who, according to Jewish lore, come from the Next World to stand under the wedding canopy of their children. Her husband, however, surpassed her dreams. She was euphoric to be marrying her gentle groom.

Her euphoria lasted 44 years. Despite the disappointment of not bearing children, despite their grueling poverty, despite his long absences abroad, as long as Yaakov Moshe lived in the same world as Chaya Sara, she lived in bliss. After he died in 1990, her trademark smile was often absent from her lips.

As Leah Landau, a friend who knew them for four decades, summed it up: "She lived for him."

While other religions exalt celibacy as the highest way, Judaism considers marriage the ultimate spiritual path. In Judaism, marriage is a conduit to bring the Divine Presence into this world.

The key to this exalted accomplishment is *shalom bayis.* Usually translated as "a peaceful home," *shalom bayis* entails a total harmony between the husband and wife. "Where the husband and wife have harmony," asserts the Talmud, "the Divine Presence dwells."

The only innate similarity between Yaakov Moshe Kramer and Chaya Sara Weiser was their common spiritual goal and their resolute zeal to attain it. In terms of their personalities and dispositions, they were essentially opposites.

The kabbalah speaks of various Divine qualities that can be found also in human beings. *Chesed,* usually translated as "lovingkindness," is the quality of unrestrained giving. In Jewish tradition, the exemplar of this quality was the Patriarch Abraham, whose generosity knew no bounds. The Torah tells of two examples of Abraham's *chesed:* When three angels disguised as itinerant idol-worshipers neared his tent, Abraham ran to welcome them, bowed respectfully before them, and personally served them a lavish feast, standing in attendance to minister to their every need. When Abraham's nephew Lot, who had opted for a life of materialism among the wicked residents of Sodom, was kidnapped during a war between "the four kings and the five kings," Abraham risked his life and the lives of his followers to rescue Lot. As these examples reveal, Abraham's beneficence did not depend on the worthiness of his recipients.

On the kabbalistic "Tree of Life" the quality that stands in opposition to *chesed* is *gevurah*. Variously translated as "judgment, restraint, overcoming, discipline," *gevurah* is to *chesed* what a dam is to a raging river. The Matriarch Sarah, wife of Abraham, is considered the embodiment of *gevurah*. Thus, when Sarah noticed that Yishmael posed a danger — both physical and spiritual — to their son Isaac, she demanded that Abraham banish Yishmael. Abraham, the embodiment of *chesed*, balked, until G-d spoke in favor of Sarah's position. "Everything that Sarah tells you, you should listen to her voice," G-d instructed Abraham.

Unmitigated *chesed* can lead to profligacy and promiscuity. Unmitigated *gevurah* can lead to stinginess and cruelty. Their balance can lead to measured, appropriate giving, like an expertly dammed river supplying power to light thousands of dwellings.

Several of their neighbors described Yaakov Moshe and Chaya Sara saying, "They were like Abraham and Sarah." They may have been referring to their astounding hospitality, but on a deeper level, Yaakov Moshe embodied the quality of *chesed*, while Chaya Sara embodied *gevurah*. As Miriam, their adopted daughter, described it: "R' Yaakov Moshe was more gentle, soft, patient. Rebbetzin Chaya Sara was stricter; she expected more of people."

A comical scene exemplifies this disparity: Among the many people who turned to R' Yaakov Moshe for financial help were several whom Chaya Sara did not consider genuinely needy. These individuals would not come to the Kramer house when Chaya Sara was home. Instead, they would hide behind bushes and only when they saw Chaya Sara, baskets in hand, leave for the market, would they venture out and knock on the door of Yaakov Moshe, who invariably would give them a donation.

Such opposing qualities can result in a strife-torn marriage. The challenge to Yaakov Moshe and Chaya Sara was to harmonize with each other. The key to such harmony was *vatranus,* the quality of submitting for the sake of peace, which Chaya Sara had seen exemplified in her mother. By nature, the quality of *vatranus* came harder to Chaya Sara than to her husband.

Whenever she disagreed with her husband, Chaya Sara chose marital harmony over victory. Because Chaya Sara was strong willed, with definite opinions, the practice of vatranus, or submission, was a constant challenge to her.

In fact, Yaakov Moshe also submitted to her. By modern standards, they had a surprisingly "liberated" marriage. He made the beds for guests and cooked when she was busy with the handicapped children, while she did most of the physical labor on the farm. When people came seeking R' Yaakov Moshe's advice, he invited Chaya Sara to sit at the table with them; she often offered her opinion, and Yaakov Moshe never publicly contradicted her. One veteran resident of their village testified: "His respect for her was ad haShamayim (sky-high)."

In most areas, however, she submitted to him, not only because she considered him wiser (she did), but also because she understood that, as the Baal Shem Tov taught, submission is the first step in spiritual growth.

In a society that equates submission with weakness and capitulation, it is not surprising that more than half of all marriages end in divorce.

For Chaya Sara, submission was a daily, sometimes hourly, choice. I once asked her how she had succeeded in overcoming anger. In a rare glimpse into the inner workings of her spiritual life, she told me: "I submitted a lot."

Over the decades she became so habituated to vatranus that she came to regard it as the most efficacious course of action. Once, in a conversation about vatranus I commented that it's hard to give in.

"Why?" the septuagenarian Rebbetzin asked in surprise.

"Why?" I laughed in disbelief at the question. "Because it's hard to give in."

Rebbetzin Tzipporah Heller, who was present, broke our standoff by explaining, "It's hard to give in because a person thinks he's right."

"Even if he's right, he can still give in," Rebbetzin Chaya Sara rejoined. She saw no contradiction. Then she continued, "I love to give in more than to argue. Discord breaks a person. My husband used to say, 'A vatron lives abundantly.' It's much better to give in than to argue."

Rebbetzin Heller, expressing the contemporary Western mind-set, remarked, "People are afraid that if they give in once, they'll have to give in over and over again."

Rebbetzin Chaya Sara assumed her "so what?" expression. "It's nothing," she insisted, "even if one gives in over and over again."

The measure of her success in vatranus is that, while she and her husband disagreed over many issues, in 44 years of marriage, they never had a single argument.

Immediately after their wedding, they moved to the farming village of Kfar Chassidim, where they rented a farm and raised chickens. R' Yaakov Moshe also worked in Haifa at a factory that produced cooking oil. At her insistence, he learned Torah early in the morning and in the evening, while she did most of the farm chores. After a year, they moved to the farming community of Kfar Gidon, which would be their home for the next 42 years.

A glimpse into the level of oneness the couple achieved was afforded me during one of my final conversations with Rebbetzin Chaya Sara. For a long time, I had been puzzled by the question of which one of them insisted on living according to the ascetic standard that always astounded their visitors, despite numerous offers to fix up their house at no cost to them. Some neighbors I interviewed insisted that it was her choice. After all, they pointed out, she came from a background of poverty, while he came from a background of relative wealth. I was dubious. I had heard stories of how she wanted to have the roof fixed, or the walls painted, and he objected that it would "disturb" his work. Moreover, one of the local women told me that when, toward the end of his life, the Kramers moved to a lovely apartment in Jerusalem, Chaya Sara showed her visitors around with obvious delight in her new surroundings.

One day I decided to resolve the issue by asking Rebbetzin Chaya Sara directly. "Which one of you," I cross-examined her, "wanted to live like that — without flooring or finished walls? Was it you or your husband?"

"I wanted it," she replied solemnly.

"*You* wanted it?" I was aghast. What woman wouldn't prefer a comfortable, pretty home! "Why did you want to live like that?"

"Because that was his will," she answered simply. "And I wanted to do his will."

CHAPTER FOUR

The Battle of Kfar Gidon

*T*HE JEZREEL VALLEY TODAY IS A VAST, verdant swathe of land in north-central Israel, running almost the whole width of the country, from Megiddo in the west to Beit Shean in the east. Famous Biblical battles were fought there — Gideon against the Midianites, Devorah against the Canaanites, the Judean king Josiah against the mighty forces of Pharaoh Necco. Little did Yaakov Moshe and Chaya Sara Kramer realize, on that day in 1947 when they drove their mule-drawn wagon up to their new home in Kfar Gidon, that they would have to fight their own battles in the seemingly idyllic valley.

Before the Zionist pioneers reclaimed the Jezreel Valley, it had been for centuries a desolate, malaria-infested swamp. The entire area was owned by a Lebanese Arab Christian merchant named Sursuk. Sursuk had purchased the valley from the Turkish Sultan when the Sultan was in financial straits, paying the paltry price of 25 *grush* (cents) per *dunam*.

A Jew named Yehoshua Hankin was determined to buy the Jezreel Valley for Jewish settlement. In 1891 he initiated his quest. It took him thirty years to succeed. In 1901 he managed to purchase land for the first two Jewish settlements in the valley, Merhavia and Tel Adass. When Hankin tried to buy the rest of the valley, however, he was thwarted, first by the Turkish authorities and then by lack of funds. Finally, in 1920, with the British controlling Palestine, Hankin succeeded in obtaining an agreement for the entire valley. The price was 300,000 pounds sterling, far beyond his means but not beyond his sights.

Hankin turned to the Settlement Department of the Zionist Organization and convinced its leader, Arthur Ruppin, of the importance of buying land for large-scale Jewish settlement. Up until that point, the Zionist ideal of settlement had been limited to towns and small agricultural collectives. Despite Arthur Ruppin's ideological support, however, the entire Jewish National Fund treasury did not contain even half the sum required to buy the Jezreel Valley.

Nevertheless, after heated debate, the 13th Zionist Congress, meeting in Karlsbad in 1921, approved the purchase, and the Jezreel Valley was acquired by the Zionist Organization. The redemption of the desolate, swampy Jezreel Valley quickly became "Zionism's greatest adventure." As one history of Zionism describes the challenge:

> *Many believed that this vast, swamp-ridden, malaria-infested region constituted the true test of Zionism. One group of chalutzim made its way to the Ma'alul area in the western part of the valley. There had been two settlements at the site — an Arab village and a German colony — but these were abandoned because of malaria. The place was called "Death Swamp" by the Arabs and the water source was called the "Well of Poison."*[1]

1. Yigal Lossin, *Pillar of Fire* (Jerusalem: Shikmona Publishing Co. Ltd., 1983) p. 129.

Within just four years, 20 collective settlements were established in the Jezreel Valley. Near the Harod spring, where the Biblical Gideon had tested his soldiers, 215 ardent young Zionists founded the country's first large-scale kibbutz, Ein Harod. The idealistic young pioneers, who thronged to the valley to turn the swampland into a socialist utopia, were galvanized by the challenge. They wrote songs and poems about the valley, romanticizing their hardships. When community planners hired by one settlement asked the pioneers to designate an area for a cemetery, the audacious young settlers replied, "We don't need a cemetery. We're not going to die."

In fact, they died in droves, felled by malaria and intermittent Arab marauders. Nothing, however, could quell the fire of their fervor. Historically, they drained the swamps with water buffalo-drawn pumps. Poetically, the swamps dried up through the sheer fire of their Zionist zeal.

The Jezreel Valley pioneers were the epitome of the Third Aliyah, those who came to Palestine between 1917 and 1923. They were young, unmarried, antireligious Socialists who had replaced the age-old Jewish value of Torah study with the value of manual labor. They scorned the hiring of cheap Arab labor and made a *cause célèbre* of "Jewish Labor." In their rucksacks they carried not the sacred volumes of Torah and *Tehillim,* which had inspired the previous generations of Jews in Palestine, but Tolstoy, Dostoyevsky, and Marx.

The pioneers of the Third Aliyah came into direct conflict with the Jews who had come to Palestine in the First and Second Aliyahs. The latter were older, married, middle class, and, for the most part, religious, or at least traditional. They had founded the villages of Petach Tikva, Rishon LeTzion, and Zichron Yaakov. They farmed the land as a necessity for their livelihood, not as an act of fealty to the glorious ideal of labor.

Yosef Gorny, professor of history at Tel Aviv University, described the conflict between the young socialists and the farmers who had preceded them to Zion:

> It was a conflict between two generations. It was an antagonism between rebellious young people, the bearers of various kinds of belief in redemption, ... and a traditional society which was becoming increasingly bourgeois....
>
> There was also a confrontation between two societies, one secular and the other devout supporters of tradition, both in maintaining a positive attitude toward religion, and in their attitude toward the institution of the family. The farmers found morally offensive the behavior of these young people, particularly the women, who left home and came to live in the villages, carrying on a kind of communal life. The farmers strove to keep their children, particularly their daughters, away from these "dissolute" groups.[2]

While this conflict raged throughout Palestine, the Jezreel Valley was a homogeneous domain of young socialists — until a group of devoutly religious Hungarians plopped themselves down in the middle of the Valley in 1924. It must have seemed as incongruous as a synagogue dropping down from heaven into the middle of a soccer field.

This unlikely intrusion was brought about by the new demographics of the Fourth Aliyah. The Third Aliyah had ended in economic failure, which reached a crisis point in 1923, when famine and unemployment racked the land. Then, suddenly, salvation came in the form of the Fourth Aliyah, a mass immigration of Jews from Poland and Hungary driven both by anti-Semitism and by the new, severe restrictions in American immigration policy that effectively closed the gates of "the Golden Medinah."

---

2. Yosef Gorny, *From Rosh Pina and Degania to Demona: A History of Constructive Zionism* (Tel Aviv: MOD Books, 1989), p. 54.

Among the Jews of the Fourth Aliyah was a group of 40 *chareidi* [devoutly religious] families from Hungary led by Dr. Chaim Weisberg. Although most of the immigrants of the Fourth Aliyah settled in the cities and towns, Dr. Weisberg's group opted to live on the land. The Zionist Organization granted them, gratis, a parcel of land in the very center of the Jezreel Valley. They named it Kfar Gidon (pronounced Gid-ohn) for the Biblical Gideon who had waged war against the myriad Midianite forces with his meager band of 300 men. The name proved somehow prophetic; it would take the faith and courage of a Gideon for these devout settlers to hold their own against the horde of antireligious secularists who surrounded them.

Yehuda Wertman, a young member of the socialist Labor Brigade (the precursor of Israel's Labor Party), contrasted himself to the Jews of the Fourth Aliyah:

> *They had no ideology. These were the same Jews we saw in Poland, before we came. ... To put it simply, they were not partners in our ideal. There was a wide gap between us. I did not even consider workers in Tel Aviv as my partners, people who could walk around in white trousers, with white shoes. I saw myself as a member of the modern aristocracy .... A man who walks around in torn pants ... that is a man! ... What made a Friday-night gathering successful? When you danced until the shirt was ripped off your back.*[3]

Contrast Yehuda Wertman's self-description with the Rosenberger family, typical residents of Kfar Gidon. Devoutly religious, Mr. Rosenberger did not work his allotted parcel of land, but rather learned Torah all day. The family had 16 children. Mrs. Rosenberger supported the family with her bakery.

The disdain of the Jezreel Valley settlers for the *chareidi* interlopers of Kfar Gidon is literally etched in stone. Even

---

3. Quoted in *Pillar of Fire*, p. 135.

today, eight decades later, a visitor to Kibbutz Mizra, which borders Kfar Gidon on the north, can see an artist's depiction of the Jezreel Valley on a giant stone in front of the communal garage. All of the Jezreel Valley settlements are included … with the exception of Kfar Gidon.

In addition to the scorn of virtually all their neighbors, the residents of Kfar Gidon had to face the harsh conditions that plagued the Jezreel Valley during that early period. The land allotted to them, while not a swamp, was like a jungle. Thistles grew higher than the makeshift cabins. When, in the middle of the night, the water buffaloes, the precursor of the tractor, would scratch themselves against the cabins, the flimsy shacks would collapse on their sleeping inhabitants. Children would take their family's flocks out to pasture only to watch wolves attack the sheep.

As surely as water flows downward, religiosity descends with the generations — unless it is bulwarked by a strong religious environment and education. The struggling residents of Kfar Gidon lacked both. Surrounded by a sea of secularists, only a rock could have resisted dissolving. That rock — or rather, pearl — was not to appear until Yaakov Moshe Kramer arrived in 1947.

Thus, over the two and a half decades that followed the settlement's establishment, the residents of Kfar Gidon succumbed. Half of them succumbed physically and left for the more hospitable environs of Jerusalem and Bnei Brak. The other half succumbed religiously, as the children of the *chareidi* parents became less and less observant. Twenty-five years after its founding, Kfar Gidon comprised an aging *chareidi* population overruled by their less religious sons, some of whom had become Mizrachi and some of whom had abandoned religion entirely and joined the socialists.

The battle that would rend Kfar Gidon in half was a microcosm of the battle that had divided Europe's Jews for half a century. Most of religious European Jewry and almost all of its Rabbinic leadership opposed the Zionist movement founded in 1897 by Theodore Herzl. Historian Rabbi Berel Wein[4] has attributed three causes to this opposition: 1) They feared that the new nationalistic movement would become a substitute for Torah, as the Second Zionist Congress idealized a "new culture" which was antitraditional and antireligious. 2) The leaders of the Zionist movement, with three notable exceptions,[5] were assimilationists and agnostics. 3) The Zionist movement had an unspoken, but nevertheless inherent, messianic quality, which had proved lethal to Jewry repeatedly in its history.

The most religious Jews of Europe, including the chassidim and the yeshivah communities, were what we now call "*chareidim,*" denoting "those who tremble in fear of God." These Jews maintained a meticulous standard of Torah observance, including a strict separation of boys and girls from the earliest school grades. Learning and practicing Torah was the goal and mode of life. Most of the men studied in yeshivah, only going out to work in order to support their families. Most of *chareidi* Jewry was represented by the organization Agudat Yisrael or, for short, the Agudah, which was founded in Europe in 1912. Though the Agudah supported settling *Eretz Yisrael,* it was ideologically anti-Zionist.

In 1909, Rabbi Jacob Reines had established the Mizrachi movement — a religious alternative to secular Zionism. Mizrachi Jews were ardent Zionists, believing that the return to the Land of Israel was God's will for the Jewish people and the first step in the process leading to the coming of the *Mashiach.* Mizrachi supported co-ed functions and included secular studies in their yeshivah curriculums. Under the ban-

---

4. *Triumph of Survival* (Brooklyn, New York: Shaar Press, 1990), pp. 239-242.

5. Menachem Mendel Ussishkin, Rabbi Jacob Reines, and Rabbi Yehudah Leib Fishman. See Wein, p. 241.

ner, "Torah and Work," they endorsed university education and professional studies.

In Palestine, and later Israel, these three groups — secular Zionists, *chareidim*, and Mizrachists — lived in separate enclaves in their own communities, settlements, or city neighborhoods. In Kfar Gidon, however, they were to become as closely positioned as warring troops in hand-to-hand combat.

In 1947, Yaakov Moshe Kramer, 37 years old, and his bride Chaya Sara, aged 23, moved to Kfar Gidon. Kfar Chassidim, where they had rented a farm for the first year and a half of their marriage, had proven a misnomer; there were few chassidim living there. When the couple heard about plots in Kfar Gidon being virtually given away, they jumped at the opportunity to own their own farm in what they thought was a genuinely *chareidi* settlement. They must have been disconcerted to discover that they were the only *chareidi* residents younger than 45 years of age.

In 1951, the Jewish Agency (which had taken over the Settlement Department of the Zionist Organization) notified Kfar Gidon that they had to absorb 20 new families to work the 20 abandoned farms. The Jewish Agency promised that the enlarged Kfar Gidon would receive more land and more water rights. They also promised every new settler a cabin and a cow.

Yaakov Moshe, who regularly met the ships of Holocaust survivors landing in Haifa in order to search for his missing relatives, offered to find new families willing to settle in Kfar Gidon. He and another resident, Yehudah Marom, brought back 20 families — all of them Holocaust survivors from Transylvania and all of them *chareidi*.

It was a quiet coup d'état. The less-religious residents apparently did not notice at first that they were now outnumbered in their own community.

When they did wake up to the new reality, they seethed with accusations. They maintained that they had been tricked, that they had agreed to absorb 20 Mizrachi families, not *cha-reidim*. As Shimon Schwartz, one of the young residents, complained: "The newcomers arrived with Poalei Mizrachi [Mizrachi Workers Party] identity cards. After they got here, they changed their skin. They were really Agudah."

Another version of the coup, told by resident Sima Rosenberg, is that the newcomers really were Mizrachi. They came with clean-shaven faces and a mitigated level of observance, but then activists from the Agudah infiltrated the moshav and influenced the newcomers to grow their beards and "to become fanatics."

A half-century later, Sima Rosenberg would give as an example of the *chareidi* "fanaticism," that they amended the *takanon* [the governing principles of the moshav] to read that only *chareidi* sons could inherit their fathers' farms. In fact, the *takanon* of Kfar Gidon, which was formulated in 1950 and never amended, has no such stipulation.

The battle lines were drawn: On the one side the *chareidim* and on the other side the secularists. While the latter group originally included Mizrachists, eventually all of them would become secular.

The first battle of the war took place immediately. The new *chareidi* families had arrived just before a *shemittah* [sabbatical] year. The Torah commands farmers in the Land of Israel to refrain from planting, growing, or harvesting crops every seventh year. *Shemittah* was an explosive issue from the earliest days of the contemporary return to the Land. Since the early agricultural collectives barely survived as it was, they maintained that it was impossible to refrain from agriculture during the seventh year. Various rabbis therefore issued a *heter* [halachic leniency] permitting Jewish farmers to "sell" their land to non-Jews and continue working it during the *shemittah* year. *Chareidi* leaders such as the Chazon Ish and Rav Binyamin Mendelsohn, however, took the position that the *heter* was invalid, and that strict adherence to the commandments dealing with agriculture would generate the spiritual merit for Jews to continue living in the Land of Israel.

R' Yaakov Moshe was determined that Kfar Gidon would abide by the strict application of the laws of *shemittah*. He managed to get all of the *chareidi* farmers in Kfar Gidon to back him, making Kfar Gidon the first agricultural collective in Israel to keep *shemittah* without leniencies. According to R' Yitzchak Mendelsohn, the son of Rav Binyamin Mendelsohn (who was eventually responsible for the widespread observance of *shemittah*), scattered farmers throughout Israel kept *shemittah* in the year 5712 [1951-52), but only Kfar Gidon kept it collectively.

This was a gargantuan accomplishment for R' Yaakov Moshe, because strict *shemittah* observance means no agricultural income for all of the seventh year and the first half of the eighth year. R' Yaakov Moshe, therefore, had to find a way to financially support all the new refugee families whom he had convinced to observe *shemittah*. In 1951, he penned a desperate plea to Rav Binyamin Mendelsohn for financial aid. It is the oldest extant letter from R' Yaakov Moshe:

> To the honor of Rav HaGaon the Tzaddik, shlita, the Rav of Kfar Ata:
>
> I am here sending the list of men who will observe shemittah without any deviation, only according to the instruction of the chareidi rabbis, for example Rav Bengis of Jerusalem, head of the Chareidi Bais Din and the Rav HaGoan HaTzaddik the Chazon Ish, and the Rav of Kfar Ata, etc. Therefore we are requesting very, very much to help us so that we will be able to receive assistance. These people are new [in Eretz Yisrael] and they don't have animals and poultry from which they can sustain themselves. They are making more and more efforts in

*order not to transgress in any way at all against our holy
Torah or Chazal. Please, please come to the aid of these
heroes as soon as possible, that the Name of Heaven not
be desecrated through us, because if, Heaven forbid, a portion of them are not able to withstand this test, what will
emerge from that is scorn and mockery and chillul shem
Shamayim, Heaven forbid, here in our area. And if we
will be able to stand, then will emerge from that a Kiddush
Hashem, and the entire area will know that it's possible to
keep the Torah also as a farmer.*

*The signers, in prayer that the Kavod of Malchus
Shamayim will be revealed swiftly.*

Twenty-four residents of Kfar Gidon appended their signa-
tures to this letter.

Given the passionate level of the *shemittah* debate even
now, a half-century later, one can imagine the response of
the not-so-religious and secular members of Kfar Gidon to R'
Yaakov Moshe's effort for collective *shemittah* observance.

Shemittah, however, was a mild skirmish compared to
the melee that ensued two years later. The children of Kfar
Gidon studied in a co-ed Mizrachi school in Afula, a town
some seven kilometers south of Kfar Gidon. In 1953, Yaakov
Moshe Kramer, who would devote the rest of his life to the
cause of *chareidi* education, started a Yiddish-speaking *cheder*
[religious elementary school for boys, also called a "Talmud
Torah"] in Kfar Gidon. This was the match that caused the
smoldering dispute to erupt into a wild conflagration.

The language battle between Yiddish and Hebrew was one
of the most explosive issues in Palestine before the establishment of the state. The secularization of Hebrew — turning it
from the language of prayer and Torah study into the language
of the cafes and soccer fields – was a flashpoint of the religious-
secular struggle. For the early Zionists, modern Hebrew was

not just a language, but a national mission. Prof. Yosef Gorny of Tel Aviv University refers to the "implanting of Hebrew" as the "life's goal" of the Zionist cultural elite.[6]

Yiddish, on the other hand, was called by the Zionists the "jargon of exile." The Yiddish-Hebrew war had raged so vociferously in pre-state Palestine that adherents of the two sides often came to blows. Even after the establishment of the State of Israel, when Hebrew had already emerged victorious as the national language, anti-Yiddish sentiment ran deep. In 1954, when the Burstein family, a troupe of secular Yiddish actors from America, staged a Yiddish play in Israel, the theater's windows were smashed and the government demanded the closing of the show. Shimon Schwartz, explaining the opposition of his faction to Yaakov Moshe's new *cheder*, commented tersely, "They studied in Yiddish. This wasn't to our liking. This was incompatible with our spirit. We couldn't live with them."

The secular faction, led by Yitzchak Beilin and Shimon Schwartz, faced a real conundrum. They believed in democracy, the rule of the majority, but in Kfar Gidon the *chareidim* were now the majority.

Instead of giving up and leaving, or giving in and co-existing, the secular group took a daring, outrageous step. They turned to the neighboring kibbutz, Mizra, for help in banishing the *chareidim*.

Mizra was a kibbutz of the Shomer HaTzair movement, the most radical leftist movement within the spectrum of Zionism. Shomer HaTzair was infamous for deliberately eating bread on Passover and pork on Yom Kippur in order to flaunt their disdain for religion. For the erstwhile religious members of Kfar Gidon to make an alliance with Kibbutz Mizra, the site of a pork-packaging plant, was akin to Roosevelt making an

6. In *From Rosh Pina and Degania to Demona*, p. 46.

alliance with the Communist dictator Stalin in order to defeat their common enemy.

The leaders of Mizra agreed to help them on the condition that in the next two elections, all the members of their faction would vote for Mapam, the Israeli Communist party. This was, of course, selling votes in the crudest fashion, but the secularists of Kfar Gidon were ready to stoop to any level in order to rid themselves of the hated *chareidim*.

They fired invectives — and finally bullets. Every moshav received a certain amount of grain, animal feed, water pipes, wood, etc. from the government. These commodities were meant to be distributed equally to all the farmers. The secular contingent of Kfar Gidon charged that they never received their share. A *chareidi* farmer named Reich was in charge of the warehouse. Shimon Schwartz said that Reich had sold the commodities on the black market and used the funds to support the *chareidi* Talmud Torah.

The charge was false. As Yaakov Moshe had arranged, the Talmud Torah was supported mostly by funds from the Satmar Rebbe in America. The shortfall was made up by tuition paid by the parents of the students.

Other disputes erupted on the economic front. Kfar Gidon was a moshav. (A moshav differs from a kibbutz. In a moshav each family lives, eats, and owns land separately, but certain buildings, equipment, and property are collectively owned. Also, they buy their seed and sell their produce collectively.) Tnuva, Israel's agricultural marketing collective, paid Kfar Gidon a lump sum for their milk and eggs according to weight. The secular farmers accused the *chareidi* farmers of producing smaller eggs, thereby reducing their income. The *chareidi* farmers had more children to feed. Before bringing their milk cans to the collection point, they would pour some milk off the top for their own families. Since the raw milk was not homogenized, the cream floated to the top. The secular dairymen accused the *chareidi* dairymen of diluting their milk cans with water to make up for the poured-off cream, thus fetching a lower weigh-in price for them all.

Accusations and counteraccusations flew until, at one meeting between the sides, one of the secular residents fired his gun and the police were called.

The peace-loving R' Yaakov Moshe was caught between his convictions and his aversion to discord. He finally went to the Chazon Ish (Rabbi Avraham Yeshaya Karelitz, 5639-5714, 1878-1953), the leading rabbi of the generation, and asked him if he and his wife should leave Kfar Gidon.

The Chazon Ish told him to stay, and that eventually good would prevail. He quoted to the beleaguered R' Yaakov Moshe the line from *Tehillim*: "These by chariots and these by horses, but we will fight by the Name of Hashem." The Chazon Ish added: "The second part of the *pasuk* will eventually be fulfilled." The second part reads: "These will fall, and we will rise."

Despite their almost visceral aversion to discord, Yaakov Moshe and Chaya Sara remained in Kfar Gidon for over 40 years, until his failing health mandated a move to Jerusalem, where top medical care was available.

The first step in facing any challenge is to <u>accept</u> the challenge. Most of us reject our challenges with an attitude of, "I shouldn't have to go through this." Thus we never summon up the mettle to pass the particular test because of our anger toward and rejection of the test itself. This is particularly true when the trial is inflicted by people, especially malicious people, rather than coming as an "act of G-d" (such as illness or a natural disaster).

The secret of accepting any challenge is to recognize that it comes from HaKadosh Baruch Hu, not from the human beings who may be its immediate agents.

Once the Chazon Ish told them to stay in the soul-racking turbulence of Kfar Gidon, both Yaakov Moshe and Chaya Sara accepted their trying situation as coming not from their bellicose neighbors, but from the one G-d. If their farm was located on the only moshav in Israel that was a permanent battleground, Hashem must have charged them with a wartime mission. If directly across the highway from their home — the northernmost plot in the moshav — stood the pork-packaging plant of Kibbutz Mizra, then the constant view was meant not to gall them but to galvanize them. Just as Kfar Gidon embodied the internecine strife that is Israel's deepest, perennial problem, so Yaakov Moshe and Chaya Sara understood that they had to embody the solution.

They stuck it out for four decades, without complaint and without vilifying the culprits who never made peace in their war against the chareidim. When, after Yaakov Moshe's death, Chaya Sara was living in the chassidic enclave of Meah Shearim, several times I asked her if she missed Kfar Gidon. She answered with a silent shake of her head, the only hint she gave at how relieved she was to finally live in a compatible environment.

As to how to settle the battle of Kfar Gidon, the Chazon Ish suggested that the two sides split into two separate moshavim, each with its own legal and financial status. This was an unwieldy solution because the farms of the secularists and the *chareidim* were as intertwined as a shuffled deck of cards.

The secularists, who by this time numbered only 14 families, rejected the idea of splitting. They wanted to get rid of the *chareidim*, not keep them as next-door neighbors. They bided their time, voted Mapam, and waited for Kibbutz Mizra to pay up.

Mizra had promised to use its clout in the government to somehow banish the *chareidim*. The government at that time (and for the first three decades of the State of Israel) was led by Mapai, the Labor Party headed by Ben Gurion. Golda Meir was the Minister of Labor, which had jurisdiction over the Registry of Moshavim. Thus the ultimate fate of Kfar Gidon lay in the hands of Golda Meir. The leaders of Mizra arranged a secret meeting at the kibbutz between Golda Meir and the secular faction of Kfar Gidon.

Now, Golda was no lover of *chareidim*, but the government coalition in 1954 included the *chareidi* party Agudah. Golda listened to the pleas of Yitzchak Beilin and Shimon Schwartz. Finally she replied, "For 14 families, I will not break up the coalition with the *chareidim*. The 14 families should leave."

This was untenable to their faction. Finally, in 1955 or early 1956, a meeting to decide the fate of Kfar Gidon was scheduled in Afula with mediators appointed by the government. R' Yaakov Moshe, ever amiable to everyone, offered Shimon Schwartz a ride to Afula in his brother Shlomo Kramer's car. All the way there, Shimon discoursed on his position, while R' Yaakov Moshe nodded silently. Shimon interpreted the nods as agreement rather than as what they were: the neutral gesture of a man who loved peace. Thus, when the meeting began, Shimon was surprised to hear R' Yaakov Moshe deliver a resolute defense of the *chareidi* position.

Disconcerted, Shimon jumped up and slapped R' Yaakov Moshe across the face.

R' Yaakov Moshe did not respond. Not physically. Not verbally. Not emotionally. Not at the time, and not in the following years.

The Talmud declares: "One who is insulted and does not insult in return, who hears himself disgraced and does not answer back, who does it out of love and is happy in affliction, of them it is written: 'and His lovers are like the sun in its full force.'"

The mediators decided that the moshav of Kfar Gidon would split into two legal entities: the *chareidi* Kfar Gidon and a new non-*chareidi* moshav named Telmei Gidon, which would govern its own affairs and economic dealings, although certain buildings, such as the synagogue, were not possible to partition.

Geographically, the two tiny moshavim were as intertwined as two hands clasped. A *chareidi* family ushering in the holy Shabbos by singing a song to the angels would be living next door to a secular family listening to the radio. Although such mixed neighborhoods exist in Israeli cities, a moshav is a homogeneous unit in terms of religion (some are secular, some are Mizrachi, etc.). Kfar Gidon is the only one of Israel's many moshavim where the schisms that divide Israeli society are etched into the hedges between front lawns.

The split should have ended the war, but it only exacerbated it. As surely as an eye will tear until it rejects a foreign body, Telmei Gidon would not rest until it drove away the *chareidim*. Every time Kfar Gidon applied for a building permit — to build a *mikveh* or a new school or to expand the moshav, Telmei Gidon vociferously opposed them in the pertinent government bodies, in the press, and in the courts.

During the 1960's, R' Yaakov Shlomo Gross, an Agudah Knesset member, succeeded in obtaining an irrigation system for Kfar Gidon. A government grant paid for half of the system, and the farmers of Kfar Gidon had to take out loans to pay for the other half. Because their fields were intertwined with the fields of Telmei Gidon, the new irrigation system also watered the fields of the secular farmers, but the latter refused to contribute anything toward its cost, insisting that the government had paid the entire amount.

The present secretary of Kfar Gidon, Mattisyahu Bohbot, who is himself not *chareidi*, summed up the moshav's history: "The whole goal of the seculars was to harass the *chareidim*."

Dealing with adversaries is a challenge that confronts everyone. The principal reasons that we dislike or even hate another person are:

∿ The other person is different (eg., more religious, less religious, different nationality, personality, or mode of conduct).
∿ The other person doesn't like us.

Of course, all such forms of hatred are forbidden by the Torah, which commands us: "You should not hate your brother in your heart." Fulfillment of this mitzvah requires much arduous inner work.

To understand how R' Yaakov Moshe and Chaya Sara dealt with their adversaries, in this case the anti-chareidi members of Telmei Gidon, we must first examine how they related to the two categories of people enumerated above.

∿ People who were different

Tzviki Shtiglitz, who was a ben bayis in the Kramers' home, said that no rabbi or Admor in Israel had such a variegated retinue: chassidim, Misnagdim, Sephardim, Mizrachim, and secularists all frequented the Kramers' home.

One member of Kfar Gidon recounted how he was accompanying R' Yaakov Moshe home from shul one Shabbos morning. They passed a member of Telmei Gidon who was working on his car from underneath. R' Yaakov Moshe's young companion averted his eyes from this desecration of the holy day. R' Yaakov Moshe, however, stopped beside the car and greeted the man with a cordial, "Shabbos Shalom." Then he stood there and waited until the man lifted his head out from under his car and returned his greeting.

Chaim Cohen described his first visit to Kfar Gidon. He was a soldier in the Israeli army and was wearing his uniform. He came to the moshav synagogue and was warmly greeted by a man in the distinctive garb of a

Satmar chassid. The chassid hugged Chaim, kissed him on his shoulders, and invited him to sleep in his home. Chaim could not figure out how a Satmar chassid, so ideologically opposed to the State and the army, could treat him so lovingly. The chassid, of course, was none other than R' Yaakov Moshe Kramer.

Even the members of pork-raising Kibbutz Mizra were not outside the Kramers' loving embrace. Obviously Mizra had no synagogue. Every Yom Kippur a handful of residents from the kibbutz would make their way to the small synagogue of Kfar Gidon. R' Yaakov Moshe would interrupt his prayers to go to the entrance and greet the men, hugging them and kissing them on their shoulders. Then he would lead them to the front of the synagogue and seat them next to himself. Upstairs, in the women's gallery, Chaya Sara would duplicate the scene. She would greet the two or three women, who usually showed up inappropriately dressed in shorts and sleeveless tops, with warm hugs, and seat them next to herself, sharing her machzor with them.

I witnessed Rebbetzin Chaya Sara's ability to love people who were so religiously different than she. Once, in the 1990's, I brought two childless couples to Rebbetzin Chaya Sara for blessings. One couple was religious, the other couple, Yossi and Rivka, were secular Israelis living in America. I told them that since we were going to the chassidic neighborhood of Meah Shearim, they had to dress appropriately. Yossi donned a kipah and Rivka covered her hair and wore a dress with long sleeves and a high neck.

Yossi's mother had grown up in Munkacs. When Rebbetzin Chaya Sara heard that, she started to converse with him in Hungarian, apparently about Munkacs before the war. While the rest of us sat there, the two of them enjoyed a convivial conversation that lasted perhaps a quarter of an hour. I thought to myself, "Because of the way he and his wife are dressed, she doesn't realize that they're secular. Otherwise, she wouldn't relate to him like he's an old friend."

Finally the conversation reverted to Hebrew and included the rest of us. I said to the Rebbetzin, "Tell Yossi and Rivka that they should move back to Israel."

Rebbetzin Chaya Sara suddenly became serious. She looked at them earnestly and shook her head. "No," she said, "it's forbidden for Jews who don't observe Torah and mitzvos to live in the Land of Israel."

❧ People who didn't like them

Apparently, there was no one who didn't like R' Yaakov Moshe. Interviews with some two dozen members of Kfar Gidon and Telmei Gidon, including octogenarians and nonagenarians who were present during the skirmishes of the 1950's, revealed that no one — including the most vociferous of the anti-chareidi agitators — disliked R' Yaakov Moshe. They all spoke of him as a "tzaddik" and an "honest man." Strangely, Shimon Schwartz claimed that "when the two sides fought, he didn't become involved. He sat aside quietly. He never took sides." Since Yaakov Moshe was the de facto leader of the chareidi faction, the founder of the Talmud Torah, and the mentor who, following the guidance of the Chazon Ish, determined their every move, Shimon's perception is astounding.

How did R' Yaakov Moshe lead the opposition without making the secularists feel that he opposed them? He embodied the dictum from Pirkei Avos: "Say little and do much." He avoided noisy confrontations, felt no compulsion to argue with those with whom he disagreed, and did what he deemed necessary in such a modest way that few knew who had done it.

R' Yaakov Moshe somehow managed to be steel in his convictions while he was silk in his relationships. Most peace lovers end up compromising their positions for the sake of harmony. For Yaakov Moshe, this was unten-

able, for his religious positions were sacrosanct to him, ordained by Hashem. Compromise would have been like negotiating over property that did not belong to him.

Instead, he pulled off a balancing act that an expert high-wire walker would have envied. While keeping his feet firmly on the wire — his religious convictions — with his hands he embraced people on both sides of the issue.

As discussed previously, Chaya Sara had a very different personality. Her innate gevurah led her to regard people through the lenses of astute judgment rather than through the love-colored lenses her husband wore. She saw people's shortcomings and sometimes disapproved of them.

As their neighbor Yossi Shtiglitz described her: "Chaya Sara was a different type of person than her husband. In the beginning, she didn't accept the way her husband was so accepting of everyone. She was a straight-shooter. If someone was bad, she said they were bad. Yaakov Moshe said that everyone was good, even someone who wasn't good."

Among the old-timers of Kfar Gidon and Telmei Gidon, several did not like Chaya Sara. They made ludicrous accusations of her supposed foibles. Shimon said, "She loved money." Another secular member of Telmei Gidon criticized the way she took care of the handicapped children. A religious woman from Kfar Gidon related to me, a half-century after the fact, an incident in which she claimed that Chaya Sara had refused to share with her her basket of carobs.

How did Chaya Sara relate to the people who didn't like her? Simply put, she did not relate to their dislike. Being popular was not one of her goals. While her astute vision easily discerned people's moral failings, she was color blind when it came to their evaluation of her.

One of the last conversations I ever had with Rebbetzin Chaya Sara took place when I was writing this chap-

ter. Having heard from the aforementioned women that Chaya Sara did not like them, I went to ask her if that were true. The Rebbetzin was already so ill and weak that she barely spoke. "Did you like _____?" I asked her.

Rebbetzin Chaya Sara's voice was faint but earnest: "I loved her."

"What about _____? Did you like her?" I quizzed her again.

"I loved her," was her final word on the matter.

The members of Telmei Gidon never succeeded in driving away the *chareidim*. In 2006, Kfar Gidon boasts nearly sixty *chareidi* families.

As for the *chareidi* Talmud Torah that had ignited the conflagration, Yaakov Moshe tended it and its sister Bais Yaakov school for girls like a precious child. When, in the 1970's, the lack of school-age children in Kfar Gidon precipitated the schools' closing, Yaakov Moshe fought to bring in new young families and to reopen the schools. In 1982, at the age of 72, he succeeded. Through what one witness described as "Yaakov Moshe's loving pressure," he got both accreditation and funding from the Israeli government for the re-opened schools (teaching in Hebrew, not Yiddish). Today over 600 students from all the towns around the Jezreel Valley learn in the *chareidi* educational institutions of Kfar Gidon.

Yaakov Moshe's impact was as deep as it was broad. His personal influence on the younger generation growing up in Kfar Gidon reversed the downward trend of religious observance. As Shmulik Heizler, who was born in Kfar Gidon in 1952, testified: "R' Yaakov Moshe operated with a very low profile, but his influence was profound. I am more religious than my father. My siblings and I are where we are religiously because of R' Yaakov Moshe."

Even the anti-*chareidi* residents were not immune to his influence. In the first house the Kramers lived in before moving to their permanent abode, the neighbors next door were a Mizrachi family named Wasserman. One day, the Wassermans' 9-year-old son Amos approached R' Yaakov Moshe and said, "I want you to give me a haircut and leave *peyot*, like yours."

R' Yaakov Moshe replied that he was willing to do it, but first Amos would need his parents' permission. He blessed the boy and sent him home. The next day an indignant Mrs. Wasserman accosted R' Yaakov Moshe and accused him of trying to influence her son. R' Yaakov Moshe responded: "I didn't influence him. He came to me of his own accord. Besides, it's too late. I've already blessed him."

Amos Wasserman grew up to be a *chareidi talmid chacham* and a *rosh yeshivah*.

CHAPTER FIVE

From Bovines to Bracelets

*T*HE MOST COMPLEX THING ABOUT THEM WAS their simplicity. The Kramers were determined to live without luxuries. Luxuries to them included electricity, a telephone, running hot water, a bathtub, a gas stove, a washing machine, plaster and paint on the walls, and flooring over the bare concrete.

For Chaya Sara personally, "luxuries" came to include any clothes fancier than a housedress and, when her teeth loosened with age, anything as image enhancing as dentures. In the early years she did wear nice outfits on Shabbos. In fulfillment of his halachic obligation, her husband bought her dresses three times a year for the holidays, and later, on his trips abroad, he brought her outfits from Europe and America. The women of Kfar Gidon ogled these dresses, with their avant-garde closures, not yet available in Israel: snaps! Was it to stave off their jealousy that Chaya Sara gave away all her nice clothes and kept nothing but housecoats? By the time she was in her late 50's, her uniform had become two housecoats, one atop the other, even on Shabbos, even to weddings.

In 1990, Mrs. Kraindy Dankovich came from London to Jerusalem to accompany Rebbetzin Chaya Sara to the *sheloshim* commemoration for R' Yaakov Moshe, a public occasion to be attended by the most esteemed rabbis. She was astounded when Chaya Sara, wearing two housecoats, announced that she was ready to go. "This," Chaya Sara declared pointing to the bottom layer, "we'll call a dress. And this," pointing to the top layer, "we'll call a coat."

As for R' Yaakov Moshe, he insisted on wearing a worn and scruffy *shtriemel*, even when wealthy admirers clamored to replace it with a fine new one. Finally one chassidic diamond merchant from Antwerp visited Yaakov Moshe in Kfar Gidon and placed a box containing a beautiful new *shtriemel* on the rickety kitchen table. When R' Yaakov Moshe declined the gift, the diamond merchant announced that he would not leave their house until R' Yaakov Moshe donned the new *shtriemel* (which in halachic terms indicated acquisition). As the hours passed and the diamond merchant did not relent, R' Yaakov Moshe finally accepted the gift. But he had the last word; he never wore the new *shtriemel* to the synagogue.

In the winter of 1985 a visitor from England was appalled to see buckets to catch the rain positioned all over the house because the roof leaked and the walls had cracks. He asked Rebbetzin Chaya Sara how she heated the house in winter. She replied, "*Baruch Hashem*, we have a lot of warm guests who warm up the house."

The Kramers' disdain for both physical comforts and outer appearances baffled some people, intrigued others, and annoyed still others. When I asked one relative if Chaya Sara had attended their daughter's wedding, she replied with barely concealed disdain, "Yes, wearing a housecoat and with no teeth!"

The Kramers' house in Kfar Gidon, with the new roof put on in 1989, the last year they lived there. The roof was put on while R' Yaakov Moshe was abroad.

The reason for the Kramers' radical nonmaterialism was a matter of constant speculation. Most neighbors concluded that it was a simple case of not wanting to spend money on themselves when other Jews needed it more. As proof, they cited incidents such as this:

A group of affluent chassidim from the United States visited R' Yaakov Moshe in Kfar Gidon. When they saw the state of his shack, they were dismayed. They asked him, "How can you live in a house without flooring? How can you receive important people in this house? We'll pay to have the whole place fixed up properly."

R' Yaakov Moshe candidly asked them, "Do you have money?"

"Yes!" they replied eagerly. "As much money as you like."

"Good!" R' Yaakov Moshe exclaimed. "Give me the money now. I have 10 poor brides to marry off."

The chassidim were disappointed, but dutifully forked over a large contribution for the brides.

A reminiscence by Rabbanit Miriam Gabbai of Afula casts doubt on this explanation for the Kramers' radical nonmaterialism. Once Rabbanit Gabbai brought a friend, the wife of a local contractor, to the Kramers' shack. The woman was simultaneously awed by the level of *simchah* in the house and horrified by its state of dilapidation. On the spot, the woman offered her husband's professional services gratis to plaster and paint the walls, lay down *ballatot*, and fix the leaky roof. Chaya Sara refused, caressing the unfinished walls and asking, "Is there any wallpaper better than this?" Rabbanit Gabbai concludes the story: "She was teaching us that simplicity is the best thing there is."

Note that Chaya Sara rejected the offer even though the poor gained nothing by her abstinence.

Another theory points to the vast amounts of *tzedakkah* money that passed through R' Yaakov Moshe and Chaya Sara's hands. The Kramers' bare-bones standard of living effectively staved off accusations that they might be using some of this cash flow for themselves. Shimon Schwartz related how once when he was visiting his uncle in Haifa, they went to the local Agudat Yisrael bank. There, much to his surprise, he saw the bank manager come out of his office and welcome Chaya Sara Kramer "as if a millionairess had arrived. She came with a bag of money. The bank manager ushered her into his private office."

Had the Kramers lived according to any but the most ascetic standard, some people might have suspected them of taking a personal cut from the *tzedakkah* money. As it was, even the critics in Telmei Gidon uniformly described Yaakov Moshe as "honest." His humble house shouted the message: You can trust your *tzedakkah* money to us.

As for furniture, the Kramers did not own a couch, and instead of a set of matching dining chairs, they had an odd collection of assorted chairs that they had picked up secondhand. Israeli homes, in lieu of built-in closets, sport free-standing wooden wardrobes. The Kramers' secondhand, broken wardrobes stood on tin cans. When the Kramers had more guests than chairs, Yaakov Moshe would bring wooden produce crates, turn them over, and cover them with towels for the guests' comfort. When the screens that kept out the Jezreel Valley's ubiquitous mosquitoes ripped, the Kramers sewed up the holes with thread. Yaakov Moshe's niece Pnina remembers Chaya Sara cooking on a primus kerosene stove when everyone else in Kfar Gidon had a gas range.

Pnina's explanation for such austerity is that her uncle regarded this world as merely (in the words of the Talmud) a *"prozdor,"* a corridor leading to the World of Eternity and Truth. One doesn't bother furnishing a corridor.

As R' Yaakov Moshe himself said, "This isn't my house; my house is in the Next World."

Chaya Sara's sisters-in-law (who were, one neighbor informed me, on a "higher social level") criticized her for the way her house looked. They told her that it wasn't proper to live like this and that she should buy nice furniture and housewares. Chaya Sara replied, "I don't want to serve material things," referring to the upkeep that even simple possessions require.

Perhaps there was yet another reason for their radical non-materialism. Some people whispered that R' Yaakov Moshe was a *lamed-vav tzaddik,* one of the 36 righteous people whose merit upholds the whole world. A *true tzaddik* must atone for his generation and their failings. Perhaps R' Yaakov Moshe sought to remedy his generation's obsession with materialism.

Unlike many religions, Judaism does not disdain the physical world and its pleasures. In fact, the objects of this world are the Jew's essential tools for the performance of *mitzvos.* Jews aim not to transcend the world, but to rectify it. Thus, in Biblical times a *nazir,* a person who chose to abstain from the pleasure of wine, was required by the Torah to bring a sin offering.

Yet, Judaism makes a distinction between physicality and materialism. From a Jewish standpoint, physicality means valuing the physical world as a means of drawing close to G-d. Materialism means valuing the physical world for itself. This distinction is often lost on Jews.

Were R' Yaakov Moshe and Chaya Sara making an unspoken statement about the relative unimportance of material things? Perhaps they were saying: If we can live without paint on our walls, you can live without imported Venetian wallpaper. If we can live without any flooring, you can live without posh wall-to-wall carpeting and marble floors. If Chaya Sara can appear for important occasions in a housecoat, do you need designer dresses?

The point was not lost on the discerning. One young neighbor, Naomi Bohbot, who moved to Kfar Gidon in 1978, told how, the first time she saw the Kramers' shack, she was shocked. But she quickly came to perceive a "certain light" in their home, "a real luminosity." The physical surroundings faded into the background as the spiritual reality predominated. It was the first time in her life that Naomi experienced spirit trumping matter.

Indeed, Chaya Sara's relationship to material assets was enigmatic. As some of the following stories show, she loathed financial loss, even to the point of disobeying her husband. On the other hand, she gave with gusto whatever she had — even her most prized possessions — to whomever needed them. Was she attached to her possessions or detached? The solution to this puzzle provides one of the most staggering insights into Chaya Sara's greatness.

When the Kramers moved to Kfar Gidon, they invested everything they had in a small dairy herd of six cows. This, more than raising crops, was to be their principle source of livelihood. They did not know that the government engaged in the spraying of pesticides on the valley's vegetation. The cows ate the poisoned grass and all six died.

Chaya Sara was devastated by this loss. She cried bitterly.

R' Yaakov Moshe bid her to stop, admonishing her, "For six million Jews, we cry. For six cows, we don't cry."

Dealing with any type of loss is a wrenching test. R' Yaakov Moshe was teaching Chaya Sara to distinguish between two kinds of loss: human loss and material loss. He was teaching her that mourning is an appropriate response only to the former, never to the latter. The loss of physical possessions never warrants our grief, because only people, not possessions, have intrinsic value.

Although this point seems rudimentary, how many parents yell at their children for breaking a valued object, oblivious to the reality that a shattered child is a worse tragedy than a shattered object? How many employers rate and berate their employees according to their productivity, disregarding their human value?

R' Yaakov Moshe was reminding the young Chaya Sara that just as she recognized the loss of her whole family in the Holocaust as coming from the hand of Hashem, so she must regard this more minor loss also as from Hashem. An ironic facet of human nature is the ability to rise to meet great, dramatic challenges and to fail at minor tests. This anomaly is often due to our failure to recognize the more minor challenges as true tests. R' Yaakov Moshe was, as it were, waving "a roadsign" in front of his young wife. He was telling her that she had the ability to choose a different, higher response to their total material loss.

Chaya Sara was so frugal that she rarely discarded anything. She even kept the labels from plastic soda bottles in order to write notes on the back. This seemingly inordinate attachment to material things is reminiscent of Rashi's commentary about the Patriarch Jacob recrossing the river on the night he fought with the angel. Rashi, quoting the Gemara, explains that Jacob went back because he had forgotten some small jars. In the Gemara, Rabbi Elazar adds the astonishing remark: "This shows that for a *tzaddik*, his money is more precious to him than his life."

What are we to make of this? And how can we reconcile such hoarding possessiveness with Chaya Sara's rampant generosity?

At another point during their early years at Kfar Gidon, the Kramers had a dairy herd of eight cows. Each cow was worth about 3,000 shekels. One day, one of the cows became sick. Chaya Sara, who took care of the dairy, found the cow lying on its side, making worrisome sounds. Afraid to lose 3,000 shekels, because a dead cow was worth only its hide, Chaya Sara suggested to her husband that if they sold the cow immediately, they could probably fetch half its value. R' Yaakov Moshe was about to depart for Bnei Brak to consult the Chazon Ish about an important matter. He told her not to sell the cow, and he left.

Every half-hour Chaya Sara checked on the cow; its condition continued to deteriorate. Chaya Sara was convinced that it would soon die, a catastrophic loss they could not afford. Suddenly a man showed up in the cowshed. He said he'd heard they had a sick cow, and he offered to buy it for 1700 shekels.

In those days long before cell phones, there was no way for her to again consult with her husband. Faced with the specter of losing 3,000 shekels, she sold the cow. It was the only time in their wedded life that she disobeyed Yaakov Moshe.

The man paid her the 1700 shekels in cash and said he would come back later to pick up the animal. "No," she protested. "Take the cow now. Later it might be dead." The man said that that would be his problem, and he left.

Chaya Sara went into the house. A half-hour later she returned to the cowshed to check if the cow was dead yet. She found the cow standing up, munching on hay, totally recovered.

She was mortified. In her fear of material loss, she had disobeyed her husband, and also lost 1300 shekels for them.

When R' Yaakov Moshe came home, he found his wife distraught and guilt ridden. Since the man had not yet returned to take the cow, Chaya Sara wanted to back out of the deal, to return the 1700 shekels and keep the cow. Yaakov Moshe told her that integrity demanded that they follow through with the sale.

At the same time, he consoled her. He told her not to fret, because this is the way it was meant to be from on high. If she had not sold the cow, he explained, it would have surely died because their decree, issued on Rosh Hashanah, was to lose this cow. Only because it was the *mazal* of the new owner to have a healthy cow did the cow recover.

The lesson is that material gain and loss have their roots in spiritual causality. Each individual receives or loses exactly what the Divine Source ordains for that individual. The ups and downs of fortune are neither random nor caused by human choices.

People may think, "I lost all that money in the stock market because I invested in the wrong stock," or, "A thief broke in and stole my valuables because I didn't install a state-of-the-art alarm system." Although Judaism obligates people to do their hishtadlus [reasonable effort] by investing wisely and protecting their valuables, ultimately all of a person's gain and loss is decreed on Rosh Hashanah, according to what Hashem perceives to be the person's spiritual needs. Loss can fortify one's humility, empathy for others, and reliance on the Divine. Acknowledging the Divine Source behind losses can ameliorate their sting.

This was a test young Chaya Sara had failed. When I heard this story from her, I thought: "If she could have failed so miserably and then gone on to become so great, there's a chance for me, too!"

While Chaya Sara never again disobeyed her husband, financial loss continued to vex her. At one point she decided to invest in chickens. Raising poultry was a profitable enterprise in those days. Chaya Sara, who ran the farm with minimal help from her husband, purchased a large quantity of chicks and tended them as they grew. It was winter, so she bought a heater to heat the chicken coop at night. One night, the heater toppled over and set fire to the hay. By the time the Kramers woke up and put out the fire, 1,000 chicks were dead. Those that remained were injured from smoke inhalation. The remedy, she knew, was milk. All that night and the next day she and Yaakov Moshe used a dropper to feed the chicks milk. Their prodigious efforts managed to save scarcely a couple hundred chicks. While telling me this story decades later, Chaya Sara's expression betrayed the grief and frustration of that winter night.

Chaya Sara feeding the chickens, 1950's

I wondered why, since the Kramers were such devoted servants of HaKadosh Baruch Hu, He didn't reward them with greater success in their agricultural efforts. When I asked Rebbetzin Chaya Sara about this, she was surprised at the question. She served HaKadosh Baruch Hu out of love, without any expectation of reward. Nor did she see any connection whatsoever between what she gave and what she got.

"Everything I didn't get," she told me, "I didn't feel like I deserved. I didn't feel that anything was owed to me. Everything is a gift. Nothing is owed."

A sense of entitlement sets most of us up for disappointment, depression, and a sense of grievance, even against G-d. Chaya Sara chose to cut the mental wire that connects giving and getting. She served G-d and man, without looking for a paycheck. Whenever she did receive something, she treated it with the ingenuous joy of an unexpected bonus.

Chaya Sara was in charge of the Kramers' finances. It was she who paid the bills and scrambled to make ends meet. Like the *eishes chayil* ("She envisions a field and buys it,") Chaya Sara was an astute businesswoman. Even when she was middle aged, she wouldn't voluntarily take a financial loss, but by that stage she accepted the inevitable with surrender and good grace.

Yossi Shtiglitz, the young farmer who rented the Kramers' land starting in 1968, paid them $2,000 a year. This was their principal source of income at that time. One year was a bad year for crops. When Yossi went to pay Chaya Sara his yearly rent, he asked her for a $400 discount — an amount the Kramers' could ill afford to lose. Chaya Sara balked. Yossi threatened to go ask R' Yaakov Moshe, who, they both knew, would acquiesce to any request. Chaya Sara retorted quickly, "No, don't go to Yaakov Moshe. I'll give you a $100 discount."

In the end, Yossi did go to Yaakov Moshe, who told his wife to accept any amount that Yossi offered. When she ran into Yossi outdoors later that day, she jokingly said to him, "You defeated me," and she laughed. This was a level of detachment from material loss that had taken her years to achieve.

Yet, even as Chaya Sara recoiled from losing money, she reveled in giving it away. Her "adopted daughter" Miriam, who lived with them in the 1950's, remembers a destitute couple coming to the Kramers' home. They sat around the kitchen table with R' Yaakov Moshe and Chaya Sara and described their desperate plight. This was before R' Yaakov Moshe set up his *tzedakkah* system with wealthy donors from abroad. He shook his head in compassion, but he truly had nothing to offer them. Then Chaya Sara suggested to him that they sell one of their eight cows and give the proceeds to this couple.

This incident transpired during the same decade that Chaya Sara disobeyed her husband rather than lose the value of one cow. She was not willing to lose a cow, but she was keen to give one away. This paradox intensifies with additional tales of Chaya Sara's wholehearted generosity.

Despite spending money on virtually nothing except food (Chaya Sara considered wholesome, nourishing food a necessity), the Kramers' coffers were often empty. Chaya Sara would save up small sums of money. R' Yaakov Moshe would give to poor people whatever he had, then Chaya Sara would happily replenish his pockets with her savings. That, too, he would give away. Once R' Yaakov Moshe was in Nazareth (perhaps during the period when he worked as a *kashrus* supervisor at the Elite chocolate factory there). He had in his pocket 15 *liras*, a respectable sum, which was all the money they possessed at that time. A poor man approached R' Yaakov Moshe and appealed for his help. R' Yaakov Moshe gave him the entire 15 *liras*. They were left with nothing.

When Chaya Sara related this episode to her neighbor Leah Landau, she told it not as a complaint, but with pride at the mitzvah her husband had performed.

Chaya Sara's ultimate test of generosity involved her gold jewelry. In true chassidic custom, Yaakov Moshe had given his bride a gold bracelet and a gold watch at the time of their wedding. It was the only jewelry she would ever own. She kept the two precious pieces in a closet, taking them out to wear only on Yom Tov and special occasions.

One day, while Chaya Sara was doing an errand in Haifa, a highly distraught young chassid came to see R' Yaakov Moshe. He was an orphan and engaged to be married, he cried, and he had no money to buy the customary gold jewelry for his bride. The stranger begged Yaakov Moshe to help him.

That day the Kramers' coffers were totally bare. He cast about for some way to help the young *chassan* [bridegroom]. Suddenly it occurred to him. He went to the closet, came back with Chaya Sara's gold jewelry, and gave them to the young stranger. The *chasan* was overjoyed.

So sure was Yaakov Moshe that his wife would approve his action and so routine for him was this act of generosity, that when Chaya Sara returned home many hours later, he forgot to mention to her what he had done.

Three weeks later was the holiday of Succos. Chaya Sara went to the closet to don her jewelry. She was alarmed to discover that they were missing. She thought they had been stolen. No, Yaakov Moshe reassured her, they had not been stolen. Rather, he had given the bracelet and watch to a young *chassan* who needed them for his bride. "I love you as you are, even without jewelry," Yaakov Moshe concluded, laughing.

Hearing this story, I was aghast. "What did you say?" I wondered indignantly.

"I didn't say anything," Rebbetzin Chaya Sara responded. "It was perfectly okay with me. I was happy to help someone who needed it."

"But your husband didn't even ask your permission," I protested. "And it was your property, your only jewelry."

"How could he ask me? I wasn't home," she explained. "Besides, he knew me well enough to know what I'd say."

"And that was it? You didn't do anything at all?"

Rebbetzin Chaya Sara probed deep into the recesses of her memory and recalled that day. "Yes, I did do something," she declared. "I laughed."

This is the ultimate level of relating to material possessions: uplifting them by using them to serve Hashem. What had been simply beautiful ornaments became a davar mitzvah, an object by which a mitzvah is performed. By using her jewelry to perform the mitzvah of hachnasas kallah [providing for a bride], she elevated it. Such elevation, according to Judaism, is the ultimate purpose of material possessions. This is the sacred potential inherent in all physical objects. This is the reason a tzaddik values his or her possessions.

Perhaps Chaya Sara did not treasure her jewelry and therefore found it easy to relinquish? Her gold jewelry was actually her most precious possession. She once told me, "My husband treated me like a princess."

A "princess" in my mind conjures up the image of a woman decked in finery and jewels, a far cry from the Chaya Sara I knew. "What did he give you?" I challenged.

"What didn't he give me?" she retorted. To prove the point she enumerated her two-item list: "He gave me a gold bracelet and a watch."

Decades after they had disappeared from her wrists, the gold jewelry continued to glitter in her memory.

That it was her husband, not she, who actually gave the indigent chassan the jewelry is a higher level of altruism. For most of us, donating something that is precious to us (our money, our time, a valued object, etc.) is both a renunciation of self-interest and an enhancement of self-interest, for the positive feeling aroused when we see the joy and gratitude of the recipient is a form of payback. That is why the Rambam considered it a higher level of giving when the recipient is unknown to the donor. Perhaps this is what caused Chaya Sara to laugh in joy when she heard that her jewelry had been given away without her knowledge.

A closer look at this story reveals an even higher level of nonpossessiveness. Even the feeling of "It's mine to give away" was absent from Chaya Sara. The jewelry was her most valuable possession, yet she had so little sense of proprietary rights over it that she considered it irrelevant if it were she or her husband who gave it away.

How can we reconcile such an exalted level of generosity with Chaya Sara's aversion to losing her property? If she could not bear to *lose* a cow how could she so willingly forfeit a cow to complete strangers? This contradiction baffled me until I confronted her with the story of the hot-water heater.

With the arrival of the handicapped children in the early 1960's, the Kramers decided that their charges' safety necessitated installing electricity to replace the fire hazard of kerosene lamps and a telephone in case a doctor needed to be called. They did not, however, purchase a hot-water heater.

For bathing the children and washing clothes, Chaya Sara heated up water on the stove. In those years, long before disposable diapers, the incontinent children (including those in their early 20's) would wear cloth diapers, easily soaked by urine and feces. At night not only the diapers got wet or dirty, but also the pajamas and the bedding. Chaya Sara would get up at 2 a.m. every night to check each child and change diapers, pajamas, and bedding when necessary. Of course, washing the children required heating water on the stove, which added many minutes to the nighttime changes.

Finally one year, when R' Yaakov Moshe was away in England, Chaya Sara decided that she would buy a boiler to provide running hot water. The potato fields that year had yielded a good crop. She decided to use the money from the sale of the potato harvest to buy a water heater.

The potatoes were duly harvested and sold. Chaya Sara put the money safely away in her closet. The next morning she intended to take a bus into Afula and buy a hot-water heater.

That night her husband telephoned from England. He told her that a family somewhere in Israel desperately needed money. He asked her to take all the money from the sale of the potato harvest and send it to that family, whose name and address he gave her.

Chaya Sara did as he asked. The next morning, she went to the post office and sent a postal money order for the full amount of the cash she had to the name and address her husband had given her. The hot-water heater would have to wait.

"How did you feel when you sent the money to the other family?" I asked Rebbetzin Chaya Sara three decades later. Having heard the story from someone else, I had gone to her to verify the details. Knowing that I, in a million years, would never have given up the water heater, I wondered how she had felt making this incredible sacrifice for the sake of total strangers.

"What do you mean, how did I feel?" she asked with a quizzical expression. While I take my emotional pulse every

15 minutes, Chaya Sara went for years without worrying about how she felt.

"You must have been disappointed," I prompted.

"No, I wasn't disappointed," she replied, surprised at the very idea. "Why should I have been disappointed?"

Yet again I felt like Rebbetzin Chaya Sara and I came from different planets. The law of gravity on my planet pulled everything toward me. The law of gravity on her planet pulled everything upward.

"You wanted the hot-water heater," I reminded her.

"Yes, I wanted the hot-water heater," she remembered, her eyes with a faraway look, remembering those years, which she considered the best years of her life.

"So you must have been disappointed when your husband told you to send the money to other people, people you didn't even know."

Rebbetzin Chaya Sara sat there puzzling over what this thickheaded American was having such a hard time understanding. Suddenly, she broke into a smile.

"You don't understand," she explained, as to a child. "The money wasn't *wasted*. They used it for something they needed."

Here was the difference between losing property and giving it away. Poisoned cows and burned chicks were a waste; no one benefited. Giving her property to others, however, was not a loss at all. Someone benefited. Suddenly I had the key to understanding her relationship to material possessions. For me, there were two modes: personal possession or personal loss. For Chaya Sara, there were two radically different modes: waste or use — it didn't matter by whom!

I inserted the key into the lock and turned it: "But you didn't have the money for what *you* needed, a hot-water heater," I insisted.

She looked at me uncomprehendingly. What was the difference?

Chaya Sara experienced the essential truth of spiritual reality: oneness. On the physical level, we are separate individuals; one body ends where another body begins. On the spiritual level, however, all Jews share one collective soul. On the physical level, the more I give away, the less I have. On the spiritual level, giving to another Jew is like transferring an object from my right hand to my left. There is no loss, only a different hand holding the object.

Chaya Sara consistently chose to focus on the spiritual reality of oneness rather than on the physical reality of separation and competition. Just as for me it is irrelevant whether my gold bracelet adorns my right wrist or my left, so for Chaya Sara it was irrelevant whether her gold bracelet adorned her own wrist or someone else's.

Her radical generosity was rooted in her consciousness of oneness with other Jews. Just as most parents experience no reluctance in sharing their property with their children, because they perceive their children as part of themselves, so Chaya Sara chose to perceive all Jews, including those she never met, as part of herself. Giving something away —whether it was a cow constituting one-eighth of her assets or her only jewelry — was to her simply "a different hand holding."

Chaya Sara's willingness to relinquish her only jewelry testifies not only to her consciousness of oneness with other Jews, but also to her victory over vanity and pride.

As a woman I can admit: All women are born vain. Chaya Sara was, by all accounts, a beautiful woman, with blue eyes and a peaches-and-cream complexion. Certainly her personal appearance must have mattered to the young wife. For her wedding, she took the money her *chassan* had given her and bought a *sheitel*. Within the first week of their marriage, Yaakov Moshe, who did not approve of *sheitels*, disposed of it. According to one account, he threw it away. According to another account, he gave it to a poor *kallah* who came to their door. When his new bride asked him why, he replied, "I like you in a *tichel*, without a *sheitel*."

Did the young bride bristle at this test? How difficult was it for her to renounce her idea of looking pretty in deference to her husband's religious preferences?

All we know is that over the years, Chaya Sara routed out vanity by deliberately relinquishing pretty clothes and ornaments. The mature Chaya Sara was a woman who cared about modesty, cleanliness, and personal neatness, but not about the trimness of her figure or the beauty of her appearance.

Perhaps she was simply born without vanity, like an albino missing the gene for pigmentation? I know she wasn't, for even in her later years she retained one small trace, like a hint of color. Twice over the years, I asked to take her picture. I wanted to capture her ebullient smile, her glowing joy. In this, as in so much, she obliged me. But in both photos, despite my call to "Smile!" she closed her lips tightly to conceal her missing teeth. For the first 15 years I knew her, the only time I saw her without a smile was when I was taking her picture — the telltale trace of vanity that testifies to what had so studiously been extirpated.

Since human beings experience their possessions as part of their identity, we can assume that pride of possession was also a natural part of Chaya Sara's constitution. In this world, where status is accorded in direct proportion to economic level, who wants to bear the stigma of poverty?

Early on, Chaya Sara must have decided to tackle such pride. Most Jewish women count among their prized possessions their Shabbos candlesticks. Even women who cannot afford expensive silver candlesticks will purchase the prettiest candlesticks they can afford. Chaya Sara's Shabbos candlesticks consisted of tin cans filled with sand into which she lodged wax candles. On the entire moshav of poor farmers, she was the only woman who lit such humble Shabbos "candlesticks." Years later, a visitor from abroad brought her beautiful silver candlesticks. She refused to accept them.

The Kramers did not own a Chanukah menorah. They dug out shallow wells in raw potatoes, filled them with olive oil, and kindled them with cotton wicks.

Chaya Sara cared greatly about hygiene, but not at all about appearances. She would scrub the *insides* of her pots until they were immaculate, but she didn't bother shining the *outside* of her pots at all. Similarly, she would wash every cup five times, but she was heedless about cleaning windows and shutters. Such housecleaning she considered a futile exercise in impressing other people.

Other women disparaged Chaya Sara for what they considered her poor standard of homemaking. While the other families of Kfar Gidon had matching chairs to go around their dining tables, the Kramers, as one neighbor acerbically told me, "had not one chair that matched another." Many of her neighbors considered such paucity shameful. Chaya Sara relinquished her pride in a hundred such matters.

Many of us, when we adopt a stringent discipline — for example, in diet or spending habits — have a subtle sense that others should conform to our standard. Although the Kramers totally eschewed material comforts, they never expected others to share their standard. Once a wealthy couple from Belgium, whom R' Yaakov Moshe had invited to stay with them at Kfar Gidon, arrived at the Kramers' shack. Perceiving that the wife was horrified and uncomfortable with their humble conditions, Chaya Sara immediately called the young couple who had the nicest home in the moshav and asked if the Belgian guests could stay with them.

During their first five years in Kfar Gidon, R' Yaakov Moshe and Chaya Sara worked together on the farm. They would ride out to their fields in a donkey-drawn wagon. Chaya Sara was always at her husband's side.

Soon, however, Chaya Sara took over all the farm chores. She fed and milked the cows, cut hay with a scythe ("like a man" as one neighbor recollected), harvested vegetables, and even taught herself to connect sewer pipes. By 1952, the year R' Yaakov Moshe started his *hatzalah* enterprise [see Chapter 7], Chaya Sara was doing all the outdoor work.

"Whatever had to be done on the farm, she did," recalls Leah Landau, who moved to Kfar Gidon in 1952. "Why didn't Yaakov Moshe do any outdoor work? Perhaps she didn't let him, because of her *kavod* for him. She went out to the fields with a wagon and a donkey, with the children in the wagon. I used to see little Miriam all the time in the wagon while Chaya Sara worked the fields. Even though it was over 40 years ago, I remember it as though it were yesterday."

According to Leah Landau, Chaya Sara was the only woman in Kfar Gidon who did the outdoor work instead of her husband. Some neighbors complained to Chaya Sara that this was not proper, that her husband should help her, but she wouldn't let him.

What was R' Yaakov Moshe doing while his wife worked the farm? Mrs. Landau assumed, "He sat in the house and learned Torah." The neighbors did not know that R' Yaakov Moshe was spending his days knocking on doors in nearby development towns, trying to enroll Sephardi children in Torah institutions.

A vignette of his life during this period reveals the essence of the man: In those days in the Jezreel Valley, the most common conveyance was not an air-conditioned car, but a horse-drawn wagon. In the summer, during the hottest part of the day, as open wagons from various settlements made their sweltering way to Afula along the road through Kfar Gidon, R' Yaakov Moshe would run out to the road with a pitcher of cold water and give drinks to the travelers.

The *shemittah* year occurred again in 5719 [1958-59]. With all the farmers of Kfar Gidon and Moshav Kommemiut intending to abstain from agriculture, the problem of their financial survival loomed. Rav Binyamin Mendelsohn, the acknowledged father of *shemittah* observance in Israel, decided to establish *Keren HaSheviis*, a fund whereby *chareidim* who were not farmers could partake in the mitzvah of *shemittah* by financially supporting the farmers who strictly observed *shemittah*. In 1958, Rav Mendelsohn asked R' Yaakov Moshe Kramer to go to America to collect funds for *Keren HaSheviis*.

It was no small request. It entailed taking a long journey by boat and being absent from home for many months. By 1957, the Kramers had two "adopted" children, one of them mentally impaired. Chaya Sara would have to tend to the farm alone and take care of the children alone. Even if intercontinental telephone service had been available in those years, the Kramers did not own a telephone. Letters, like people, traveled slowly by boat.

For 34-year-old Chaya Sara, it meant relinquishing not only her husband's presence, assistance, and guidance, but something even more precious. By that time, they had been married 12 years without children. Over and over, they had consulted specialists in this area, but to no avail.

At the end of 10 years of marriage, as the Talmud suggests, R' Yaakov Moshe had offered Chaya Sara a *get* [divorce], so that she would be free to marry a man with whom she might have children. She categorically refused. As much as she yearned for children, her devotion to her husband was the paramount emotion in her heart. His leaving for America was a *de facto* admission of defeat in their heartrending struggle to have children.

Not having children was undoubtedly the hardest test of Chaya Sara's life. It challenged her on many levels. Although she had a lifelong fear of doctors and clinics as a result of her trauma with Dr. Mengele, during that first decade after the Holocaust she sought and endured whatever tests and treatments were then available to help her bear a child.

Anyone who has been unable to have children can testify what a test of faith it is. Other misfortunes, such as not getting married or undergoing financial losses, can be blamed on a multitude of circumstances, but the keys to children are exclusively in Hashem's hands. Chaya Sara unceasingly prayed to Hashem for children. She constantly repeated the prayer of the Biblical Channah.

Chaya Sara never got over the pain and disappointment of not bearing children. In her final years, this was the one ache in her heart that she spoke about to those closest to her. Yet, incredibly, she never allowed that pain to interfere with her love and gratitude to G-d for His abundant goodness.

To have the deepest desires of our hearts satisfied is a choice usually not in our hands. The choice we do have is whether or not to become embittered by our disappointments.

R' Yaakov Moshe and R' Yehudah Weiss from Kommemiut left in 1958. Their mission was to collect money for *shemittah* farmers from all segments of the American *chareidi* population. This included both Satmar and Agudat Yisrael, who were warring camps. The measure of their success is that both parties received them enthusiastically.

While R' Yehudah Weiss returned to Israel after several months, R' Yaakov Moshe stayed for a year and a half, probably to collect funds for his incipient *hatzalah* venture. He got a job in a kosher butcher shop. Only Chaya Sara's frantic telegram regarding their "adopted" daughter Miriam's abduction by her natural mother brought him hurtling home.

Although Chaya Sara had ceased her formal education at the age of 14, she became a woman well versed in Torah. Her conversation was always spiced with verses from Torah, *Tehillim* [Psalms], and *Mishlei* [Proverbs], as well as *aggados* [the story parts of the Talmud] and *mussar* [ethics] books. A child growing up in Migdal HaEmek, a development town in the northwest part of the valley, recalls coming home from school one day in the 1980's and finding the Kramers in her apartment. They had come to visit her ailing father. R' Yaakov Moshe was at her father's bedside, and Chaya Sara was discoursing to the women gathered in the living room on the meaning of the *Iggeres HaRamban*. "She could quote *pesukim* [Scriptural verses] from everywhere," one neighbor testified.

Where did Chaya Sara acquire her Torah education? Her husband taught her. Their relationship was not only that of a husband and wife, but also of a rebbe and disciple.

Notwitstanding, R' Yaakov Moshe had enormous respect for his wife and her opinions. He called her an *"ishah pikchis* — an astute woman." When people came to him for advice, he would ask them if they wanted Chaya Sara to sit in, because she was "very wise."

Years later, in England, R' Yaakov Moshe told Sheindy Leiber about Chaya Sara: "Her *davening* helps more than anyone's *davening*." When chassidic women in England went to him for advice and blessings, he would tell them: "Don't go to me. Go to my wife. She has the power."

R' Yaakov Moshe had such high esteem for his wife's prayers that, when a woman in London was having trouble in childbirth, he phoned his wife in what was the middle of the night in Israel, often waking her up, because, as he told his hosts, "Her *davening* is the most powerful."

To Shimon Dankovich, R' Yaakov Moshe disclosed that the Satmar Rebbe, Rav Yoelish, had told him that Chaya Sara was one of the "*nashim tzidkanios* [righteous women] of the generation."

R' Yaakov Moshe's regard for his wife translated into very practical terms. If he saw her standing, he would bring her a chair. And he always asked her softly, "What can I bring you? How can I help you?"

A salient aspect of the Kramers' first decade in Kfar Gidon was the arrival of Yaakov Moshe's relatives. In all, six of Shmuel Zanvill and Chaya Kramer's 14 children survived the Holocaust. Avraham Mendel, the oldest, had emigrated to America decades before the war. Peretz, born in 1906, had married and was living with his wife Yehudis on the family homestead when he was drafted into a labor battalion. After the war, he located Yehudis in Bergen Belsen. The couple, who never had any children, made their way to the shores of Palestine in 1946 and joined Yaakov Moshe in Kfar Gidon. Staunchly Torah observant, Peretz and Yehudis felt so at home in Kfar Gidon that they purchased a farm there.

Chaim, three years Yaakov Moshe's senior, had a wife and three children before the war. They were all murdered in Auschwitz. Chaim married again and subsequently had three daughters. In 1951, Chaim, his second wife Hanna Leah, and Pnina, the first of their children, migrated from Romania to Israel. The nascent state was in the throes of absorbing an immigrant population equal to the entire population of the country. Most newcomers were consigned to tent camps, where they lived under the most primitive conditions. To save Chaim and his family from such a fate, Yaakov Moshe brought them directly from the port to Kfar Gidon.

Shlomo, Yaakov Moshe's younger brother, was also married with three children before the Holocaust. His wife and children were likewise murdered in Auschwitz. Shlomo married Margalit in 1947, and they eventually had three children. Shlomo and Margalit arrived in Israel late in 1951 on a ship with 3,000 other refugees. Yaakov Moshe and Peretz had come to meet the boat, searching for family members who had survived. Shlomo spotted Peretz. The two older brothers brought Shlomo and his family home to Kfar Gidon.

Yosef Efraim, the youngest Kramer brother, immigrated to Israel much later, in 1958. He chose not to come to Kfar Gidon, but moved directly to Lod, then to Netanya. He did not figure in the family saga that unfolded in the Jezreel Valley.

Although better than a tent camp, Kfar Gidon in those days had little to offer the new immigrants. Chaim's family and Shlomo's family each lived in a quarter of a barn, separated by a cloth partition from the other half of the barn, which was occupied by the barn owner's family.

Why did R' Yaakov Moshe not invite his brothers to share his own tiny shack? Unbelievably, he and Chaya Sara were already sharing their puny premises with other relatives. R' Yaakov Moshe's first cousin had come to Israel in early 1951 and was living with his wife and two children in Kfar Ata. R' Yaakov Moshe found them there, brought them back to Kfar Gidon, and gave them half of his tiny home. He relinquished to them one of the two rooms and hung a sheet as a divider in the hallway and makeshift kitchen.

When I first heard this story, I asked, "How long did the Kramers endure such crowded conditions?" I would have been impressed with any answer over two weeks, and expected the narrator to say, "A couple of months." Instead, he thought for a minute and replied, "Well, the relatives had

R' Yaakov Moshe (left), Chaya Sara (right), and the family that stayed with them for two years

two children while they were living with the Kramers."

I was skeptical and decided not to use the story. Months later, while interviewing a relative of R' Yaakov Moshe who lived in New York, I asked her when she had become acquainted with Chaya Sara. She replied that in 1951, when she was a child, her family had moved into the Kramers' house, dividing the house down the middle. How long did they live that way? For over two years, as both her brother and her sister were born in the Kramers' house. She went on to mention that she never once saw Chaya Sara angry. "She laughed a lot," was her predominant recollection.

Living in such close quarters with her husband's relatives must have been a test for Chaya Sara. Not only did she have to relinquish what little physical comfort she had, but she had to forfeit her privacy as well. An even harder test must have been to watch the cousin's wife give birth to child after child while she herself remained barren.

Ironically, as our houses have grown bigger, our willingness to share our living space has diminished. We are tested at every stage: whether to invite guests to stay with us; how long to let them stay; how to respond to incompatible personalities; how graciously to put up with their foibles; etc. The image of Chaya Sara squeezing down the hallway on her side of the white sheet, hearing the cries of a newborn baby and laughing, is a powerful expander to the lack of space in our hearts.

As much as Yaakov Moshe's brothers must have suffered from the physical conditions in Kfar Gidon, they suffered more from their own religious turmoil. In the wake of the Holocaust, both Chaim and Shlomo had lost their faith. The devout brothers whom Yaakov Moshe had known in Transylvania were not the same men who alighted from the ships in Haifa.

The murder of their beloved children had plunged both Chaim and Shlomo into lifelong mourning, but they responded in diametrically opposite ways. Chaim, for the rest of his long life, arose every morning and stood before the photographs of his dead children. He never stopped speaking about them. Shlomo, by contrast, never spoke of his loss. So total was his wall of silence that when his second set of children became adults they were surprised to learn for the first time that their father had had previous offspring.

Almost six decades after the Holocaust, while being interviewed for this book, the taciturn Shlomo declared: "Movies and documentaries don't begin to describe the horror of Auschwitz. The Germans threw children alive into the fire. They said to us, 'Where is your G-d now?'"

This was a question Shlomo couldn't answer. Is it possible that he was describing the murder of his own children?

After the unspeakable horrors he witnessed, Shlomo, unable to bear his loss, left Auschwitz stripped of his piety as surely as others were stripped of their valuables and eyeglasses.

As for Chaim, his wife Channa Leah, who had come from a more modern Orthodox background, anchored him to a minimal level of religious observance. While still in Communist Romania, Channa Leah had made a vow: If her family made it to Israel safely, she would keep a kosher kitchen and cover her hair. This was all they observed when they came to Kfar Gidon.

Six months after their arrival, Shlomo and Margalit, feeling out of place on the religious moshav, moved to the town of Afula. Shlomo came to Kfar Gidon to visit his brothers virtually every weekday for the next 50 years. He and Peretz would sit around Yaakov Moshe's kitchen table at night and talk.

Chaim decided to buy a farm on Kfar Gidon, but he had not even one *grush* to put down for a deposit. The operating committee of the moshav decided that since he was Yaakov Moshe's brother, they would dispense with the deposit and sell him the farm for monthly payments. Chaim stayed in Kfar Gidon for four years. Then what his daughter Pnina would call "the religious wars" of the mid-50's put him into an untenable position. On the one hand, he disagreed with the *chareidim*. On the other hand, he would not say a word against their leader, his beloved brother Yaakov Moshe. Therefore, he sold his farm and moved to Sdei Ilan, a Mizrachi moshav near Tiberias. Every week Chaim and his family traveled to Kfar Gidon to visit.

Relating to nonobservant family members is a challenge that faces many religious Jews. Responses often fall into two categories: the disapproving, distancing approach and the "I'll convert you to the truth" approach. Yaakov Moshe was a paragon of a third approach: "I'll love you so much that you'll want to be close to me, and somehow, gradually, my love of G-d and Torah will rub off on you."

Yaakov Moshe never directly chastised his brothers nor discussed theological issues with them. Instead, he treated his errant brothers and their families with such affection and warmth that they were drawn to him as bees are drawn to the flower's nectar. And, just as bees engaged in drinking nectar inadvertently brush against the stamen's pollen and pollinate the flowers, so his brothers, unintentionally, subconsciously, picked up Yaakov Moshe's devotion to Hashem and His Torah. Shlomo eventually returned to full observance; Chaim made some movement toward observance, but while the post-Holocaust Chaim could not give his heart to Hashem, he did encourage his daughter. When his oldest daughter Pnina chose a very frum lifestyle and married a chassid, Chaim supported her choice.

Pnina Kramer lived in Kfar Gidon from the age of 4 to 8 (1951-55). She gives us a child's view of R' Yaakov Moshe during that early period. "My uncle was warm and loving. He spoke so tenderly to everyone. He called me, in Yiddish, 'Chaya Perela.' He often called family members by their Yiddish names; it was more endearing. He taught me to make *berachos*. I followed him everywhere."

Pnina recalls that R' Yaakov Moshe never directly corrected her or anyone else. If someone had done something wrong, he would tell a story or parable. "Those who wanted would understand the point."

Although Pnina and her sisters called their other aunts and uncles, "Aunt Yehudis," "Uncle Shlomo," etc., Yaakov Moshe and Chaya Sara insisted on being called by their names without any title. Their humility could not tolerate even the minor honorific of "Uncle" and "Aunt."

When Chaim's family made their weekly visits to Kfar Gidon, they never left Yaakov Moshe's house empty-handed. He always had something to give them, such as matzah at Pesach time.

By the time Pnina was 12 years old, she decided she wanted to be *chareidi* like her aunt and uncle. Yaakov Moshe was making his first trip to America. He asked his "Chaya Perela" what she wanted him to bring for her. She replied, "Dark-gray stockings." Two years later, when Pnina was ready to enter high school, she asked to go to Bais Yaakov [the *chareidi* school system for girls]. Yaakov Moshe and Peretz's wife Yehudis arranged for her to enter Bais Yaakov in Bnei Brak.

At the age of 16½, Pnina felt ready for a *shidduch*. Yaakov Moshe heard about a Chassidic *bachur*, Dovid Kubitchek, who he felt would be perfect for her. They met for the first time in Shlomo's apartment in Afula, with all the uncles and aunts in attendance. When she was 17, Pnina and Dovid married.

"I am where I am religiously only in Yankel Moshe's merit," declares Pnina, the true fruit of the bee's attraction to the sweetness of the nectar.

R' Dovid Kubitchek, R' Yaakov Moshe and R' Shlomo Klein at Pnina's wedding, 1964

How did Chaya Sara relate to her husband's large and ubiquitous family? Having no living relatives of her own, she could have felt jealous or infringed upon by them. Or, given the tremendous honor she accorded her holy husband, she could have been embarrassed by his less-observant relatives.

Pnina testified that Chaya Sara was always welcoming and friendly to Yaakov Moshe's family. She had a good relationship with Pnina's mother, and never disapproved of less-observant relatives. Even when Yaakov Moshe did not attend the mixed weddings, because of the proscription against men watching women dance, Chaya Sara, who was not bound by any such proscription, did attend. As out of place as she must have felt — and was! — she insisted on affirming her bond with her husband's family.

Yehudis, Peretz's wife, died in 1961. From that time until Yaakov Moshe and Chaya Sara left Kfar Gidon in 1989, a period of 28 years, Chaya Sara shopped for Peretz, did his laundry, had him as a guest every Shabbos and holiday, and looked after his other domestic needs.

Some altruistic people treat strangers like family, and family like strangers. Yaakov Moshe and Chaya Sara treated strangers like family and fami ly like their own bodies. What else could we expect from souls who never noticed the distinction between themselves and other Jews?

CHAPTER SIX

The Train to Greatness: Avramele and Miriam

O NE MORNING IN 1950, 26-YEAR-OLD CHAYA Sara, following her usual routine, rose early in the morning and milked the cows. She had no idea that that day would prove to be the most momentous day of her life.

Late in the morning, a neighbor approached, pulling a red-headed 2½-year-old boy behind her. She asked Chaya Sara to do her a favor. She was taking care of this mentally handi-capped child, the son of her cousin, who had divorced his wife shortly after their brain-damaged baby was born. Now she had to do an errand in town, and couldn't take the child with her, because he was too unruly. He was so unruly, she told Chaya Sara, that she often had to tie him to the bed. Would Chaya Sara watch the boy for the afternoon?

Chaya Sara gladly agreed to care for the child, whose name was Avramele. When the neighbor returned several hours later, she found Avramele clinging to Chaya Sara's skirt, crying, and refusing to leave her. The neighbor, tantalized by the prospect of ridding herself of this unwanted burden, gazed at Chaya Sara and remarked: "Living with you would be *Gan Eden* for him."

Chaya Sara looked at the frightened, clinging child, then looked back again at the neighbor who had been tying him to the bed. She made her decision. She agreed to take the child.

She would care for him, day in and day out, for the next 55 years, until her death. It was the most significant decision of her life.

Looking back on the life of Rebbetzin Chaya Sara Kramer, it seems like she made many choices that were even more difficult. She undertook the care of many children who were much more debilitated than Avramele, children who were both physically and mentally handicapped, who needed to be spoon-fed and lifted from bed to chair, incontinent adult "children," even violent children who sometimes attacked her physically.

Compared to the children who would come later, Avramele was easy. While mentally impaired, he was physically healthy. He even helped Chaya Sara. He often took out the garbage and would hang laundry on the line. He would go on the bus with Chaya Sara to do the grocery shopping in Afula, and would help her carry home the heavy baskets of food and produce. Avramele grew up to be a placid, unobtrusive personality, who would stand off to the side and observe, rocking from side to side, occasionally muttering short sentences, his long red peyos swaying.

If, however, we watch the film of her life starting not from whom she subsequently became, but rather in its proper sequence, the 26-year-old housewife, farmer, and Holocaust survivor who stood facing her neighbor could easily have chosen to say, "I'm sorry, but no." After all, she had been married barely four years. She still intended — and certainly hoped — to give birth to her own children. She had no idea how this mentally defective toddler would develop and what impact his constant presence would exert on the family she hoped to raise.

Had she asked for a few hours to consider her decision, had she calculated the pros and cons, Chaya Sara could have come up with several compelling reasons to decline to take Avramele:

- ✺ *Raising a retarded child is an onerous job with little emotional fulfillment. The satisfaction of watching a child advance from milestone to milestone and eventually to marriage would never accrue from this child. This was precisely the reason his own parents had given him away. Why volunteer to undertake such a thankless task she had not been assigned?*
- ✺ *Financially, she and her husband could not afford the extra expense this child would entail. With the losses incurred by the disasters to their livestock chronicled in the previous chapter, the Kramers barely had enough money to feed themselves. Contrary to what some neighbors whispered, Avramele's father, who lived in Meah Shearim and rarely made contact with his son, never contributed any money toward his upkeep.*
- ✺ *Raising a normal child requires approximately 20 years' investment of energy and resources until he can stand on his own. A child like Avramele would never achieve independence. Saying "yes" was a lifetime commitment that would never be discharged. In fact, even on the last day of her life, Rebbetzin Chaya Sara had to admonish the 57-year-old Avramele to behave nicely and not be "chutzpadik." Unlike today, when schools for special needs children care for them for a*

good portion of the day, in 1950 there was no facility nor support system to share Chaya Sara's 24-hour-a-day job. Taking responsibility for Avramele would never allow for vacations, days off, nor retirement.

If the young Chaya Sara did make any such calculations, she did it instantly, and immediately made her decision: She welcomed Avramele. Decades later, she explained to me why: "He needed someone who could be like a mother to him, without any sense of estrangement." Notice that her reasoning had only to do with his needs, not her own.

This was the fundamental choice she made on that day in 1950: to put the needs of another — a complete stranger — above her own needs. All of the subsequent choices she made in her life were simply variations — albeit more complex — on this theme.

Chaya Sara the wonder-worker was born in Rapide in 1924, but Chaya Sara the tzaddekes was born in Kfar Gidon in 1950, on the day she chose to adopt a frightened retarded child who needed a mother.

When we think of making choices, we envision a fork in the road. The traveler on life's journey can choose to walk east or west. If he later changes his mind, he can simply turn around and backtrack, or even cut a path between one road and the other. In reality, our life's journey proceeds not along a road, but along a railroad track. Once a person has boarded the train going west, it will inexorably take him in that direction. That is what Pirkei Avos means when it asserts: "One mitzvah leads to another; one sin leads to another." Once a person is on a train, turning around or changing directions is difficult — and unlikely.

When the young Chaya Sara Kramer chose to adopt a mentally deficient 2½-year-old, she boarded a train called "Selfless Giving." That train took her up a steep mountain toward spiritual greatness. We can only won-

der whether she would ever have been handed the greater challenges she later faced had she not chosen selfless giving that day in 1950.

Most of us, as we stand on the train platform of choice, choose to board the train that looks sleekest and most comfortable, without even bothering to check on its destination. Chaya Sara chose to board a dilapidated train that promised a bumpy, sooty ride; its destination was spiritual greatness. She was, in fact, not self-conscious enough to notice the train's destination. She boarded only because she heard the cries of a little child issuing from within.

The polarity between giving and taking is the essential choice that confronts all of us, many times a day. Hashem's fundamental attribute is that He is a Giver. We emulate Hashem whenever we choose to give without thinking, "What's in it for me?"

We don't have to undertake a 24/7 commitment that goes on for the rest of our lives, but we could choose to be givers by: contributing more to charity than we can easily afford; giving our time to listen to and empathize with people with whom we don't naturally resonate; volunteering for a good cause; helping our child/spouse/ friend even when it feels like a one-way street; and not making our continued giving contingent on receiving acknowledgment and gratitude. Any of the above choices means boarding the train heading toward higher and higher levels of selfless giving.

While physically normal, Avramele was severely mentally impaired. Tested as a teenager, he was found to have the intelligence of a 3 or 4-year-old. Despite attending the first grade of R' Yaakov Moshe's *cheder* year after year after year, he never learned the *alef-beis*. One neighbor recalls watching R' Yaakov Moshe trying to explain something to Avramele. R' Yaakov Moshe patiently repeated the point perhaps a hundred times. Still, Avramele didn't get it.

And, as the neighbor had testified, the child was unruly. He would roll in the mud and tear his clothes. Once, when Avramele was in his teens, Chaya Sara ordered the services of a *shochet* to slaughter some chickens. Avramele stood by and watched. Later that day, trying to imitate the *shochet*, Avramele killed 18 chickens. Yaakov Moshe cautioned the abashed Chaya Sara not to reprimand Avramele because he was incapable of understanding. A full week later she had recovered from the loss enough to say to him nicely, "We don't do things like that."

Yet, as the neighbor had also predicted, living with the Kramers was *Gan Eden* (Paradise) for Avramele. Neither of his adopted parents ever raised a hand or voice to him, no matter how uncooperative his behavior. Yossi Shtiglitz remembers once coming upon R' Yaakov Moshe in a field as he tried — unsuccessfully — to convince Avramele to come home. Avramele was 10 years old and decidedly overweight. Finally R' Yaakov Moshe fetched their donkey with the wagon and gently lifted the heavy child and set him into the wagon.

Miriam, the only child they ever raised who was neither physically nor mentally challenged, used to complain that Chaya Sara would discipline her but not Avramele. Chaya Sara would reply, "There's no one there to discipline."

Many of the neighbors, rather than admiring the Kramers for their 24-hour-a-day *chesed*, criticized them for keeping the unkempt, difficult boy. Members of Telmei Gidon sometimes upbraided Chaya Sara saying: "Why do you keep that dirty, dim-witted kid? He's an embarrassment to the moshav."

Chaya Sara, who had learned to control her temper, reserved her rare bouts of indignation for those who abused Avramele. Once the boy happily brought home a piece of cake a neighbor had given him. Chaya Sara looked at the cake and saw that it was all moldy. Chaya Sara was irate that someone could so heartlessly take advantage of a helpless child.

Yet Avramele was not totally untrainable. When he was fully grown, he would still play with the little children of the moshav. This was a potentially explosive situation, because the children often teased Avramele, and if he had hit them, he could have seriously harmed them. The Kramers, however, taught Avramele never to hit. And he never did.

In fact, he once saved a person's life. In the 1980's, a bus stopped at Kfar Gidon and Avramele and several other passengers descended. Only Avramele noticed one of the passengers, a deranged man, lie down in front of the bus's wheels. Even his limited intelligence understood what had to be done. He yelled to the driver, "Don't go! Don't go! There's somebody under the wheels!" and thus saved the man's life.

Like so much in the Kramers' life, Avramele was not what he appeared. Once R' Yaakov Moshe gave the Belzer Rebbe a *kvittel* with Avramele's name on it. The Rebbe, who did not know the boy at all, told R' Yaakov Moshe: "Be very careful with this child. He's a holy child. Don't ever hurt him."

Indeed, as Avramele grew up, both Kramers showed him an inordinate amount of respect. Sometimes, when people would come to R' Yaakov Moshe for a blessing, he would send them to Avramele.

During the 1980's, Zalman, a man in a religious community abroad, went missing. Every day one of his worried friends phoned R' Yaakov Moshe to ask for a blessing for

Avramele and Avigdor Galandauer in Kfar Gidon

Zalman's safe return. One day, when Zalman had been missing for about seven weeks, R' Yaakov Moshe told his friend that he could stop worrying. Avramele had had a dream and had announced, "Zalman is coming home tomorrow." The next day, Zalman returned.

Once, a visitor to the Kramers' home noticed Avramele *davening* in a corner. Having heard that Avramele was "crazy," the visitor was surprised to see him davening with fervor and exalted intensity. Suddenly Avramele became aware that he was being watched. Immediately, he reverted to his usual simple-witted behavior.

In 1980, a young couple named Eliezer and Naomi Gevirtz moved to Kfar Gidon. They were highly committed Chabad Chassidim. Eliezer befriended Avramele, who decided that he also wanted to be Chabad. Although R' Yaakov Moshe was a staunch Satmar chassid, and Satmar and Chabad were involved in an ongoing feud, R' Yaakov Moshe never uttered a word against Chabad and accepted with good grace that his only "son" had chosen to align himself with the rival group.

Years later I was taking a Chabad friend of mine to get a blessing from Rebbetzin Chaya Sara. My friend was worried that when this Satmar-affiliated rebbetzin would find out that she

Kfar Gidon; Avramele is in the center

was Chabad, she would balk at conferring her blessing. I had never seen Rebbetzin Chaya Sara hold back her blessing from anyone, but I was clueless as to the scope and depth of the Satmar-Chabad feud. When we got there, Rebbetzin Chaya Sara received my friend lovingly. Upon hearing that she was Chabad, the Rebbetzin laughed and remarked proudly, "Avramele is also Chabad."

When Rebbetzin Chaya Sara was in her 70's, I interviewed her for this book. (She had given me permission to write it during her lifetime as long as I didn't use her real name.) Since I had learned that every soul comes to this world to effect a particular *tikkun*, I was trying to ferret out what Rebbetzin Chaya Sara's own *tikkun* was. Despite my searching questions, I kept hitting a brick wall. Finally, frustrated, I asked her, "So why did you come to earth in this lifetime?"

She gave me a clear-as-the-nose-on-your-face look, and answered matter-of-factly, "Why, to take care of Avramele."

"To take care of Avramele?" I asked, thunderstruck. This great soul, this spiritual master, had come into this world just to take care of a brain-damaged boy?

"Yes," she answered simply. "He's a *tzaddik*."

I had heard chassidic stories about *tzaddikim* coming back to this world as persons who are exempt from *mitzvos*, so that they could fix the one small mistake they had made in their previous *gilgul* without accruing any new sins. Hearing Rebbetzin Chaya Sara assert that Avramele is a *tzaddik*, I stammered, "Y-you mean he was a *tzaddik* in his last *gilgul*?"

"Yes," she answered. "And in this *gilgul*, too."

I wasn't going to let her get away with this. The 52-year-old Avramele, who usually greeted me with a smile, rocking from side to side repeating, "Rigler, Rigler," had that day locked himself into the kitchen because he was afraid of the unknown woman I had brought with me. I pressed on: "In what way is Avramele a *tzaddik* in this *gilgul*?"

"He does only good and never does bad," she answered with a shrug. She couldn't understand why I was having such a hard time grasping this.

"What good does he do?" I insisted. I had never seen him do anything at all.

"He says '*shalom*' to people. That's an act of *chesed*."

"What else?" I challenged.

"Avramele does not like to touch or be touched," she explained. "But once when I fell, he put out his hand and helped me up."

I left her apartment in a state of total cognitive dissonance. How could it be that Rebbetzin Chaya Sara Kramer came into this world only to take care of this mentally impaired person, who is a *tzaddik* because he once reached out his hand and helped her up? I kept turning the idea over and over in my mind, but could not solve the enigma of Avramele and his part in Rebbetzin Chaya Sara's life.

What is certain is that she loved him very much. In 1984, Chaya Sara underwent an emergency hernia operation in Jerusalem's Hadassah Hospital. After her release, Yaakov Moshe took her for recuperation to the nearby apartment of their niece Pnina Kubitchek. Pnina remembers Chaya Sara

Avramele and Reb. Chaya Sara with a young visitor — 2000

lying in bed crying, "Avramele! Avramele! He's a *yasom chai* [an orphan whose father is still living]!" Despite her infirmity, she wanted to immediately return to Kfar Gidon in order to take care of the 36-year-old Avramele, who had been left in the custody of Yaakov Moshe's brother Peretz.

Indeed, even at the end of her life, when she was ill and needed total care, she continued to place Avramele's needs above her own. I asked her why she didn't go live in Bnei Brak with her adopted daughter Miriam, instead of being taken care of by strangers. After all, Miriam was clamoring to take care of the Rebbetzin. Rebbetzin Chaya Sara replied simply, "Avramele doesn't want to go to Miriam's." And that was that.

Avramele, 1999

Close to the end of her life, when Avramele had taken to locking himself in the kitchen most of the time, rendering it impossible for any of the Rebbetzin's caregivers to cook for her, she finally revealed an insight into the part he played in her life. She said to me, "Avramele helps me."

"How does he help you?" I challenged.

"He helps me because I love him," she replied. "A person cannot live without loving."

If Avramele arrived in Chaya Sara's life as a test, Miriam arrived as a reward.

One day in late 1951, a taxi pulled up to the Kramers' shack. A dark-complexioned young woman holding a 9-month-old baby girl emerged from the cab. She told Chaya

Sara her name and the child's name, and offered the baby to Chaya Sara.

By that time, Chaya Sara had been married for five years. All her prayers and all her medical attempts to have children had so far proven fruitless. With soaring heart, she took the baby from the woman's hands, and thanked *HaKadosh Baruch Hu* for this gift from Heaven. The woman got back into the taxi and drove away — without even leaving a telephone number.

The young woman, whom I will call by the pseudonym Batsheva Levi, had recently made *aliyah* from Afghanistan with her entire extended family — parents, siblings, husband, 2-year-old son, and this baby, born en route. Batsheva was feeling overwhelmed by having to adjust to living in the fledgling State of Israel, with its tent camps and new language. Then she discovered that she was expecting again. When she heard about a righteous couple living in the Jezreel Valley, she decided to entrust them with her daughter. She was sure she would have many more babies in the future. She was right. She subsequently gave birth to 13 more children.

Miriam grew up as the Kramers' daughter, with no inkling that she was not their biological offspring. Her first language was Yiddish. She called Chaya Sara "Mommy," and Yaakov Moshe "Tatty." The Kramers, however, did not bother to go through any formal, legal process of adoption. This omission would later come back to haunt them.

Miriam's reminiscences provide a rare glimpse into the intimate home life of two *tzaddikim*. Looking back as an adult, Miriam characterized their home as redolent with "tranquility, tolerance for all, holiness, purity of speech, modesty, fairness, unconditional love, and the desire to make others feel good and loved."

She reports that she never saw her parents argue. She did see them disagree, always about the same issue: Mommy

Left to right: Avramele, Miriam, Chaya Sara

would worry that Tatty was overexerting himself and would bid him to rest, but he refused. When R' Yaakov Moshe was sick, he would try to hide it from his wife, lest she insist that he stay in bed. One time, for example, R' Yaakov Moshe, burning with fever, fell on his way to the bathroom. When Chaya Sara ran to help him, he gave the excuse, "I merely bumped into something." His astute wife checked and discovered that he had a high fever. She raised her hands to heaven and cried, "Master of the worlds, help me!" After putting her husband to bed, she ran to a neighbor to telephone a doctor.

R' Yaakov Moshe's trademark kiss on the shoulders was also the result of his wife's concern about his health. He used to kiss men on the cheeks, but Chaya Sara protested, "How can you kiss everybody like that? Some people are ill, and you could catch it." To please her, he began kissing the less-contagious shoulder area.

After they installed a telephone, R' Yaakov Moshe would

receive calls from abroad throughout the night. Chaya Sara appealed to him to disconnect the phone at night so he could sleep undisturbed. He refused, pointing out, "*HaKadosh Baruch Hu* doesn't disconnect Himself from us at night."

In this as in everything, Miriam reports, Chaya Sara accepted her husband's word as final. She accepted his word not as a loyal citizen accepts the edict of the government, but as cotton cloth accepts dye. Over the years Miriam witnessed Chaya Sara changing, absorbing Yaakov Moshe's way of interacting with people. During the last years of Chaya Sara's life, her caregiver told me, the Rebbetzin, despite her infirmity, took phone calls throughout the night. "The Rebbetzin said," quoted the caregiver, "'*HaKadosh Baruch Hu* doesn't disconnect Himself at night. How can we?'"

Miriam testifies that Chaya Sara never once answered her husband back. "He would say what he would say, and she would laugh, and that would be the end of the discussion. If she said she wanted curtains or tiles like in every other home, he would reply, 'What do we need these things for?' And she accepted his decision without question."

Once little Miriam said to her mommy, "Tatty doesn't want these things, but women want them, so why not get them?" Her mommy, however, always accepted Tatty's word as final. "She accepted everything with *simchah*," recollects Miriam.

The Jewish ideal of marriage is that the primary role of the husband is to be the mashpia, the one who bestows; the wife's primary role is that of the mekabel, the one who receives. Receiving is a difficult challenge for many women, especially strong women such as Chaya Sara. For a vessel to receive, it must be empty.

Chaya Sara had a strong personality, and entertained definite ideas and opinions. Leah Landau testified: "She *learned from him and obeyed him. But in many ways, she wasn't like him."*

In Chapter 3, we discussed their essential polarity as chesed versus gevurah, unrestrained giving versus setting boundaries. Kfar Gidon resident Naomi Gevirtz explained: "We could say R' Yaakov Moshe was absolute chesed. He was like Avraham Avinu — giving to everyone. But Chaya Sara was like Sara Imeinu. She had unbelievable gevurah, strength. She knew how to establish boundaries to giving in order to protect her husband. He appreciated Chaya Sara's role as a housewife, and said she had a discerning eye. She distinguished between the good and the not good."

Their disparity was epitomized in a nightly ritual: When their home became infested with mice, Chaya Sara would put down mousetraps every night. After she went to bed, R' Yaakov Moshe would remove them.

Although she perceived the world from a virtually opposite perspective than her husband, she received from him, learned from him, and obeyed him. By her own admission, the only time she ever disobeyed her husband was when she sold the sick cow. That was a test she failed. The Talmud declares: "A tzaddik falls seven times and gets up." A remorseful Chaya Sara moved on and made herself into a wife of whom one neighbor testified: "His words were kadosh kedoshim [holy of holies] to her." This was a choice she made.

Yaakov Moshe used to affirm: "A man who hits another is wicked, but a man who hits his wife is crazy. Because his wife is *himself*. A person who beats himself is crazy."

Miriam recalls how thoroughly Yaakov Moshe lived up to his own dictum. "The *tzaddik*," she testifies, "respected his wife like his own body." When Chaya Sara would get up from her afternoon nap, Yaakov Moshe would run to bring her her slippers. "Everything he saw that she needed, he ran and got."

Although Chaya Sara did most of the housework and cooking, R' Yaakov Moshe frequently helped. He swept the floors, made the beds, and assisted in the Pesach cleaning. Chaya Sara was very concerned about cleanliness, but cared little about neatness. Thus, she did the cleaning while he did the straightening up. As soon as he left for shul in the predawn hours, Chaya Sara would wash the floor. When an occasional crisis with the handicapped children kept her from cooking, Yaakov Moshe would prepare the meals. "And his cooking was so delicious," Chaya Sara herself testified, "that everyone would lick their plates!"

R' Yaakov Moshe taught his daughter Miriam: "When we daven *Shemoneh Esrei*, as we pray, '*Oseh Shalom*,' we take three steps backward. The meaning of this is that if a person wants to live in *shalom*, peace, he must take three steps backward, that is, he must compromise, he must give the other person the feeling of satisfaction."

Miriam had ample opportunity to put this teaching into practice. Whenever she and Avramele, three years her senior, quarreled, Chaya Sara told her that, since Avramele was less intelligent, she must be the one to give in. Her parents taught her that giving in was not an act of capitulation, but rather an act of transcendence.

In terms of service to himself, R' Yaakov Moshe was a man with no expectations. Miriam never saw him get annoyed if dinner wasn't ready or if Mommy made something that he didn't like. Once he returned home tired and hungry from a long trip to Jerusalem and found that his wife had not cooked dinner. "It doesn't matter, *mein tyre kind* [my dear daughter]," he assured Chaya Sara. "Whatever there is in the house, just serve it." She was a simple cook, but whatever she prepared satisfied him. His older brother Peretz told Miriam that even as a child Yaakov Moshe would never ask his mother, "What's for dinner?" He was content with whatever was on his plate.

In terms of service to *HaKadosh Baruch Hu*, by contrast, R' Yaakov Moshe had definite expectations. And because he regarded his wife "like his own body," the standard he applied to himself he applied to her as well. Whenever the young Chaya Sara bought herself a new dress, she would come home and try it on for her husband, asking, "How does it look, Yankel Moshe?" She meant aesthetically, but Yaakov Moshe looked only at how much the dress conformed to the Torah's standard of *tzenius* [modesty]. Was it long enough? Till where did the sleeves reach? Was the color unobtrusive? Was the material tightly woven so that one couldn't see through it? Was it at all tight? Was there, heaven forbid, any semblance of a cross in the printed design? If Chaya Sara had missed something, Yaakov Moshe would ask her to exchange the dress [Israeli stores do not generally give refunds] and pay extra money to the salesperson for the inconvenience.

While a less self-confident woman might have been miffed or hurt by her husband's rejection of her selected dress, Miriam relates that Chaya Sara always reacted with good-humored acceptance. Miriam remembers one time, for example, when Chaya Sara bought a dress in Afula. When she tried it on for him, R' Yaakov Moshe gently told her, "Chaya Sarala, it's a little small on you; it's not so modest."

Chaya Sara laughed and asked, "*Nu*? So, what should I do with it now?" When her husband instructed her to take it back, she did so without fussing. She had wanted to wear a pretty dress only to please him; if it pleased him more for her to return it, it made no difference to her.

Both of the Kramers were exceedingly stringent about *tzenius*. Yet, when it came to his beloved wife, R' Yaakov Moshe sometimes made leniencies. Since Chaya Sara always suffered from problems with her feet (no doubt exacerbated by the Jezreel Valley's steaming hot weather), R' Yaakov Moshe permitted her to go without stockings in the house, as long as her dress reached her ankles and she wore shoes. Although R' Yaakov Moshe himself held by only one *hechsher* [*kashrus* certification], that of *Badatz Eidah Chareidis*, if Chaya Sara liked some foods that were available only with a different good *hechsher* (such as Chug Chasam Sofer), he had no problem with her buying those foods.

Miriam loved her mother, but she idolized her father. His gentle, soothing manner made the little girl want to emulate him in everything. She needed no persuading or reminding to fulfill religious obligations, such as washing hands for *netilas*

R' Yaakov Moshe, Miriam, Chaya Sara, 1957

yada'im, saying blessings, or *davening.* Whatever Tatty did, that's what she wanted to do.

For example, Miriam loved to eat bread with margarine. Chaya Sara always bought margarine with a *Badatz hechsher,* but one day the store was out of their regular brand. Chaya Sara decided that since little Miriam loved margarine so much and she was, after all, only 5 years old, it would be okay to feed her margarine with a different *hechsher.* When she got home, Chaya Sara put bread spread with that margarine on the table and called Miriam to come and eat lunch. Miriam washed for bread, sat down, and took a bite. "I was a girl who always liked to look at *hechsherim,*" she recalls. Examining the package of margarine, the 5-year-old noticed that it did not have the *Badatz hechsher.* Horrified, she cried, "I'm not going to eat it!"

The endemic hand-wringing among religious parents desperate for ways to convince/cajole/compel their reluctant children to fulfill religious obligations could learn much from Yaakov Moshe's child-rearing technique. His unwavering love, gentleness, and encouragement were an adhesive that bonded his daughter to him so thoroughly that she replicated his every movement, like a label glued to wind chimes. For example, even inside the house, little Miriam would not go without stockings. "I *wanted* to follow his *chumrahs* [stringencies]," she explains.

As an adult, Miriam recalls essential advice she received from R' Yaakov Moshe: "He would tell me, 'Dear daughter, before everything you do, stop and think whether you're bringing *nachas* to Hashem by your actions. In this way you'll be able to save yourself from sinning.'"

As for how to relate to secular Jews, R' Yaakov Moshe told Miriam, "Secular Jews are people who have distanced themselves from Hashem, and we have to bring them closer."

Her parents also instructed her in how to deal with non-Jews, such as the local Arabs: "They said we must relate to them cordially, and not cause them to hate us. And they cautioned me to be careful." If the Kramers saw needy Arabs, they would give them bread and vegetables.

Miriam was still a young child when she realized that people were calling her father a *tzaddik*. She went to him and told him, "Everyone says you're a big *tzaddik*."

Her father answered, "Look, my dear child, people make a mistake about me, but you know the truth."

Miriam giggled and replied, "I really do know the truth."

Miriam's upbringing provides a glimpse into the educational methods of two *tzaddikim*. In general, their way was abundant positive reinforcement, such as the following story shows:

Chaya Sara and Yaakov Moshe would rise very early to milk the cows. One winter morning Chaya Sara didn't feel well. She told her husband that he'd have to milk the cows by himself. Little Miriam couldn't bear the thought of her beloved father having to do all the work on his own. Although it was barely dawn and bitterly cold, Miriam jumped up out of bed and announced, "Tatty, I'll come with you."

R' Yaakov Moshe bid her to go back to bed. "No, my dear daughter, go back to sleep. It's very cold outside." Miriam, however, insisted on helping him. He gave her a stick and instructed her to herd the cows so that they entered the milking area one at a time. When they finished the milking and returned to the house, R' Yaakov Moshe effusively praised Miriam to his wife over and over again: "How much Miriam helped me today!"

Miriam adds: "He always made a big deal out of every good deed I did. His way was to encourage rather than to reprimand." Chaya Sara would join in his praise, a two-tiered cheering section for their child's every commendable action.

Notice that their positive reinforcement was entirely verbal, augmented by loving caresses and occasional treats. They felt no need to buy toys and games to reward their child. Although the Kramers could not afford presents, Miriam never felt deprived. When she played at a friend's house and saw her dolls, she would go home, take a pillow, tie a piece of string around it to make a neck, and be happy with her homemade "doll." Her life was so full of love that she never noticed her lack of toys.

In terms of Miriam's upbringing, Chaya Sara was stricter than R' Yaakov Moshe. She didn't punish, but she sometimes yelled. She made few demands on Miriam, but when she did ask her to do something, such as going to the grocery store or watching Avramele when they had guests, she expected to be obeyed.

Kfar Gidon resident Chaim Cohen was once asked to describe Chaya Sara. He replied, "Chaya Sara's greatness was in her patience." He went on to describe how patient she was with the handicapped children she cared for.

This description is a far cry from the short-tempered child Chaya Sara Weiser had been. Miriam, however, described her adopted mother's patience more precisely: "With the sick children, she had unbelievable patience. With normal people, she didn't have such patience."

Many people testified that Chaya Sara never ever lost her temper with the sick children. Since anger is usually the result of frustration, and the handicapped children provided countless daily occasions for frustration, I once asked Rebbetzin Chaya Sara how she refrained from succumbing to the urge to yell at even the most rambunctious of the children or young adults. She replied, "There was no one there to yell at." Clearly, yelling for her was a conscious and calculated choice.

For most of us parents, yelling is an expression of our own frustration disguised as a didactic tool. For Chaya Sara, yelling was truly a didactic tool and therefore useless on children who could not be taught. The proof of this is that she did occasionally yell at Miriam, her only normal child, but she never used the tool of anger on the intractable, troublesome, often wild children under her care.

Once — just once — she spanked Miriam. Miriam was in second grade in the girls' school her father had founded in Kfar Gidon. She always went right home from school, but one day a classmate invited her over to see some beautiful pictures. Miriam thought it would take only five minutes, but when she was fifteen minutes late, her worried mother went out to look for her. Chaya Sara went from house to house in the moshav searching for Miriam. When she found her, she took her home and spanked her. Both Chaya Sara and Miriam remembered — and spoke about — that spanking for decades afterwards.

The story does not end there. When R' Yaakov Moshe came home, Miriam tearfully told him what had happened. Clearly, Yaakov Moshe did not approve of hitting children. He said to his wife ever so gently, "Chaya Sarala, why?" Then he asked her to remedy the situation by giving Miriam some candy. But he certainly didn't want to leave the child with the impression that he had sided with her against her mother. Once Miriam was sucking the candy, he said to her, "You have to understand your mother. She was very worried. She didn't do it out of anger, but rather so that you'll be more careful in the future."

Chaya Sara's father had both yelled and spanked, but Chaya Sara's husband guided her along a different child-rearing path. When Chaya Sara became annoyed because Miriam didn't come the first time she called her, Yaakov Moshe would tell his wife: "Chaya Sarala, my dear, with Miriam it's possible to talk. She's a girl who understands. Talk to her and she'll listen to you." Chaya Sara overcame her own nature and chose to follow her husband's educational approach.

Although, unlike hitting and yelling, such gentle methods do not produce instant results, their impact is deep and lasting. Not only did Miriam grow up to be an exceptionally good and devout woman, but she perpetuates her father's techniques with her own seven children: "I continued in his way," she testifies. "In my home, my children know that I don't get angry. Rather than yelling or hitting, I deal with them with darchei noam [ways of pleasantness]. I learned from R' Yaakov Moshe that a child obeys more by a soft approach. And always I ask myself, 'If the tzaddik were here now, how would he react?'"

For all parents, the training of their children is an ongoing challenge. To restrain one's hand and voice when facing a disobedient child requires both self-discipline and a strong commitment to gentle child-rearing. Perhaps it also requires the example of a Yaakov Moshe Kramer.

According to Miriam, R' Yaakov Moshe was by nature more serious, while Chaya Sara had a better sense of humor, but both of them had a playful streak. Almost every Purim residents of the neighboring Kibbutz Mizra, notorious for its pork-packing plant, would come to R' Yaakov Moshe and ask to borrow his *shtriemel*. Although he understood that the kibbutznik dressed in the chassidic costume would be the brunt of their jokes, he invariably lent them the *shtriemel*.

Chaya Sara was quick witted and often came back with a humorous repartee. Miriam remembers a not-so-religious neighbor excoriating Chaya Sara: "If you want to be so *chareidi*, why don't you go live in Meah Shearim?"

Chaya Sara retorted: "If it bothers you so much that I'm *chareidi*, why don't you go live in Kibbutz Mizra?"

When it came to the welfare of her family, on the other hand, Chaya Sara was extremely serious. In truth, she was an overprotective mother. Miriam was afraid to reveal to her when she didn't feel well, because the inevitable consequence would be layers of warm wrappings, especially around her throat, cups of hot tea, and bed rest, which meant she couldn't go outside to play.

Only once during the years she was growing up did Miriam see Chaya Sara erupt in fury. An unemployed, indigent man used to come every week to the Kramer home. Chaya Sara would give him food, then send him to collect alms among the other residents. One day, when Chaya Sara was out of the room, the man spoke inappropriately to young Miriam.

At that moment, Chaya Sara returned. Outraged, she yelled at the man, "Get out of here, and never come back!"

He tried to defend himself with, "But I was just telling her that I like her." Chaya Sara's tolerance did not extend to those who could endanger the welfare of others. She wrathfully chased him out of the house, shouting after him, "You will never come back here!" He never did.

One day in 1959, when R' Yaakov Moshe was in America and Miriam was 7½ years old, a car pulled up to the Kramers' shack. A dark-skinned woman and man got out. The woman greeted Miriam, "*Shalom*, sweetheart," and asked her where her mother was.

"Working in the fields," Miriam replied.

"Go and call her," the woman commanded.

Miriam ran to her mommy and told her that a woman wanted to see her. "How does she look?" Chaya Sara asked, an ominous feeling creeping up in her heart.

"Dark, like an Arab," Miriam replied.

Chaya Sara intuited immediately that Miriam's mother had returned. She hurried back to the house with Miriam at her heels and dread in her heart.

Whatever she was feeling, Chaya Sara greeted the woman warmly and naturally, as if seeing her after a hiatus of seven days rather than seven years: "Ah, *shalom*, Mrs. Batsheva. How are you?"

The man accompanying Batsheva was her brother. He asked Miriam, "Do you know how to write?"

Miriam said she did. "Come," they said, handing her a pencil and a piece of paper. "Write down these names."

Miriam wrote as they dictated: "Yael, Rivka, Menachem ...." She thought it was an exercise in writing. When she finished, they said to her, "All these names, they are your brothers and sisters."

Miriam was confused. She had no brothers except Avramele, who, unlike her, had not been born to the *tzaddik* and *tzaddekes*.

Then the strange man said: "I'm your uncle, and this is your mother."

Miriam, terrified, ran to Chaya Sara and cried, "What do these people want?"

Chaya Sara tried to reassure Miriam — and herself — that everything would be all right. She turned to Batsheva and spoke in calm, measured tones, suggesting that if she wanted the child back, the proper way to go about it would be to gradually build up a relationship with Miriam by visiting regularly over a period of a few months.

Batsheva agreed, and they left. Visiting regularly, however, proved too difficult. Batsheva by now had several young children at home, and Kfar Gidon was an hour and a half's journey from the Levis' home in Tel Aviv.

A few months later, with R' Yaakov Moshe still abroad, Batsheva and her brother returned. Ignoring Chaya Sara, they told Miriam that they had come to take her home. Miriam refused to go with them. Her uncle picked her up, kicking and screaming, and forced her into the car. They drove off, with the cries of "Mommy! Mommy! Save me!" reverberating down the dirt road.

Chaya Sara stood there, helpless. She couldn't save Miriam and she couldn't save herself.

Telling me the story decades later, her face reflected the palpable anguish she reserved only for speaking about her losses in the Holocaust. Chaya Sara concluded her account with the bewildered musing, "She didn't even say, 'Thank you.'"

Chaya Sara immediately sent a telegram to her husband. Then she closeted herself in the house and cried for three days, without eating or drinking.

The neighbors, meanwhile, told Chaya Sara that it was her own fault for not signing legal papers to adopt Miriam at the beginning. The bereft Chaya Sara, however, believed that biological parents, no matter what, retained an absolute right to their children. She responded: "Even if I had signed legal papers, if her true parents came to ask for their daughter, I wouldn't be able to refuse them." This was the reason she didn't fight for Miriam.

Batsheva Levi had reclaimed her daughter not only because she felt guilty. Rather, she had done it to vindicate her own reputation. Her neighbors used to gossip about her, "See that woman? She sold one of her daughters." For years, Batsheva disregarded this *lashon hara*, but one day her own mother lashed out at her. Batsheva arrived at her mother's home to find her arguing with one of her grown sons. Batsheva tried to quell her mother: "It's enough already! He's a grown man! How much are you going to quarrel with him?"

Her mother fired back at Batsheva: "I'm not like you. If you don't manage with a child, you throw her away."

Deeply hurt, Batsheva resolved at that moment to reclaim her daughter. After she got Miriam back, she took the child to her friends and crowed, "See, this is the daughter you said that I sold. Here she is!"

Suffering — large or small — is a fiery ball that is thrown at us. As our hands burn from the heat, we have a choice: to throw it at someone else or to keep it, however much it hurts. Throwing it at someone else is called anger; we blame others in order to rid ourselves of the pain. Keeping it, regardless of the pain, is the opposite of anger; the antonym for "anger" in Hebrew is "savlanus," which literally means "suffering."

Hit in the solar plexus by the fiery ball of losing her only daughter, Chaya Sara could have easily reacted with anger, blaming Batsheva. Batsheva, after all, had cruelly wrested Miriam away with no consideration for Miriam nor gratitude to Chaya Sara for seven years of devoted care. Instead, Chaya Sara chose to hold the pain. Despite her own anguish, she never uttered an angry nor critical word against Miriam's biological mother.

Years and decades later, Chaya Sara would still cry whenever she remembered the terrible day they took Miriam from her. Only after 40 years had passed could Miriam report, "Today, she can speak about it without tears, just with great pain."

Nevertheless, rather than blaming Batsheva, Chaya Sara refused to assign fault. She believed absolutely that everything that happened to her came from the one G-d, the G-d of justice and love. Even during the first years, when her heart was still blistering from the searing pain of her anguish, Chaya Sara would say of Batsheva, "Perhaps in my last gilgul I had children, and she didn't have children, and I did to her what she's doing to me now."

Given that Chaya Sara, the daughter of the quick-tempered Mendel Yosef, knew herself as a woman who was by nature prone to anger, this accomplishment is astonishing. It also proves that the indignation she felt when Miriam was threatened was indeed ego-less. When she herself was the target of the fiery ball, she never threw it back at the one who had pummeled her with it.

For all of us, anger is a recurrent challenge. The fiery ball comes in many forms: a spouse belittling us, a child disobeying us, a friend ignoring us, a neighbor disturbing us. Those raised to regard life like a game of volleyball — "Thrust the ball away as soon as it touches your fingers" — may not even realize that there is another choice: We can catch the pain and hold it. In this, Chaya Sara, weeping for her only daughter without blaming the agent of her loss, is our paradigm.

Miriam, meanwhile, thought she had been abducted by Arabs. She, too, cried and refused to eat. No doubt Miriam's anguish must have added many degrees of heat to the pain Chaya Sara was suffering.

It was summer, in the sweltering heat of Tel Aviv. The Levis' neighbors, seeing the child dressed in stockings and long sleeves, yelled at Batsheva: "She looks like an old woman. Roll up her sleeves! Take off her stockings! Give her a little air!" But Miriam held her ground, and the Levis, who were a religious (but not *chareidi*) family, did not insist on undermining the lifestyle she had imbibed in the Kramers' home.

As soon as the news reached R' Yaakov Moshe in America, he boarded a plane for Israel. Rushing directly to the Levis' home, he spoke to them kindly, telling them *midrashim* to illustrate the harm that ensues from acting too hastily. He managed to convince them to allow the process of reclaiming Miriam to proceed gradually by letting the child go back and forth between Kfar Gidon and Tel Aviv. That very day, he returned Miriam to Chaya Sara's embrace.

Miriam, sure that these strangers were not her family, inferred that Chaya Sara must have sold her to them. Hugging Chaya Sara, she cried, "Mommy, what? You want to sell me to other people?"

A tearful Chaya Sara replied: "Heaven forbid! If I had given birth to you, then even if they filled up this room with gold and silver, I wouldn't give you to them even for one minute."

The next two years was a tug-of-war between the Kramers and the Levis. Once, when R' Yaakov Moshe came to Tel Aviv to take Miriam back for a few weeks, the Levis told him that the child was sleeping, and besides, she was finally getting used to her biological family. They prevailed on him to let her stay. R' Yaakov Moshe had brought a bag of sweetened puffed wheat and a little box of lemon candies for Miriam. These were the only two kinds of treats with a *Badatz hechsher* available in Afula, and therefore they were the standard sweets that the Kramers always bought for Miriam. After getting the Levis to agree that they would relinquish Miriam for the Chanukah vacation, R' Yaakov Moshe left the package and returned to Kfar Gidon.

When Miriam woke up, Batsheva told her that she had bought her some treats. She handed her the bag of puffed wheat and the box of lemon candies. Miriam instantly recognized the sweets. She fell on the floor and cried hysterically, "You didn't buy it! My Tatty was here!"

In addition to his personal loss, R' Yaakov Moshe was worried that Miriam's spiritual progress would be compromised by her living in the Levi home. Thus, when Miriam was 10 years old, R' Yaakov Moshe came up with a solution that, while it would not return Miriam to the Kramer home, would ensure her spiritual stability. He suggested enrolling Miriam in Bayit Lepleitot, a *chareidi* dormitory school in Jerusalem. "Not with you, and not with us," was the maxim that sold the idea to the Levis.

So that Miriam would not be alone among strangers, R' Yaakov Moshe, whose full-time work it was by this time to register children in *chareidi* institutions, persuaded the Levis to also send Miriam's sister, one and a half years younger. He would, of course, foot the bill for both girls.

Yaakov Moshe's work frequently brought him to Jerusalem. Whenever there, he would visit Miriam, bringing treats and coins not only for the two sisters, but also for all of their friends, "to eliminate the possibility of jealousy on the part of our fellow students," Miriam recalls.

Since the Levis, whose family continued to grow, rarely came to Jerusalem, after two years they decided that the supposedly equal compromise was not equal at all. Resenting R' Yaakov Moshe's more frequent contact, they yanked the two sisters out of Bayit Lepleitot, and brought them home to Tel Aviv. There Miriam lived until she married at the age of 18.

Miriam did, however, spend all her school vacations with the Kramers, always bringing with her two or three of her brothers and sisters. The result was that all of the Levi children became imbued with the religious values of R' Yaakov Moshe and Chaya Sara. All 15 of them remained religious and married observant spouses, an astounding record in those days for a non-*chareidi* family. The younger sister who had accompanied Miriam to Bayit Lepleitot married a man who subsequently became a *Rosh Yeshivah*. One of Miriam's brothers became a *Rosh Kollel*.

As for Miriam herself, she established her own home in the mold of "the *tzaddikim*" whom she continued to call "Mommy" and "Tatty." At Yaakov Moshe's behest, she sent her children to Satmar schools. Her husband is a *ben Torah* who learned in *kollel* for many years. Until the end of Chaya Sara's life, whenever she saw her "son-in-law," she would tell Miriam in Yiddish, "I see the *Shechinah* on your husband's face."

The most remarkable part of Miriam's story she herself was unaware of. When Miriam related to me the tale of Chaya Sara's gold jewelry, I asked her, "Did R' Yaakov Moshe ever buy her any other jewelry? For example, did she wear jewelry to major occasions, like your wedding?"

Miriam's answer shocked me. "They didn't come to my wedding."

Naturally, I had assumed that Miriam's wedding must have been the high point, the most joyous occasion, of their otherwise difficult life. "What do you mean?" I asked, incredulous. "You were their only daughter! How could they not come to your wedding?"

Miriam answered matter-of-factly: "They had a cow that was about to give birth. They had to stay home and help the cow deliver. Otherwise, it would have been *tza'ar ba'alei chaim* [the prohibition of causing pain to animals]."

"They missed your wedding to help a cow deliver?" I

Reb. Chaya Sara and Miriam at the wedding of Miriam's daughter

asked in disbelief. Rebbetzin Chaya Sara once laughingly defined her role in life: "I was a midwife to cows." But to miss the wedding of their only daughter? "Couldn't they have asked a neighbor to take care of the cow?" I insisted.

"No, all the neighbors had their own farms and their own duties," Miriam answered simply.

"Well," I continued to object, "why didn't one of them stay home with the cow, and the other one attend your wedding?"

"They couldn't," Miriam naively replied. "It took both of them to help the cow give birth."

I knew it couldn't be true. R' Yaakov Moshe had been abroad for a year and a half; Chaya Sara had helped birth many calves by herself. And to miss Miriam's wedding for the sake of a cow? I hurried to Rebbetzin Chaya Sara's Meah Shearim apartment to ferret out the truth.

"Why didn't you go to Miriam's wedding?" I asked as soon as I was seated opposite the Rebbetzin at her dining-room table.

She gazed at me and replied, "We couldn't. Miriam called us 'Mommy' and 'Tatty.' It would have embarrassed her parents in front of all their relatives and friends if we had been there, with Miriam treating us like her mother and father."

I knew that this was the truth, but Chaya Sara's answer astounded me even more than Miriam's. After the Holocaust, no one in Chaya Sara's life had caused her as much pain as Batsheva Levi. Although surrounded by her own brood of children, Batsheva had wrested away Chaya Sara's only child for self-serving reasons, had refused even to equally share Miriam's time, and had, out of jealousy, yanked Miriam out of Bayit Lepleitot. For the honor of this woman, who had so ruthlessly and cruelly broken Chaya Sara's heart, they decided to forgo their greatest joy, Miriam's wedding.

I sat there in silent awe. Did I have even an inkling of the greatness of the woman sitting across the table from me?

CHAPTER SEVEN

Even a Small Amen

*T*HE MASSIVE SEPHARDI IMMIGRATION WAS both the triumph and the disgrace of the State of Israel's early years. Of the one million Jews who inhabited the Oriental Diaspora, all but a smattering emigrated between the years 1949 and 1956. Most of them made *aliyah* to Israel.[1] They came from Morocco, Tunisia, Egypt, Iraq, Yemen, Syria, Turkey, Persia, and Bucharia.[2] With European Jewry destroyed and American Jewry ensconced, the "Ingathering of the Exiles" of which the Zionists boasted came to mean the mass *aliyah* of Sephardi[3] Jews.

---

1. A significant minority of North African Jews went to France.

2. The Jews of Algeria left in 1962, and the vast majority of them went to France.

3. The term "Sephardi" properly refers to Jews who were exiled from Spain. While North African, Turkish, and many Syrian Jews were descended from Spanish exiles, the Jews of Iraq had lived there since the destruction of the First Temple and the Jews of Yemen had left ancient Israel probably during the Second Temple period. Nevertheless, since it is common to divide Jewry into the designations "Ashkenazi" and "Sephardi," we will refer to all the Jews from Moslem lands as "Sephardim."

While the population of the State of Israel in 1948 was for the most part Ashkenazi and secular, the new Sephardi immigrants were religious. They spanned the spectrum from devoutly religious to "traditional," meaning that they observed Shabbos, *kashrus*, and the laws of family purity [*mikveh*]. They regarded themselves as a proud link in an ancient chain, as Jews who had valiantly maintained their commitment to G-d and Judaism in the face of persecution and exile.

The secular establishment in Israel regarded them very differently. In fact, a controversy raged about whether the Jews of Moslem countries should be welcomed into the Zionist state at all. The European elitists who ruled the nascent state considered denizens of Moslem countries to be "primitive," both culturally and religiously. Ben-Gurion, in his book *The Individual and His Destiny*, compared the Sephardi communities to "dust — without a language, without education, without roots. Turning this dust into a cultured nation is not an easy task."

The cultural imperialism that pervaded the Zionist leadership assumed as a sacred tenet that the only respectable culture was secular European culture. If Sephardi Jews did not know who Shakespeare and Mozart were, then they were primitives, no matter that they were well versed in Rambam and Ohr HaChaim. As Amnon Raz-Karotzkin,— Professor of History at Ben-Gurion University and a secular Jew, explained:

> *Where the oppression was felt the most was in relation to the eastern Jews, because they were the ultimate: they were outside of European culture and they were religious. ...*
>
> *The discussion [among the Zionist elite] was whether you could "rehabilitate" them. The debate was between those who said it was impossible to "rehabilitate" them and*

*the liberals who said it was possible to "rehabilitate" them.
In any case, no one accepted them as they were.*

*The theory was that in order to "rehabilitate" them, you
had to separate them from their parents, to separate them
from their traditions. That was the basis for advanced
educational schemes, that only if they would separate
them from what the Ashkenazim viewed as their primitive
homes, cut them off from their primitive traditions, would
it be possible to shape them into human beings. ... Their
absorption involved cutting off peyot and negating their
culture and their Jewish identity.*[4]

The antagonism that the secular Zionists felt toward
Judaism and those who practiced it is explained by secular
Israeli historian and journalist Tom Segev: "Zionism saw
itself as in competition to religion. ... One of the first struggles
within the Zionist movement was internal, not external — to
convince the Jews to believe in Zionism. And the main opponent of Zionism was *chareidi* Judaism."[5]

Against this hostile background, hundreds of thousands
of naive Sephardi Jews poured into the fledgling state. They
were assigned to tent camps, where they were easy prey for
those whose goal was to divest them of their religion and culture. The adults were told that work, money, and even food
would be made available only to those who joined the socialist Histadrut labor union, which was aligned with the ruling
leftist Labor Party.

But it was the children who were the real target of the
elaborate scheme to "rehabilitate" the Sephardi immigrants.
Antireligious kibbutzniks were sent into the tent camps to
act as teachers and youth counselors. The official guide of

---

4. From the documentary, *Herzl and Zionism*, produced by Four Fingers Productions
and Shofar.

5. Ibid.

the extreme leftist Shomer HaTzair movement, published in 1956, is a blatant training manual for how to strip their young charges of their religious beliefs and practices:

> *How shall we treat the religious scouts in the youth move-ment? Among our trainees we often see religious trainees, especially in the tent camps. Obviously, our mission is to bring them to a recognition that their faith in G-d is totally illogical, and there is no place for it in a modern, enlight-ened regime. ...*
>
> *In short, at this point, the counselor should act with tolerance and try to abnegate the importance of religion, defining it as a disturbing element for the membership in the youth movement. ... In this way, by not attacking reli-gion directly, but undermining its basis, the trainee will understand by himself and will leave the religious faith.*[6]

Gradually the tent camps emptied as the large families of immigrants moved into cramped apartments in existing cities or in new development towns in remote locations far from employment opportunities. When kibbutz activists offered Sephardi parents free room, board, and tuition for their chil-dren in kibbutz schools, most parents gladly accepted the chance to relieve the crowding at home and at the same time provide their children a "modern" education.

These efforts to "rehabilitate" the Sephardi immigrants succeeded on a grand scale. Almost the entire younger gen-eration of Sephardim, including those born in Israel during the first decades after their arrival, shed their religious practice as if it were a fur coat in the steaming Levant sum-mer. They were unaware that the sweltering temperature came not from the climate, but was artificially induced by

---

6. *HaMadrich HaShomri L'Shaylot B'Chinuch HaShomri,* published by the Union of the Shomrim, December, 1956.

a sophisticated machine powered behind the scenes by the antireligious establishment.

Yaakov Moshe Kramer witnessed this unfolding cataclysm and decided to do something about it. He realized that the same forces tapped by the secularists — peer pressure and the incentive of free education and relief of crowding at home — could be utilized in the service of Judaism.

One day in 1952, R' Yaakov Moshe took a bus to Beit Shean, a newly-built development town on the eastern edge of the Jezreel Valley, populated by poor Moroccan immigrants. He knocked on a door, asked to speak to the parents of the family, and convinced them to entrust their school-age children to him. He promised to provide them with a good education in a religious institution, and assured them that the costs of tuition, room, and board would be paid for by him. He left with the children in tow, and took them to a *chareidi* school with dormitory facilities, sometimes as far away as Bnei Brak or Jerusalem. There he enrolled the children, provided them with books and school supplies, and made sure that they had the clothes they needed to fit in with their peers.—

R' Yaakov Moshe repeated this procedure thousands of times during the next four decades. He knocked on doors in Beit Shean, Afula, Migdal HaEmek, Pardes Hanna, Haifa, Nazereth Ilit, and Kiryat Ata. He devoted the rest of his life to rescuing Sephardi children from the anti-religious whirlpool that threatened to drown their souls.

Kfar Gidon resident Yossi Shtiglitz gives a firsthand portrayal of R' Yaakov Moshe's *hatzalah* [rescue] work. In 1968, fresh out of the army,[7] Yossi bought an old car. R' Yaakov Moshe immediately employed him as a driver. Yossi would drive R' Yaakov Moshe to a designated address in Beit Shean,

---

7. Although Satmar Chassidus is vehemently opposed to the secular state and its army, R' Yaakov Moshe never said anything critical to the Shtiglitz brothers about their serving in the army.

explaining to Yossi that these were religiously weak homes or homes where one parent was religious and the other was not. R' Yaakov Moshe would disappear into the house. An hour or an hour and a half later, he would emerge with one, two, or three children, sometimes accompanied by one or both parents. Yossi would then drive them to Ohr Chadash in Kfar Chassidim or another *chareidi* institution, an hour's drive away, where R' Yaakov Moshe would enroll them at his own expense. Then they would return to Beit Shean and repeat the process.

No part of the process was easy. R' Yaakov Moshe had to convince the parents — and the children — to transfer from a secular or government religious school (90 percent of whose graduates would not be Shabbos observant) to a *chareidi* school. He had to convince the *chareidi* schools to accept children whose lifestyle by then wreaked of Torah desecration. And then he had to find the finances to pay for the entire project which, at its height, supported over 300 children a year in *chareidi* education.

How did R' Yaakov Moshe, in his foreign-looking, long black coat and chassidic hat, convince Sephardi parents to entrust their children to him? According to Zev Shtiglitz, who worked for R' Yaakov Moshe in the early 1980's, the incentive was twofold. First was the financial incentive. The families were poor. Getting free education and having two or three less mouths to feed was a powerful enticement. The second reason went deeper. The parents, many of whom had themselves allowed their religious observance to slide, saw the devastating consequences of secular culture. Their children were becoming involved in petty crime, not-so-petty crime, alcohol addiction, and, in later years, drug addiction. The prospect of returning their children to the pure and holy lifestyle they themselves had known in Morocco or Iraq won over many parents.

Zev Shtiglitz recounts one experience that by then was certainly typical. Zev went to a Yemenite family on a moshav in the Jezreel Valley. In the house he saw no sign of religion. The mother, who was wearing a sleeveless shirt, told Zev that she had wanted her children to have a "modern" education, but the secular schools were a big disappointment to her. She was alarmed when her oldest son dropped out of school and spent all day riding his motorcycle. This was not how she wanted her children to turn out. Zev succeeded in registering five children from that family in *chareidi* education. Today all five children are married and raising their own children in religious homes.

Once R' Yaakov Moshe had the children in tow, he had to convince the *chareidi* schools to accept them. This was decades before the movement of *kiruv rechokim* made a cherished goal out of bringing secular Jews back to religious observance. In general, between 1952 and 1977, the Rabbinic leaders of the *chareidi* world decided that the only way to protect Torah Judaism from the corrupting influence of the secular world was to isolate it from all contact. Mixed neighborhoods, once the norm, disappeared, as *chareidi* enclaves in Meah Shearim and Bnei Brak drew up the drawbridges to protect their religiosity from the kind of infiltration that had wreaked havoc in Europe and Israel. Thus, the idea of enrolling nonreligious students in *chareidi* dormitory schools must have seemed like introducing cholera patients into the carefully sanitized and sequestered domiciles of healthy children.

Little wonder that, in the early years, the principals of the *chareidi* schools initially refused to enroll the children R' Yaakov Moshe brought. Although R' Yaakov Moshe always stopped en route to outfit the children in appropriately modest clothes, their interviews with the principals revealed how immersed they had been in the secular culture. R' Yaakov Moshe was not one to argue. He simply sat down and informed the principal that he would not move until the children he had brought were enrolled. Sometimes it took many hours, but by nightfall the children were accepted.

R' Yaakov Moshe's role in the children's lives did not end there. He visited often, looking after all their needs. He supplied them with books, pencils, notebooks, and erasers. He bought them clothes and shoes, so that they would not stand out as the destitute immigrants they were. Aliza Kevisa, an orphaned girl whom R' Yaakov Moshe placed in a *chareidi* dormitory high school, recalls: "I remember that when I was in high school, he came to visit me to make sure that everything was all right with me. When he arrived, he would ask, 'Where is my daughter?' Everyone was amazed that I had such a special father!"

Moshav Adirim in the Jezreel Valley was founded by religiously traditional Moroccan Jews. As new immigrants, they were naive and unsuspecting when the Labor Party arranged that children from Adirim would attend the Jezreel Valley Regional School, located near Afula. As one girl from Adirim later explained: "Our parents were *temimim* [naive, unsophisticated]. They didn't understand that the Regional School was a *secular* school. They thought it was a *Jewish* school. Little by little, they saw the bad impact it was having on their children."

Eventually a religious elementary school (Chinuch Atzma'i) was opened in Adirim. Almost all of the children of Adirim transferred to this school. One particularly religious family sent their daughter Tamar[8] to Ohr HaChaim, a *chareidi* high school in Bnei Brak. Tamar was distressed that one Shabbos-observant family in Adirim continued to send their children to the secular regional school, claiming that it offered a higher standard of education. Tamar suspected that finances were the real motive, since the Regional School was free, while

8. This is a pseudonym, as the source prefers to remain anonymous.

religious schools, only partially funded by the government, always charged tuition.

In 1970, when she was in 11th grade, Tamar went to Ohr HaChaim's principal Rav Hillel to ask if this recalcitrant Adirim family could get a discount to send their oldest daughter to Ohr HaChaim. Rav Hillel could not authorize a discount, but he sent Tamar to R' Yaakov Moshe Kramer in Kfar Gidon. R' Yaakov Moshe promised to pay the entire tuition, room, and board for the girl. Armed with this offer, Tamar went to speak to the father of the family. As soon as he heard that he wouldn't have to pay tuition to send his daughter to Ohr HaChaim, he consented. Today that girl is the principal of a Bais Yaakov school.

"It was not that R' Yaakov Moshe paid for these children and that was it," Tamar remembers. "He kept continual contact with them. He gave them money for coats, eyeglasses, and pocket money. He treated them as his own children, inquired after them, and visited them."

And, like an astute father, R' Yaakov Moshe tried to satisfy not only these children's physical needs, but also their emotional and psychological needs. When the girl from Adirim asked R' Yaakov Moshe for a coat like the other girls had, he bought her one, despite Tamar's objection that a coat was an unnecessary luxury in the warm climate of Bnei Brak. R' Yaakov Moshe told Tamar: "If a person says he needs a white horse, you have to buy him a white horse, and not what you think he needs."

The official receipts that R' Yaakov Moshe had printed for his *hatzalah* work identified it as, "*Tomchei Dalim*, Institution for Refugee Children of Sephardic and Oriental Communities." R' Yaakov Moshe, however, ended up adopting not just the children, but their entire families, not just when they were in school, but forever. In addition to paying for the children's education, he also helped the families financially, found *shidduchim* for the children when they grew up, helped pay for their weddings,

R' Yaakov Moshe at the bris
of Yehudah Michaely

served as *sandak* at their sons' *brissos*, counseled them when they had *shalom bayis* problems, and gave them spiritual encouragement and blessings throughout the ups and downs of their lives.

The following case is typical: A religiously traditional family, who had emigrated from Morocco, lived in Afula Ilit. The children attended the government religious school there. In 1968, the father of the family died at the age of 38, leaving a widow and seven children, the youngest of whom was 2 years old. Someone apprised R' Yaakov Moshe of the plight of this family. R' Yaakov Moshe immediately became involved. He enrolled all the children in *chareidi* schools and paid all their expenses, but he didn't stop there. He stepped into the breach and supported the family in a myriad of financial and psychological ways as well.

Aliza, the oldest daughter, was 14 years old when her father died. R' Yaakov Moshe sent her to a dormitory high school and visited her there. She forged a close relationship with the Kramers. When she graduated, she went to them in Kfar Gidon to get their advice about where she should look for a job appropriate for a religious girl. Without a word, R' Yaakov Moshe ordered a taxi and traveled to Migdal HaEmek in the northwestern corner of the Valley, where he went straight to the home of Rav Yitzchak David Grossman. R' Yaakov Moshe appealed to his younger colleague to find some kind of work for Aliza in the local Bais Yaakov school that Rav Grossman had founded. Note that although the Kramers owned a telephone by this time, R' Yaakov Moshe did not take the easier route of phoning Rav Grossman, but rather went to see him personally to underscore how very important this matter was to him.

The Kramers' efforts continued long after Aliza had become an adult. They found her a *shidduch*, and continued to help the new generation of her family both materially and spiritually. Even after the Kramers moved to Jerusalem and R' Yaakov Moshe left this world, Aliza and her husband continued to visit Chaya Sara every year, seeking her advice and blessing.

In 1982, a 16-year-old boy from a Sephardi family in Afula Ilit won third place in the prestigious International Bible Contest. His family, beaming with pride at their son's brilliance, had ambitions that he be the first in the family to study in university and become a professional. The boy, however, longed to go to yeshivah and study Torah. His parents vociferously refused to pay for yeshivah tuition — even if they had had the money. It seemed like this bright boy with so much promise would be unable to study in yeshivah. Then, somehow, he found R' Yaakov Moshe Kramer, who financed his complete education in Torah institutions. The indigent Sephardi boy grew up to become the rabbi of his town, a *Rosh Yeshivah*, and the father of eight children, who also excel in their Torah studies.

R' Yaakov Moshe did not just change people's lives; he changed their generations.

For some 25 years, R' Yaakov Moshe ran what one Kfar Gidon resident called "a one-man show." When he was nearly 70, R' Yaakov Moshe started hiring a few people to knock on doors in his stead. Some of those who worked for him were themselves people whose education he had financed. He paid them per capita for every student they enrolled.

Yet, from the beginning, it was not "a one-man show," but "a one-couple show." According to R' Yaakov Moshe himself, everything he did was in the merit of his wife.

This was true both passively and actively. Chaya Sara's passive participation was obvious for all to see; she permitted him to spend his days doing something (the neighbors were not sure what) other than working on their farm or taking a paying job elsewhere. (Although R' Yaakov Moshe did work in a cooking oil factory in Haifa during the late 1940's and as a *mashgiach kashrus* [*kashrus* superviser] at the Elite chocolate factory in Nazareth for a period during the mid-1960's, these seem to be the only paying jobs he held during the four-decade period that they lived in Kfar Gidon.) The neighbors testified that she did all the work on the farm from 1952, which happens to be the year he started his *hatzalah* work. When they badgered Chaya Sara that her husband should help her, she never revealed what he was doing instead of tending to the cows and harvesting the vegetables.

The greater secret was Chaya Sara's active, behind-the-scenes participation in her husband's work. Their adopted daughter Miriam testifies: "He always said that whatever he succeeded in doing was in the merit of his wife. He said that the idea to help others was hers. ... He always stressed: 'If Mommy didn't help me, it would be very difficult for me.' Actually it was the Rebbetzin who initiated and directed him in his acts of *chesed*."

According to, R' Yaakov Moshe's niece Pnina Kubitchek, "R' Yaakov Moshe always said that his *koach* came from her."

Rav Yaakov Deutsch, the highly respected kabbalist and *Rosh Kollel*, was a young *bachur* learning in Kfar Gidon when he met R' Yaakov Moshe Kramer. In the beginning, the young man would go to R' Yaakov Moshe with personal questions, but soon R' Yaakov Moshe enlisted him in helping to place children in Torah institutions. Young Rav Deutsch found the work daunting. He was hesitant to ring the doorbells of strangers, especially those ensconced in a nonreligious lifestyle. R' Yaakov Moshe would encourage him. As Rav Deutsch recalls: "He would say, 'You go and you'll succeed.' And I did."

Sometimes Rav Deutsch faced grueling opposition from certain parents. R' Yaakov Moshe would not let him become discouraged. He would point out that granting a Torah education to a single child was worth all the effort. He would say to Rav Deutsch, "Even a small *amen* is worth struggling for."

Over the years, the scope of the work grew to include virtually the entire country. One woman who as a child had been educated by R' Yaakov Moshe and who went on to work for him wrote: "I was sent by Rav Kramer to addresses and families in Pardes Channa, Haifa, Migdal HaEmek, Nazareth, Kiryat Ata, Afula, Safed, Kiryat Shemonah, and more. Even though the traveling was difficult for me — sometimes I was traveling for hours — I couldn't refuse."

A list of 276 students supported by R' Yaakov Moshe in 1989, the last year before his death, enumerates dozens of different schools and yeshivos in which R' Yaakov Moshe and his workers had enrolled these children. The locations span all of Israel, from the Galilee to the Negev. Another list of 64 individuals to whom he distributed money in January 1990 records addresses in such far-flung locations as Acre, Ofakim, Kiryat Shemonah, and Ashdod.

As one woman who was spiritually rescued by the Kramers wrote: "I myself feel as if I am their daughter, and my husband feels as if he is their son. If there ever is a meeting of all the children the Rav and Rabbanit helped, I'm sure the numbers would reach the hundreds if not the thousands."

R' Yaakov Moshe with a family he helped.
Rebbetzin Chaya Sara is in the back, center.

Who covered the expenses for the *hatzalah* work? In the early years, the Satmar Rebbe, who had established a thriving movement in Williamsburg, Brooklyn, supplied the funds. In 1968, the Satmar Rebbe suffered a serious stroke. Although he lived for another 11 years, he was no longer the dynamic activist he had been. Instead, he appointed two of his chassidim, R' Nachman Landau and R' Shulam Lauffer, who had been closely associated with R' Yaakov Moshe back in Satu Mere, to collect funds for his *hatzalah* work.

Eventually, in the mid-1970's, R' Nachman Landau convinced R' Yaakov Moshe that much more money would be

R' Yaakov Moshe (circled) at Lod airport

raised if he himself would travel to America to collect funds. Sometime between 1974 and 1978, R' Yaakov Moshe, carrying his food with him, boarded an airplane for New York.

He soon established an annual schedule. He left home every year after Pesach and spent three months raising money in New York, then went to England for two or three more weeks of fundraising, then to Antwerp for one week. He always returned to Israel right after Tishah B'Av, so that he could make sure all of his children were properly registered in their respective institutions before the new school term began on the first of the Hebrew month of Elul.

Chaya Sara not only gave her physical and emotional support to her husband's work but, when he started traveling abroad, she also gave what was most precious to her in this world: her husband himself. His extended fundraising forays abroad were a sacrifice she made with love — and tears.

"To stay at home alone with Avramele and Hindele when R' Yaakov Moshe traveled abroad was very hard on her," relates their neighbor Esther Schutz. "My husband also goes abroad, but, *Baruch Hashem*, my children are healthy and they are my own children. She never said to him 'Don't go.' And those trips weren't even for her benefit. He didn't go to raise money for his own family."

Another neighbor, Chaim Cohen, reports, "When Yaakov Moshe left for the States, Chaya Sara began crying." R' Yaakov Moshe wrote to her three times a week, and sometimes sent packages containing clothes and salamis. Miriam remembers that when Chaya Sara opened his letters and packages, "She would cry. She missed him so much." Miriam adds: "She didn't have her own children. Her joy in life was her husband. Yet, she let him go, once for a whole year and a half. This was her *mesirus nefesh*."

R' Yaakov Moshe's yearly trips to America and Europe kept him away for one-third of every year. While history is full of husbands absent for prolonged periods — merchants seeking their fortunes or, in the beginning of the 20th century, Eastern European immigrants to the United States working for years to bring over their wives and children — Chaya Sara's situation is different in that her husband's absence brought no personal gain to her.

Most of us take the fabric of our lives and cut from it a coat for our personal use. Then, from the remnants, we salvage a piece here, a corner there, to contribute to the community. The Kramers took the fabric of their lives and cut from it a coat for the community. The only scrap they kept for themselves was their marriage. Yet, in the 1970's, one-third of this tiny remnant of personal life was requisitioned by the community. And Chaya Sara gave it.

She could have refused and, without a doubt, R' Yaakov Moshe would have respected her wishes. After all, R' Nachman Landau in New York had for years done a conscientious job of raising funds for R' Yaakov Moshe's work. The problem was that, as the years went on, more people were turning to R' Yaakov Moshe for help. Chaya Sara's "no" would have meant saying "no" to children stranded in secular schools, to young brides whose wedding depended on a dowry, and to families who couldn't afford a washing machine (although Chaya Sara herself never had one).

Letting her husband go abroad for one-third of every year was a choice that Chaya Sara made. It was her "akeidah." She was asked to sacrifice the presence of the person she most loved in the world to the world. Her consent probably cost her more anguish than any other choice she ever made.

The choice "for me" or "for them" confronts all of us every day. It is probably not possible and certainly not *healthy for any of us to choose the totality of self-sacrifice that Rebbetzin Chaya Sara chose. But the choice is open to all of us to sometimes sacrifice our personal good for the good of the community: by volunteering at a hospital during the hour we were planning to cuddle up with a good book or by giving to charity the money we'd rather spend on a night out. Putting the collective first can be as simple as the example set by Rabbi Yaakov Kamenetsky, who, when stopped at a red light beside a city bus, told his driver to let the bus go first because it held more people.*

Enrolling children in Torah institutions was the essence but not the extent of R' Yaakov Moshe's work. Because he loved every single Jew he encountered or even heard about, he intuited their unspoken needs and exerted himself to help each one in every way possible. R' Yaakov Moshe did not help charity cases; he forged relationships. This was his "unofficial work" and his lifetime passion.

An example: Moshe Yunion was a 19-year-old soldier, the son of traditional Persian immigrants who lived in Beit Shean. Moshe had attended a co-ed government religious school. On a furlough from the army in 1976, Moshe and a friend were hitchhiking home from Eilat. They were given a ride as far as Kfar Gidon, arriving there at sundown. A bearded chassid in a threadbare long coat greeted them warmly, took each of them by the hand, and led them into the synagogue for the evening prayers. Afterward, he invited them to his home for supper.

That was the beginning of the relationship between R' Yaakov Moshe Kramer and the young soldier. Moshe Yunion visited the Kramers often after that and, under their subtle influence, became more and more observant. When he was 23 years old, the Kramers made him a *shidduch* with Yaffa, a religious girl from Tiberias. Two years after the wedding, Moshe fell ill with a spinal malady. Throughout the crisis, R'

Yaakov Moshe supported them emotionally with letters and financially with money.

Another example: Naim Benino was shopping in a clothing store in Afula one spring day in 1964. Suddenly R' Yaakov Moshe entered the store. Calling Naim, "*Yehudi hayakar* [precious Jew]," R' Yaakov Moshe hugged him and kissed him on the shoulders. Then he invited the erstwhile stranger to visit him in Kfar Gidon. "I'm asking you to come to me tomorrow," R' Yaakov Moshe told him, "and I'll give you handmade matzah." When Naim came the next day, R' Yaakov Moshe gave him not only matzah, but also wine.

Thus was launched a relationship that Naim cherished for the rest of his life. When Naim went to R' Yaakov Moshe to tell him he was marrying off his eldest son, R' Yaakov Moshe immediately zeroed in on the worry behind the good news. "First of all, do you have any debts in the bank?" R' Yaakov Moshe asked.

When Naim admitted that he did, R' Yaakov Moshe offered, "I'll give you the money to pay back that debt. And for the wedding I'll give you monthly checks from someone, but you must pray for that person every day."

When Naim turned to R' Yaakov Moshe for help in marrying off his second son, he lent him a large sum of money. Every month Naim paid back 60 shekels.

R' Yaakov Moshe, who was a genius at giving, understood that the greatest gift he could give others was the opportunity to be a giver. Thus he enlisted Naim Benino in his *hatzalah* work. He would send him to buy books in Bnei Brak to distribute to the many students he supported. He would also send money to Naim and would instruct certain boys and girls to pick up their stipends from him. "He wanted to give me merit," Naim reminisces.

Rather than having donors and recipients, R' Yaakov Moshe set up pairs of "mutual givers." This was the trademark of his *chesed* work. When someone came to him and offered *tzedak-kah* money, R' Yaakov Moshe would give him an envelope addressed to a needy family and ask him to send the money directly to that family. Inside the envelope R' Yaakov Moshe would insert a hand-written note to the family asking them to pray for their benefactor.

Meir Shalom Tanzee was a young student who frequented the Kramer home. His memoirs describe how R' Yaakov Moshe would intuit his unspoken needs, whether for clothes or for traveling expenses. The Rav would give him the necessary funds, at the same time asking him to pray for a *shidduch* or for children for individuals whose names he would give him. "Once a letter arrived from a couple from Jerusalem," writes Meir Shalom. "Inside it was a written note from Rav Kramer asking me to pray that they be blessed with children. I prayed, and they were indeed blessed with children."

R' Yaakov Moshe understood that even the poorest person has something to give, and that a person's prayers and blessings are no mean contribution. Aliza Kevisa remembers: "Wherever he went, he carried a list of names of ailing people who needed to be healed, and he would ask ordinary people to pray for them. Simple people would come to him and the Rav would ask them to bless him. Yes, *they* should bless *him*! How great was his humility!"

According to Kfar Gidon resident Chaim Cohen, R' Yaakov Moshe tried to preserve the dignity of those he helped by giving indirectly. For example, there was a widow with many children who lived in Migdal HaEmek. R' Yaakov Moshe asked Rav Grossman to hire this widow to clean one classroom in his Bais Yaakov school. The job took her less than 30 minutes a day, but she received a handsome monthly salary for it. The "salary" came from R' Yaakov Moshe, funneled through Rav Grossman.

The Kramers' cramped house was full of notebooks in which R' Yaakov Moshe kept the names and addresses of virtually everyone he met. He would initiate correspondence with these people, inquiring about their problems and needs. "Every day he would get a lot of letters from all over Israel," Aliza Kevisa recalls. "The Rav never took any of them lightly. He sat and answered every single letter, and also invited the petitioners to his house. He would ask everyone who came to him if they knew anyone who needed a *shidduch* or a *yeshuah* of any kind. He would take down their address, and he would work for their good."

Without the benefit of a computer or filing cabinet, R' Yaakov Moshe would tie every pile of letters with a rubber band, and would file them in cartons according to his own system. He saved every letter for decades, and never forgot a single correspondent.

Chaya Sara was an indispensable participant in this work. When R' Yaakov Moshe was abroad, he would write out checks and send them to his wife for her to distribute to people and schools throughout Israel. It was Chaya Sara who traveled by bus to Haifa to deposit the money that her husband collected. According to Aliza Kevisa, who stayed with Chaya Sara while R' Yaakov Moshe was abroad in 1978, "during the periods when he went abroad, his wife would take his place." The people kept coming and asking for help, and Chaya Sara would deal with each of them.

Even when R' Yaakov Moshe was at home, Chaya Sara was his visible partner. When people came for help or advice, both Kramers usually sat down at the table with them. Whether or not R' Yaakov Moshe agreed with his wife's advice, he never contradicted her. Kfar Gidon resident Eliezer Gevirtz witnessed many such sessions: "He would want to give money to everyone. She would want to ask questions to ascertain the details of their situation." Eliezer adds: "I was on her side."

According to Eliezer, "Whenever they disagreed, he gave in to her."

How often did that happen? "Every day."

Over the years, the Kramers made 405 *shidduchim*. Sometimes a *shidduch* was jeopardized by the inability of one side to come up with enough money to pay for the wedding or to outfit the prospective home. In such cases, R' Yaakov Moshe would save the *shidduch* by paying the money from his own pocket.

R' Yaakov Moshe understood that many battered wives stay with their husbands because they feel unable to support themselves and their children independently. Whenever an abused wife came to R' Yaakov Moshe for advice, he never told her to go back to the husband who was beating her. Instead, he would undertake to support the wife and her children in a separate living situation.

Once, a yeshivah *bachur* came to R' Yaakov Moshe for money. He gave him 100 shekels. A few days later, the *bachur* returned, claiming that someone had stolen the money from him. R' Yaakov Moshe said, "I'll give you another 100 shekels, and if you know who stole the money, I'll give you also 100 shekels for him. Because obviously he needs money, too."

R' Zalman Leib Waldman of London related this story: When one of his daughters became a *kallah*, he traveled with her to Eretz Israel to visit the graves of *tzaddikim* and also to get a blessing from R' Yaakov Moshe Kramer in Kfar Gidon. R' Zalman Leib brought with him four $100 bills, which he folded up and handed to R' Yaakov Moshe. R' Yaakov Moshe didn't even look at the money. He put it into his pocket, gave him a "*yasher koach*," and then sat his visitors down and talked with them. While they were talking, a poor man arrived at the

Kramer home. He told R' Yaakov Moshe about his desperate situation and how he needed money. R' Yaakov Moshe put his hand into his pocket and, without looking at the amount, gave all four folded bills to the stranger.

Yaakov Moshe's unrestrained generosity masked his shrewdness, but he knew how to be clever when necessary Once an Arab man from the locality, who had heard that Yaakov Moshe doled out funds, came to him and appealed for money. Yaakov Moshe was in a quandary. If he gave the Arab money, he would certainly return every week for more, but Yaakov Moshe knew that his donors had intended to support Jews, not Arabs. On the other hand, if he refused, he feared what the Arab might do. Yaakov Moshe came up with an ingenious solution: He told the Arab that he couldn't *give* him money, but he would *lend* him money, to be repaid next time he came. The Arab was never seen again.—

By contrast, when it came to giving to Jews, R' Yaakov Moshe made no distinction between one needy Jew and the next. As someone who knew him well testified, "To him a *Yid* was a *Yid*." Or as the Kramers' neighbor Simcha Heizler reported about them: "Whoever came and asked, they gave. They didn't 'check people's *tzitzis*.'"

One woman from a nearby town came to Kfar Gidon every week to collect *tzedakkah*. Her children were dropouts and her family was immersed in a dissolute lifestyle. Oblivious to the religious level of the moshav, the woman came wearing pants, with her hair loose. The other residents of the moshav were repelled by her appearance and didn't want to support her unsavory lifestyle. The Kramers, however, gave her money every week — for years. Every time she appeared at their door, they received her warmly, sat her down, offered her food and drink, and talked with her.

A chassidic visitor from abroad remembers sitting at the Kramer table in Kfar Gidon. "A woman wearing red pants came to the door. They warmly invited her in and sat her down at the table." Just as the Kramers' table was big enough to accommodate a chassid and a woman in red pants at the same time, so the Kramers' hearts were big enough to accommodate a chassid and a woman in red pants in the same love.

The quality, more than the quantity, of the Kramers' *chesed* reveals their greatness. People left their presence feeling not only helped, but loved. Their *chesed* was akin not to feeding a hungry person at a soup kitchen, but to inviting the hungry person to one's own table and sitting with one's arm around him while he ate.

As Avigdor Galandauer, who worked closely with R' Yaakov Moshe during his final years, testifies: "Every *Yid* was to him like his *ben yachid*, his only child." Yaakov Moshe Kramer, who was never blessed with any children of his own, became a loving father to virtually every Jew he met.

Thus, when an orphaned young woman came on a rainy day to seek the Kramers' advice, R' Yaakov Moshe's first question to her was: "Do you have an umbrella?" (When she admitted she didn't, he gave her his own.)—

Another time, upon enrolling an indigent girl in a dormitory high school, he realized that she would be embarrassed because she didn't own a suitcase. (He gave her his own suitcase.)

I myself experienced R' Yaakov Moshe's astute attentiveness. In the summer of 1986, shortly after I made *aliyah*, I traveled to Haifa to pick up my lift. Having made careful inquiries about all the many technicalities of getting a lift through customs, I had heard that all the taxes and costs had to be paid in cash, so I was traveling with the requisite sum of money. On the way to Haifa, I stopped by the Kramers to get a blessing for a *shidduch*. R' Yaakov Moshe gave me his blessing, but he was also concerned that I might not have enough cash to release my lift.

I will never forget the scene: I was standing in the Kramers' ramshackle shack, with rags stuffed into the holes in the roof and pieces of string holding the shutters together. R' Yaakov Moshe reached under his dilapidated table and pulled out a plastic bag full of 50 and 100 shekel notes. He insisted on giving me 50 shekels in cash for unforeseen costs in releasing my lift. I was overcome by the irony: this impoverished *tzaddik* was forcing money on me, "the rich American." I kept refusing, but he would not relent until I took the cash. "Releasing a lift requires more money than you may realize," he kept saying. I had come to a holy *tzaddik* for a blessing, and had found a doting father worried about my running short of cash. When I left, in my purse I carried the extra 50 shekels, and in my heart I carried the feeling that I was precious and beloved.

Every time R' Yaakov Moshe sent people a letter inquiring after their needs, he enclosed a stamped, self-addressed envelope so that they would not have to incur any expense or trouble in answering him. Whenever he asked someone to come to see him *so that he could help that person*, he enclosed enough cash to cover the person's bus fare — both ways.

Perhaps the most amazing aspect of R' Yaakov Moshe's work was how well he kept it hidden. Lifetime neighbors in Kfar Gidon knew that he helped people but, except for those few he enlisted to assist him, the neighbors had no idea about his *hatzalah* work. And even the most probing chronicler will never uncover the full extent of his *chesed*. Yet, here and there, like the sun shining through slits in the cloud cover, R' Yaakov Moshe's deeds sometimes reveal themselves. Kfar Gidon resident Esther Schutz related this story:

> I was once in a wig shop in Bnei Brak. The owner of the shop asked me where I was from, and I told her, "Kfar Gidon." Suddenly, she hugged me and kissed me and said that I come from a place imbued with the holiness of the

tzaddik Rav Kramer. She said she had lived in Migdal HaEmek. Her sister was widowed and left with six children. Every month a messenger arrived with a sum of money. For years, there was never a month that passed without the messenger arriving with that sustenance. She never knew who sent the money. Only after he left this world did she find out that her benefactor was Rav Kramer of Kfar Gidon.

In R' Yaakov Moshe's own eyes, he was a simple farmer. In the eyes of his contemporaries in Kfar Gidon, he was an exceedingly good man. In the eyes of those he encountered on the street and helped, he was Eliyahu HaNavi. Still others whispered that he was a *lamed-vav tzaddik* – one of the 36 righteous people on whose merit the world stands.

His niece Pnina Kubitchek remembers someone in the family referring to R' Yaakov Moshe as a *lamed vavnik*. Her father, R' Yaakov Moshe's brother Chaim, quickly silenced the suggestion. He said that he knew someone who was considered a *nistar* [a hidden *tzaddik*], and when the word got out, the man died. Chaim forbade his children to ever endanger their uncle by calling him a *lamed vavnik*.

Still, many people were suspicious. "R' Yaakov Moshe used to tell stories about *lamed-vav tzaddikim*," Avigdor Galandauer recalls. "It seemed to us that he was one of the *lamed-vav tzaddikim*, because he knew too much about them."

Indeed, Rav Chaim Kreiswirth, Chief Rabbi of Antwerp, held that R' Yaakov Moshe Kramer was a *lamed-vav tzaddik*. In the summer of 1989, during R' Yaakov Moshe's last trip to London, R' Moshe Markovich held a dinner to which he invited many distinguished rabbis. Rav Kreiswirth was in attendance, and was speaking to a colleague when R' Yaakov

Moshe walked in, leaning on his cane. "That Yid," declared Rav Kreiswirth, "is a *lamed-vav tzaddik.*"

"Why, that's a contradiction in terms," objected the other rabbi. "By definition, the *lamed-vav tzaddikim* are hidden. If you know who he is, then he can't be hidden."

Rav Kreiswirth shook his head. "'Hidden *tzaddikim*' doesn't mean that we don't know that they are *tzaddikim,*" he asserted. "'Hidden' means that most of their greatness is hidden."

R' Yaakov Moshe was adamant about keeping his powers hidden. One day in the late 1980's, R' Avigdor Galandauer was sitting in the Kramer home in Kfar Gidon when he witnessed this scene: The esteemed Rav Kreiswirth came to R' Yaakov Moshe to wrest a blessing for a critically ill man in America. R' Yaakov Moshe declined to bless the man (which was usually a sign that the person's destiny could not be changed). Rav Kreiswirth begged him to promise that the man would recover. R' Yaakov Moshe denied that he had the power, saying, "I can't do that. I'm not a great man. I'm just an ordinary farmer."

Rav Kreiswirth pleaded, "I know that whatever you ordain will be fulfilled. I know that you're the *tzaddik hador* [the primary *tzaddik* of the generation]."

"No, no," R' Yaakov Moshe refuted him. "I'm just a simple farmer."

R' Yaakov Moshe was, in fact, a *tzaddik's tzaddik.* The greater the status of a particular rabbi, the more he seemed to know about R' Yaakov Moshe Kramer. When young Moshe Bunim Kraus of Zurich arrived in Eretz Yisrael in the summer of 5739 (1979), he went to pay his respects to his Rebbe, the Krepschnever Rebbe. The Krepschnever Rebbe asked him if he knew R' Yaakov Moshe Kramer. When the young chassid replied that he didn't, the Rebbe exclaimed: "Go to him in Kfar Gidon and meet him, because one-third of Eretz Yisrael stands in his merit!"

A man from England who needed a *yeshuah* went to see the esteemed Rav Wozner in Bnei Brak. Having decided to seek blessings from all the great *tzaddikim* in Eretz Yisrael, the man showed Rav Wozner a list of *tzaddikim* he had been given. He asked Rav Wozner to check the list and tell him if everyone on it was worth visiting. Rav Wozner inspected the list, crossed out some names, then added at the top one more name, "R' Yaakov Moshe Kramer." Handing the list back to the suppli-cant, he asserted, "R' Yaakov Moshe Kramer should be at the top of the list. To him you should go."

Shlomo Kramer relates that his brother Yaakov Moshe once asked him to drive him to the Baba Sali. When they arrived at the Baba Sali's residence, the line of people waiting to see the illustrious *tzaddik* and miracle worker stretched for half a kilometer. R' Yaakov Moshe and Shlomo took their place at the end of the line. When Shlomo noticed one of the Baba Sali's attendants surveying the crowd, he told him, "Go tell the Baba Sali that R' Yaakov Moshe Kramer from Kfar Gidon is waiting to see him." The attendant went. Minutes later, the hundreds of people standing in line "split like the sea" and cleared the way for R' Yaakov Moshe to go right in to the Baba Sali.

One night in 1984, at 2 a.m., a man knocked on a door in Kfar Gidon. He asked urgently, "Where does the Rav live?" The unsuspecting farmer sent him to Rav Ackerman, the offi-cial Rav of the moshav. When Rav Ackerman realized that the supplicant was none other than the *gabbai* of the Baba Sali, he showed him the house of R' Yaakov Moshe. Only several days later, when they heard the news of the Babi Sali's pass-ing, did the people of Kfar Gidon realize that the *gabbai* had come to enlist R' Yaakov Moshe's prayers in a desperate effort to save the Baba Sali.

According to Avigdor Galandauer, the great *tzaddik* Reb Yankele, the Rebbe of Antwerp, used to call R' Yaakov Moshe when he was presented with difficult *kvitlach*. Reb Yankele would turn to R' Yaakov Moshe "to help him solve the problems in heaven."

After the passing of the Chazon Ish, Yaakov Moshe used to go regularly to Rav Elazar Menachem Mann Shach, the Ponovezher Rosh Yeshivah, to consult with him about his *hatzalah* work. Rav Asher Gabbai recalls that he once accompanied Yaakov Moshe to Rav Shach's residence on a Thursday night, when Rav Shach usually received the public. When they arrived and knocked on the door, they were told that Rav Shach was sick and was not seeing anyone. Rav Gabbai announced that he was with R' Yaakov Moshe Kramer from Kfar Gidon. Immediately the door opened and the pair was ushered into Rav Shach's presence. Despite his infirmity, Rav Shach stood up in respect for R' Yaakov Moshe.—

Rav Shach was known to have said that R' Yaakov Moshe Kramer was a "*tzaddik gamur* [a complete *tzaddik*]."

And this man, whom the greatest rabbis honored, whom did he honor? Every single Jew. Although he helped thousands of people, his devoted efforts were always aimed at individuals — this particular child, this particular widow, this particular Jew.

R' Nissan Taktuk, who served as R' Yaakov Moshe's assistant in the later years, recounted an incident that reveals what R' Yaakov Moshe's true focus was. R' Nissan was complaining about a glitch in the system. R' Yaakov Moshe surveyed the list of over 300 children for whose education they were paying. "Tell me, Reb Nissan," he asked, "from all these names, are there two children who are true?"

Reb Nissan was puzzled. "What do you mean 'two'? We've got hundreds of children here."

"But," persisted R' Yaakov Moshe, "are two of them *emes*? Have we saved two children?"

"Much more than two!" exclaimed Reb Nissan. "We've saved hundreds of children."

"Well," R' Yaakov Moshe concluded, "if we had saved only just two children, it would have been worth all the money and more."

The same Sephardim whom the secular Zionists scorned and looked down on were honored and cherished by R' Yaakov Moshe Kramer. He spent most of his life serving them.

CHAPTER EIGHT

Handicapped Children

The Surprising Secret of Her Happiness

*T*HE *MAGGID* RAV SHABSI YUDELEVICH WAS once in Kfar Gidon. Having heard about the *tzaddik* who lived there, he went to visit him. When he entered the Kramers' shack, he encountered a piteous sight: The couple had, he counted, "seven children, and not one of them was whole in body or mind." Although R' Yaakov Moshe received him with love and joy, and offered him a meal, Rav Yudelevich could not bear to eat while viewing the Kramers' horrific burden. *What tzaros this couple has!* he thought. Only afterward did he learn that not one of the children was the Kramers' own offspring.

In 1960 or 1961, with Miriam gone, Chaya Sara started taking care of severely brain-damaged and mentally ill children from religious families. This was long before there was any institution for these children in Israel. They came for many reasons and for one reason. Hindele's family, for example, was emigrating to America, and the American immigration authorities would not accept a child so handicapped that she would be a lifetime drain on the American economy. Other parents sent their children away because in the *chareidi* community of that time a brain-damaged or mentally ill child was a stigma that jeopardized the *shidduch* possibilities of the other siblings. Still others sent their children away because they were simply too difficult to care for. These were the many reasons.

The one reason behind the many reasons was that the parents, simply unable to cope with the awesome challenges of dealing with those special-needs children, did not want them. According to Miriam, "Most of the parents, when they saw how bonded Rebbetzin Chaya Sara was with their child, forgot they had a child. They rarely came to visit. The parents would often give the child to the Kramers and bid him farewell."

Chaya Sara accepted them all: Shamaya, Hindele, Shimale, Volbe, Yechezkel, Shiyala, and more than two dozen others over the next two decades. Some stayed for a year; Yechezkel stayed for 15 years, Hindele for 20. Some were physically as well as mentally handicapped; others were so able bodied that when they hugged Chaya Sara they nearly choked her. Some were little children; others were 18 or 20 years old with the minds of little children. Most came from Israel; Volbe and two mentally ill teenaged brothers came from chassidic families abroad. One mentally ill 20-year-old was so high functioning that he attended synagogue services; others were totally bedridden. Some were passive and sweet; others were wild and dangerous to themselves, to the other children, and to Chaya Sara. The only thing they all had in common was that they needed someone to take care of them, and they found a common shelter under the wings of Chaya Sara Kramer.

Why did she do it? Although some of the neighbors whispered that she was being well compensated, the truth is that she received barely enough money to pay for the children's food. While the Kramers themselves never applied for nor received any financial benefits from the Israeli government, most of the children's parents had registered them with *Bituach Leumi,* the Israeli Social Security, so that they received monthly disability payments. These sums were forwarded by the families to Chaya Sara. She received no additional payment for her 18-hour workday, nor any compensation for their medicine nor for taking them to the best doctors, whom she paid privately.

Why did she undertake such a gargantuan task? Leah Landau, Chaya Sara's longtime neighbor and friend, answers simply, "She did it for the mitzvah."

I once asked Rebbetzin Chaya Sara, "When the yetzer hara [evil inclination] speaks to you, what does it say?"

She replied: "It says not to do good."

She had long since passed the spiritual level where the yetzer hara could tempt her to do bad. Instead, the voice of the lower self tried to seduce her into refraining from performing acts of goodness.

Her yetzer hara certainly had no shortage of true and compelling arguments not to take in handicapped children: Her house was too small and ill equipped to handle them; she was not trained in dealing with medical problems; she had already done a lifetime's worth of chesed by taking in Avramele; her hernia precluded lifting heavy loads (such as children who were not ambulatory); her chronic leg ailments precluded standing on her feet all day to take care of such children; and, most cogent of all, her temperament was not suited for the task.

Despite this onslaught of perfectly reasonable reasons not to undertake the massive task, this chorus of practical voices urging her to refuse the next child, Chaya Sara consistently chose to do good. It was a choice she made

*every time a distraught parent knocked on her door car-
rying a bundle of human misery or holding the hand of a
rambunctious mentally ill teenager. She fought her own
yetzer, and she chose to do good.*

*This master of Jewish martial arts once explained to
me how she defended herself against the yetzer hara.
She said that whenever she felt the pull of the yetzer
hara, she would say to herself, "I want to fix it." And
she would ask Hashem for the strength to do so. This
was a two-step maneuver: 1) Consciously wanting to
resist the blandishments of the yetzer hara, rather than
docilely yielding to its voice, and 2) appealing to Hashem
Yisbarach to grant her the victory, rather than depending
on her own strength.*

*I proceeded to ask her: "What middah helps us win
when we're in conflict with the yetzer hara?"*

*To this she replied: "Not to think of yourself, not to
be absorbed in yourself." The third step in her defense
against the yetzer hara: Swing your mind around from the
mirror and face the person or situation that requires help.*

*The choice to do good despite all the cogent reasons
not to is a choice that all of us encounter. We all have
compelling reasons to decline requests for help, whether
they be a friend on the phone or a charity appeal in
the mail. Of course, we owe our dedication to our own
family first. Assuming, however, that our primary obligation to our spouse and children is taken care of, how
do we respond to the challenge to do good? We can all
legitimately cite our limitations of time, energy, financial
resources, and even our own nature. "I'm not the type to
take care of the elderly." "I faint at the sight of blood."
To choose to do good over the chorus of our true and
convincing excuses not to is within our free choice.*

While a lesser person might have harbored some resentment
toward the parents who had cast their burden on a stranger's

shoulders and then virtually disappeared, Chaya Sara not only didn't bear negative feelings toward the parents, but also went out of her way to protect their reputations. She kept the background of the children secret, lest anyone impugn the parents or reveal the secret stigma they hoped to hide.

"The Rebbetzin never told us who these children were," relates Miriam. "Their identities were kept totally secret." During the two years that Miriam boarded in Bayit Lepleitot in Jerusalem, she became acquainted with two sisters. One of the sisters suddenly came down with high fever and, so the school grapevine had it, "went crazy." A while later, Miriam went to the Kramers for a school vacation. A new girl was in Chaya Sara's care. Miriam recognized her. "Oh, I know her," she told Chaya Sara. "Didn't she study at Bayit Lepleitot?"

The Rebbetzin answered: "Of course not, she's not even from Israel."

Miriam, a determined 12-year-old, was not so easily deterred. "I spoke to the girl, and asked her her name and her sister's name, and I saw that it was the same girl." When she proved to Chaya Sara that she did, indeed, know the girl's true identity, Chaya Sara admonished her not to reveal it to anyone.

While our mental picture of taking care of handicapped children is probably painted in pastels, Leah Landau's memories paint a portrait in dark purple with streaks of black:

> How she cared for those children! And it wasn't easy. There was one boy of 8 or 9 who would consistently take off his clothes and run outside. There was another boy, bigger. She suffered a lot from him. She was afraid that he would hit her. It was very, very hard for her. They were violent. Despite her fear, she kept them, and she took care of them.
>
> She never lifted her hand against any of these children. Real parents hit their children, and especially children who misbehave like this, but Chaya Sara never did.

According to R' Yaakov Moshe's niece Pnina, one of the more violent boys once turned on R' Yaakov Moshe with a knife. "Anyone who didn't see the way those children were and the way the Kramers handled them," testifies Pnina, "couldn't believe it."

Even the children who were easy were difficult. Hindele, a sweet-natured child, lived with the Kramers from the age of 10 until she passed away at the age of 30. Hindele's body was grotesquely deformed. Her arms were shriveled and she walked with difficulty. Her face was covered by red, scaly skin, and she drooled (with R' Yaakov Moshe and Chaya Sara running after her to wipe her face). She made hideous sounds that only Chaya Sara could decipher as speech. "It was frightening to look at her," Esther Schutz recalls, "really frightening. Once I came, and she pulled me so hard. She apparently wanted to hug me, so she pulled me. I was scared."

Another child, Avraham Shaya, was a teenager. "All day he jumped around," recalls Miriam. "He ate very little, but took lots of pills. The Rebbetzin took him to the best doctors and paid a lot of money for those doctors. The doctors said that people with a condition such as Shaya don't live long, but because he was under Chaya Sara's dedicated care, he lived longer."

Chaya Sara cooked and fed them three meals a day. Those who were incapable of feeding themselves, such as one girl without hands, she spoon-fed. Those who were capable of stating their preferences would tell her what they wanted to eat. After she made the food, sometimes they would change their minds. With infinite patience that did not come naturally to Chaya Sara, she would ask them, "So, what do you want?" Then she would cook that for them. Sometimes a child would wake up during the night and ask to eat. No matter what the hour, Chaya Sara would prepare what the child wanted.

She got up every night at 2 or 3 o'clock and made the rounds of the children, changing their diapers and bedding.

She feared that Heaven would judge her negatively if she ever let a helpless Jewish child lie wet or dirty.

Rather than feeling that she had toiled enough for these children throughout the long day and that she deserved an uninterrupted night's sleep, the twin thoughts, "I've done enough" and "I deserve," found no place in Chaya Sara's mind or heart.

A recurrent theme in this book is that, in her inner plumbing system, she paid scant attention to the inbound pipes, and focused instead on the outbound pipes. As quoted above, she once told me, "I didn't feel that anything was owed to me. Everything is a gift. Nothing is owed."

Eliminating the ogre-voice of "I deserve" is a vaulted spiritual accomplishment, but it must not be confused with the negative state of self-deprecation. For some people, "I deserve nothing" is synonymous with "I'm bad; I'm worthless." How did Chaya Sara achieve humility without self-abasement?

There was another pipe in her inner plumbing system. It ran perfectly vertical. This was the pipe that connected her to HaKadosh Baruch Hu. The contents of this pipe flowed in both directions; gifts of Hashem's love were always descending and Chaya Sara's gratitude was always flowing upward. How could she feel worthless when it was so clear to her that G-d loved her? How could she feel prideful when it was so clear to her that everything she had and gave to others flowed from the Divine Source?

We all have the choice to expunge the sense of entitlement from our psyches. This does not require installing the vertical pipe, but rather recognizing that it was always there. We are being deluged at every moment with Hashem's love and largesse. The more we notice this, the less we will harp on what is owed us and the more we will connect the L-joint that allows that bounty to flow outward to others.

The children needed constant supervision. Those who were physically fit threw things, broke things, threw food, even dirtied the bathroom with their own excrement.

Once an irate worker from the Department of Health arrived without prior warning. She had heard that one Chaya Sara Kramer was running a home for handicapped children without a license. As soon as she got out of her car, she smelled the odor of urine from the blankets hanging on the clothesline, proof enough to her that the proper standard of cleanliness was not being met. When Chaya Sara came outside to greet her, the incensed health worker announced that she was closing down this illegal institution and would find other, more suitable homes for the children.

She demanded to see the inside of the house. Chaya Sara stepped aside and motioned to her to enter. The health worker took two steps inside. The sight that greeted her was not of the handicapped children she was used to, but children so twisted and deformed that she recoiled in horror. At that moment, the bathroom door swung open and an older child, his hands smeared with his own excrement, emerged. The health worker turned and fled, and was never heard from again.

Although it was not her nature, Chaya Sara was punctilious in administering the children's medication. This, too, was not easy, as the youngsters often refused to take their pills. They had to be cajoled in a myriad of creative ways. One young visitor, Meir Shalom Tanzee, remembers: "I was amazed at R' Yaakov Moshe's and Rebbetzin Chaya Sara's devotion, the undivided attention they gave their adopted children. When one of the children had to take medication, they never forced him to take it. They would say, 'Here, Rav Meir (meaning me) will give it to you,' as if that were a special treat."

The Kramers didn't own a bathtub, but after the arrival of the handicapped children, they did install a showerhead.

Bathing the seriously deformed children was a strenuous undertaking. Miriam remembers watching Chaya Sara bathe one deformed girl. "She would put the child in the shower, soap her, shampoo her, rinse her off, dry her, and dress her. It really required at least two people, but she did it all herself."

Chaya Sara suffered from a hernia, but, afraid of doctors and hospitals after her experience with Dr. Mengele, she refused to undergo a hernia operation. Nevertheless, she lifted not only the heavy pots of food, but also the children themselves whenever necessary, from bed to chair and back. While R' Yaakov Moshe helped her whenever he was there, his *hatzalah* work kept him out of the house most of the day. Chaya Sara was a one-person staff comprising nurse, orderly, cook, laundress, and janitor.

But most of all, she was a mother. She loved these children. Rather than maintaining any clinical distance from them, she bonded with them. She gave them not only her time and dedicated care, but also her heart. When they refused to eat, she would run to the grocery and buy the most delicious (and expensive) fruits to tempt their appetites. When Hindele could no longer eat solid foods, Chaya Sara splurged on a food grinder for her, and would go out to the fields and pick fresh tomatoes to prepare nutritious juice for her.

Still, convincing Hindele to eat was a major project. One of the most enchanting vignettes of the Kramers' life was described by Esther Schutz. Esther visited the Kramers one day at lunchtime. She found Hindele propped up in a chair and witnessed R' Yaakov Moshe "singing, dancing, and clapping his hands," enacting a whole performance, in an effort to get Hindele to open her mouth so that Chaya Sara, poised ready with a spoonful of food, could slip it in.

Hindele spent the last two years of her life confined to bed. When, toward the end, she was admitted to the hospital in

Afula, the doctors and nurses were amazed that she did not have a single bedsore. They exclaimed that no professionally trained nurse could have taken as good care of her.

Esther Schutz recalls visiting the hospital during the final phase of Hindele's life. When she entered the hospital room, she found Chaya Sara sitting beside the bed, "kissing Hindele and stroking her."

Chaya Sara paid the emotional price for that love. Most of the children suffered from serious physical ailments; they died young, and she was left to bury them and grieve for them. Women in the moshav testified that the only time they ever saw Chaya Sara cry was after the death of any of the handicapped children. Miriam adds that even years after a child's death, whenever Chaya Sara spoke about that child, she wept.

Yet the hardest part of this unrelenting 20-year-long job, without vacations or days off, was not the physical labor it entailed nor the emotional heartbreak when a child died. The hardest part for Chaya Sara was overcoming her own fear of calamity. Taking care of such seriously ill children, she was always afraid that something would happen to them.

Sometimes it did. Once Hindele, who suffered from severe epilepsy, had an epileptic fit while eating. Food was lodged in her throat. Chaya Sara was frantic that Hindele would choke to death. Yaakov Moshe, who happened to be present at the time, managed to dislodge the food and save the girl's life.

Another time, a child stuck a sharp metal object into his mouth, cut himself and began to bleed. Chaya Sara panicked. Yaakov Moshe removed the metal, and calmed his frantic wife.

Whenever a child became ill in Yaakov Moshe's absence, a frenzied Chaya Sara would grab the child and run for the nearest doctor, which meant taking a taxi to Afula.

She had undertaken the responsibility to care for these children. She was like a sentry posted to guard a structure that held a precious treasure. She would be held accountable if the treasure was stolen, but the structure itself had gaping holes and massive cracks on every side. How could she possibly keep the treasure safe?

"Did Chaya Sara's fear of impending catastrophe come from the Holocaust?" I asked Leah Landau.

"It came from her heart," she responded.

Yet, despite her implacable fear, Chaya Sara opened her home to one sick, unwanted child after another.

Why was Chaya Sara not cowed by the staggering difficulty of the task she undertook? The answer is as deep as it is simple: Chaya Sara did not subscribe to the concept, so prevalent in the Western world, that life should be easy. "When a person comes to this world, it's hard," she used to say. "It's meant to be hard. You don't suck honey in this world."

Ease has become a predominant value in Western society, to the extent that corporations spend millions of dollars in research and development in order to save two flicks of an index finger on a potential customer's computer keyboard. How often, in all of our lives, has the difficulty of a prospective course of action been the deciding factor in our choosing against it? The false god of ease seduces our hearts into a sense of grievance over every hindrance, complication, and inconvenience that we encounter on our path, as if the smoothness of the road is more important than where it leads.

Chaya Sara, by contrast, was not deterred from any course of action by its difficulty. Although caring for the handicapped children is the most salient example of this, her life is replete with other instances. For exam-

ple, after her traumatic experience with Dr. Mengele, Chaya Sara was afraid of doctors and hospitals. Naomi Gevirtz, who moved to Kfar Gidon in 1980, related that Mrs. Haas, a childless widow in the moshav, became sick and was hospitalized. Chaya Sara asked Naomi to accompany her to the hospital to visit Mrs. Haas. "I saw that Chaya Sara was very scared of the place," Naomi recalled, "but she forced herself and went anyway. I saw how she overcame her personal fears for the sake of another person. It was hard for her to enter the hospital room, to see her friend lying in bed, but she did it anyway."

Chaya Sara was also afraid of dogs. Tamar Cohen, another young wife in Kfar Gidon, had two dogs. The Kramers always gave a gift for every child born in the moshav. One of Tamar's sons was born in the winter. She describes Chaya Sara walking through the moshav's muddy roads in the rain, umbrella in hand, bringing a gift of money for the new baby. When she reached Tamar's house, she stood in front and called out, "Are the dogs here?" Tamar assured her that the dogs were tied up, and Chaya Sara, visibly struggling against her fears, entered the house to deliver the gift and bless the child.

Not only did she undertake actions regardless of their difficulty, but once she decided to do something, she did it well, not grudgingly or halfheartedly. "If she had to do something," Miriam summed up the Rebbetzin's approach, "it would not make a difference if she were tired. She did it with zeal."

To refuse to kowtow to the false god of ease is a choice that all of us can make.

Tackling what is difficult for the sake of others is a spiritually high level. I understood that Chaya Sara had achieved this level, but I was not prepared for the conversation that ensued one day when we were discussing her care of the handicapped children. "It must have been hard," I remarked, stating the obvious.

"No, it wasn't hard," she replied simply.

"Of course it was hard," I insisted. "For years you had on average three or four handicapped children whom you were taking care of all by yourself when your husband was away. It must have been very hard."

Rebbetzin Chaya Sara shook her head. "It wasn't hard," she repeated.

I was annoyed. The Rebbetzin had this maddening habit of turning my reality upside down. I wasn't going to let her get away with it this time. "You had to cook for them, bathe them by heating up water on the stove, change their diapers before the days of disposable diapers, even change the diapers of grown children, keep them from hurting themselves and each other —"

"And do the laundry," she chimed in.

"Yes! The laundry! How could it not have been hard?" I asked petulantly.

"For meals, I would just take a big pot, fill it with vegetables or chicken or noodles, and cook it up," she chuckled. "It wasn't hard."

Aha! I had done my research, and now I had her. "Isn't it true," I asked like a wily lawyer, "that Hindele had to be spoon-fed? It wasn't just a matter of cooking up the stew and calling, 'Come and get it!' You had to sit and spoon-feed her."

"Yes, I spoon-fed her," Rebbetzin Chaya Sara admitted.

I continued my cross-examination. "Were there other children who had to be spoon-fed?"

By now her face was shining and she was smiling broadly as she remembered those years. "Yes," she replied simply.

Checkmate! "You had to feed four handicapped children,

and spoon-feed more than one of them. Then it must have been hard!" I proclaimed triumphantly.

"No," she shook her head, and repeated, not insistently, just matter-of-factly. "It wasn't hard."

I left her Meah Shearim apartment that day in a state of total cognitive dissonance. Why didn't she perceive her task of taking care of the handicapped children as hard? And how did she manage to do it so cheerfully? Neighbors had testified that Chaya Sara was always smiling and happy. How could she spend years drudging away at the thankless task of taking care of people who never progressed nor said "thank you," and still be joyful? This mystery vexed me, her perception that her job was not hard irritated me, and her joy in the face of such a job positively baffled me.

I spent years trying to ferret out the secret of her constant joy. Here was a Holocaust survivor, the sole survivor of her family, a barren woman, who lived in poverty. Her beloved husband was absent for months at a time, and she had spent the prime of her life taking care of brain-damaged children who either died or departed. Any one of these circumstances would have been enough to plunge an ordinary person into unremitting depression. But here was Rebbetzin Chaya Sara, always joyful.

Once, during the brief period that the Kramers were living in Jerusalem prior to R' Yaakov Moshe's passing, I brought several of my friends to receive his blessing. As each woman went into a side room to describe her problem to the *tzaddik*, the rest of us sat in the living room with Rebbetzin Chaya Sara. We must have looked like a glum bunch, because the Rebbetzin tried to cheer us up. "Don't worry," she told us, "each of you will get the blessing you came for."

One of my friends asked her earnestly, "But how do we remain *b'simchah* [joyous] while we're waiting for the blessing to come down?"

I glanced around the room. Every one of us came from a salubrious American background, had children, and enjoyed material prosperity many times more affluent than Rebbetzin Chaya Sara, yet here we were asking *her* how to be happy!

"How do you stay *b'simchah?*" she incredulously repeated the question. "How can you <u>not</u> be *b'simchah?* You have eyes and they see! You have ears and they hear! You have legs and they take you wherever you want to go! How can you *not* be *b'simchah?!*"

I left her that day excited that now I knew her secret of *simchah*. She didn't look at what she lacked — parents, children, money. She looked at what she had — eyes, ears, legs — things that the rest of us barely notice. This mind-set is what the sages call, *"sameach b'chelko,"* being joyous with one's portion — however meager that portion might be — by noticing and amplifying its every tiny constituent. This means being grateful not only that one can see, but also that one can see color, movement, depth, and detail.

As the years passed, however, and I also tried to focus on the oft-ignored blessings of good health, being married, having healthy children, and living in a Torah environment, I realized that such consciousness could make one happy, but not outright joyous, not beaming with the glowing-face-and-broad-smile *simchah* that was Rebbetzin Chaya Sara's trademark.

Then I learned something that unraveled the mystery. I realized that, paradoxically, taking care of the handicapped children was not an *impediment* to her *simchah*, but rather the *cause* of her *simchah*.

In the *Da'as Te'funah*, Rabbi Moshe Chaim Luzzato ponders the meaning of the Torah's statement that G-d "had heartfelt sadness" [*Bereishis* 6:6] at the state of mankind before the Flood. What could Divine sadness mean? Surely G-d does not feel human emotions! Rabbi Luzzato answers that Divine sadness is a state of cutting off the flow. Rabbi Friedlander, in his commentary, adds that the converse must also be true, that Divine happiness must mean a state of abundant flow from G-d to His world.[1]

Since "Divine happiness" is the prototype of human happiness, this teaching reveals that the essence of human happiness is also free flowing — from one person to another. Therefore, Chaya Sara's abundant, 18-hour-a-day giving was the cause of her abundant, glowing *simchah*.

Joy is a choice. On the simplest level, happiness is a result of one's attitude, of one's appreciation for whatever one has. Yet Rebbetzin Chaya Sara's glow-in-the-dark joy went much deeper than seeing her glass as half full. In her spiritual plumbing system, the tap was always open and flowing, indeed, gushing out. That was a more profound choice than attitude. It was the choice to be a giver, like G-d Himself is a giver. Chaya Sara did not choose happiness. She chose giving. Happiness was the natural result.

In fact, she paid no attention to the intake pipes. When I asked Miriam what Chaya Sara used to do for "fun," she replied, "Nothing. She was always doing for others."

Miriam offered as an example that Chaya Sara never took walks for pleasure; she walked only when she needed to get somewhere to do something for someone. She also never visited her friends for pleasure. (Once her friends in the moshav complained that she didn't visit them. In a rare moment of humor, R' Yaakov Moshe counseled her, "Better they should be angry that you don't visit than that you do visit.")

In the Western world, we have been indoctrinated with the concept that "getting" breeds happiness — the proverbial, "When you're depressed, go out and buy a new hat."

---

1. I am grateful to Rabbi Leib Kelemen for pointing out this teaching to me.

The result of this inverted philosophy is that people spend much money and energy acquiring a profusion of material objects, and the next day they are as depressed as ever.

According to Judaism, the antidote for depression is not, "go out and buy something," but rather, "go out and help someone."

Each of us has the choice to be a giver. We have copious opportunities to give to our parents, spouse, and children. Even people who live alone can give — to friends, neighbors, co-workers, and a host of needy causes. We do not have to give on the scale of Chaya Sara Kramer; every small act of "turning on the faucet" brings a proportionate simchah.

This point, that Chaya Sara's *simchah* derived from her loving altruism to the handicapped children, begs a deeper question: How could she love children who were so inherently unlovable? Children who were grotesquely deformed? Children who were wild and even dangerous? Children whose own parents didn't even love them?

Here we hone in on the true greatness of Chaya Sara Kramer: She managed to look past the physical bodies and personalities of each child to the soul within.

Although society regarded these handicapped individuals as unproductive, the Kramers considered their lives both important and meaningful. Thus, when their lives were in jeopardy due to their illnesses, R' Yaakov Moshe added names meant to increase their longevity. Hindele became "Alte Hinda." Shiyala became "Chaim Yehoshua."

Shiyala, who was both physically and mentally impaired from birth, died after 18 years without ever walking or speaking. "He didn't talk, but he did laugh," Miriam remembers. Apparently the love the Kramers showered on him elicited such joy-induced laughter. Despite Shiyala's not having done anything perceivable by ordinary vision during his 18 years of life, R' Yaakov Moshe had inscribed on Shiyala's tombstone a lengthy epitaph fit for a *tzaddik*:

> *Chaim Yehoshua the son of _____ and _____*
> *was requested by heaven and passed away*
> *and was buried on the tenth of Iyar in the year 5734*
> *in his 18th year.*
>
> *He is an intercessor for his dear parents _____ and*
> *_____, and his dear grandfather Reb _____*
> *_____ and his dear grandmother _____,*
> *and his dear brother _____ and his sister ___*
> *_____ and his sister _____ and for Yaakov*
> *Moshe ben Chaya Kramer and for his wife Chaya Sara*
> *bas Malka and for the members of their household with*
> *which his precious soul in faith was among them for*
> *many years as a dear son and a delightful child.*
>
> *May his soul be bound with the righteous.*
>
> *And may it be His will that the verses may be fulfilled*
> *speedily and easily, "And then you shall know that I am*
> *Hashem when I open your graves and when I bring you*
> *up from your graves, My people" (Yechezkel 37:13) and*
> *"And my servant Dovid will be a king over them ...."*
> *(Yechezkel 37:24).*
>
> *The King Mashiach is Dovid himself.*

When Yaakov Moshe was asked why he bothered to inscribe the names of Shiyala's grandparents and siblings on his tombstone, he replied that the family had not come to the funeral, but someday, when Yaakov Moshe himself would no longer be there, members of the family would come looking for Shiyala's grave, and in this way they would be able to identify it with certainty.

Yaakov Moshe's prediction was fulfilled several years after his death. A chassidic woman and her daughter came to Kfar Gidon, searching for the cemetery. The woman explained to Naomi Bohbot that her brother had been one of the handicapped children cared for by the Kramers, and that he was buried somewhere in the cemetery of Kfar Gidon. Now her daughter was engaged to be married, and it was their custom to come to the graves of their relatives to invite them to the wedding. Naomi took them to the cemetery and, sure enough, the bride's uncle's grave was unmistakable.

Hindele spent the last phase of her life in the Afula hospital. There Chaya Sara sat with her all night, and R' Yaakov Moshe, after *davening Shacharis*, would sit with her all day. "They had no time to sleep," recalls Esther Schutz. "And they never complained. They did it all with *simchah*."

Two weeks before Hindele died in 1982, she said several times to Chaya Sara that she wanted to play in the *chatzer* [yard] of Shiyala. Shiyala had died years previously. Chaya Sara was alarmed by this repeated statement, fearing that it meant that Hindele would soon follow Shiyala to the Next World.

After Hindele passed away, Chaya Sara told Miriam: "Who knows, but perhaps in their previous *gilgul* Shiyala and Hindele were husband and wife, and thus they both came together to me, and therefore she wanted to play in the *chatzer* of Shiyala."

Hindele's last words were: "Mommy, I love you very much." After she died, R' Yaakov Moshe said *Kaddish* for her and learned *Mishnayos* for her. Both Kramers grieved greatly for Hindele. "After Hindele died," recalls one neighbor, "it took them a long time to return to normal life." Although, especially in her final phase in the hospital, Hindele had required absolutely all of Chaya Sara's and R' Yaakov Moshe's time, energy, and devotion, neither of them felt relieved by the demise of this 30-

year-old woman who could not move and could barely speak. On the contrary, they treated her death as a real tragedy.

Despite their total incapacity, Shiyala's tombstone proclaims that he was a "dear son and a delightful child," and Hindele's tombstone identifies her as a "good intercessor" before the Heavenly Throne. Obviously, the Kramers, while so thoroughly engaged with their charges' broken bodies, were always focused on their perfect souls.

Looking at another human being as a soul rather than according to his/her appearance, aptitudes, talents, and productivity is an exalted level of spiritual accomplishment. That Chaya Sara consistently chose to look at people with spiritual X-ray vision is evidenced by her treatment of the handicapped children.

But is this choice available to the rest of us? When our own child is throwing a tantrum, can we remember the immutable soul within? When an employee is involved in protracted personal problems, necessitating missing lengthy periods of work, can we focus on the soul and its needs over our business and its needs?

Unlike most other choices, which can be made swiftly and often dramatically, spiritual vision must be cultivated gradually. The more we perceive Divine Providence behind events large and small, the more we credit prayer as an effective agent of change, the more we appreciate Torah study as the basis of the world's existence, the more we'll be able to perceive the spiritual essence within other people. It is not a matter of choosing to put on special glasses, but rather of choosing to do daily eye-exercises that, in small increments, will ultimately confer spiritual vision. Every small choice to see the eternal soul over the appearances of the moment brings us closer to spiritual X-ray vision.

It's ironic that a soul as exalted as Chaya Sara Kramer devoted her prime not to expounding spiritual truths but to the physical drudgery of taking care of incontinent people incapable of understanding even the most rudimentary Torah concepts. Then again, perhaps it's not so ironic. G-d picked Moshe to lead the Jewish nation not because he expounded spiritual truths to Yisro's family, but because he physically picked up a tired stray lamb and carried it on his shoulders back to the flock. In Judaism, hands-on giving is the measure of greatness.

CHAPTER NINE

Hospitality, Chesed, and Humility

O NE NIGHT, AT ABOUT 2 A.M., R' YAAKOV MOSHE
and Chaya Sara were awakened by a loud knock on
their door. When R' Yaakov Moshe opened the door,
he found two women standing there. Asking no questions, he
immediately invited them in and gave them something to eat,
as Chaya Sara, fearful of nighttime intruders, timidly helped
him. The women explained that they had wanted to stay with
someone else in the moshav, but the other family didn't let
them in. As R' Yaakov Moshe and Chaya Sara were making
up their own beds with fresh linen for the women (they themselves would sleep on the concrete floor), she whispered to
him, "Why did they come so late at night?"

R' Yaakov Moshe answered, "Why do we need to know? If
someone comes to you for something, you give to them."

The Kramers turned giving into a fine art. Just as a work of
art has many different dimensions — color, form, style, mood
— so the Kramers' hospitality had many different dimen-

sions: *how* they gave; *how much* they gave; *to whom* they gave; *at what cost to themselves* they gave.

The Kramers' hospitality was not reserved for Shabbos guests. Any person who came to their house at any time was treated like an honored guest. "The way they received everyone was unbelievable," recalls Esther Schutz. "The two of them literally *ran* to the door. They would exclaim, 'Oh! What an important guest has arrived!' Every guest was made to feel so very important."

"Guests" included even people from Kfar Gidon whom they saw daily. Tamar Cohen, a moshav housewife 40 years Chaya Sara's junior, remembers: "Chaya Sara would announce each visitor before they entered, calling each person 'dear.' When I came, even just to borrow a cup of sugar, she would announce, 'Dear Mrs. Tamar Cohen has arrived.'"

As soon as the guest entered their humble abode, the Kramers would serve liquid refreshment and something to eat. "Sit down. What will you drink?" they would ask and, without waiting for an answer, they would start pouring cola and loading the table with food. "Everything they had in the house, they set out on the table," another young neighbor testifies.

Chaya Sara feeding visitors c. 1983

Rebbetzin Chaya Sara, R' Yaakov Moshe, and R' Avigdor Galandauer
in the Kramers' home in Kfar Gidon

R' Yaakov Moshe's niece Pnina recalls, "In their house, you couldn't empty your cup, because they would immediately refill it."

According to Miriam, if the guest had come from afar, the *tzaddik* would whisper to him, "Perhaps the guest needs to use the bathroom." Miriam adds: "He would whisper so as not to embarrass him."

The Kramers made no distinction between one guest and another. Great rabbis, ordinary people, wealthy visitors from abroad, poor beggars, old and young, Ashkenazim, Sephardim, Chasidim, Litvaks, religious and nonreligious —all were received with honor, joy, and love.

The Kramers' *ahavas Yisrael* [love for other Jews] was expressed through every part of their bodies: their eyes, their smiles, their voices, their hugs. R' Yaakov Moshe typically kissed on the shoulders the men who arrived, while Chaya Sara often hugged the women.

Their legs also took part in the mitzvah. "They were always waiting for guests," Simcha Heizler remembers. "Chaya Sara would look out the window to see who was coming. As soon as she saw me, she would run outside to greet me."

Meir Shalom Tanzee recalls his first meeting with the Kramers:

> When the Rav heard from my father that he had a son who studied in a yeshivah (this was very rare during those years in the Afula area), he asked to meet me. The first meeting was very moving. The Rav received me with kisses and great love. From then on and on every occasion that permitted, I would visit the Rav and Rabbanit. The Rav would sit with me and we would expound Torah. And the Rabbanit loved our family.

Any person who missed the last bus that passed Kfar Gidon would be invited to spend the night at the Kramers. One evening Chaya Sara and Tamar Cohen were conversing near the bus stop. A young girl, a stranger, was standing and waiting for the bus. Chaya Sara did not consider it safe for a young girl to travel alone at night. She invited the girl to sleep at their house.

R' Yaakov Moshe was especially zealous in preparing the beds for overnight guests. He never asked his wife to do it. Meir Shalom Tanzee describes one night in the 1970's when he slept at the Kramers' house:

> Once the Rav and I were at a wedding in Bnei Brak. On the way back, there was private transportation to Kfar Gidon. Because my parents lived in Afula Ilit and it was too late at night to get a public bus there, I was compelled to stay at the Rav's home. The Rav prepared my bed for me. Of course, I didn't agree that he should make up the bed for me. I was a young man and the Rav was elderly. I wanted to make the bed myself, but the Rav insisted that he do this mitzvah. Then he waited for me to get into bed. He wouldn't go to sleep until I was in bed.

The Kramers, who lived so sparsely, loved and gave so profusely. When one couple from England arrived to visit, Chaya Sara put out drinks and grapes for them. "Massive amounts of grapes," remembers Sheindy Leiber. "You'd think they had a lot. Of course, they had nothing. But they gave us massive amounts of grapes and other fruit."

According to Aliza Kevisa, who spent considerable time in the Kramers' house, R' Yaakov Moshe's own diet was usually restricted to bread, garlic, and salt. On special occasions he would eat boiled potatoes. But the Kramers fed guests according to a completely different standard. "His wife the Rabbanit would make and serve others what they themselves never ate. He always had canned goods he would open for visitors who came from afar."

And the visitors would relish both the food and the holy atmosphere. "Even when the food was simple, visitors would taste a special taste that they had never tasted before," Aliza reminisces.

"The Rebbetzin was a wonderful cook," recalls Miriam. "Anyone who came into their house said, 'Rebbetzin, what a wonderful smell in your house!' One guest said, 'Even a slice of bread with margarine and a slice of tomato in your house tastes better than a kabob in my own house.'"

When guests from afar left, Chaya Sara would give them provisions for the journey home. Rebbetzin Baila Berger from Jerusalem remembers: "They could only give to us. We couldn't leave without getting a box of cookies — not a couple of cookies, but a whole box."

Starting in 1980, R' Yaakov Moshe became recognized more and more as "a hidden *tzaddik*." For the last decade that they lived in Kfar Gidon, a steady stream of visitors made their way to the Kramers' home, to receive blessings, to ask advice, and to simply bask in their holy radiance. Their neighbor Yossi Shtiglitz remembers: "The road to their

Chaya Sara seeing off visitors, 1980's

house had cars going on it all night — 1 a.m., 2 a.m., all night until morning."

On *Chol HaMoed* of the final years, over 100 people came each day to visit the Kramers. R' Yaakov Moshe built a large sukkah in his yard to accommodate all the guests.

Tviki Shtiglitz, who was a *ben bayis* in the Kramer's home, declared:

> *Why do I say that R' Yaakov Moshe was the greatest of the generation? Other gedolim have a seder yom [daily schedule]— so many hours for learning, so many hours for sleeping, so many hours for receiving the public. R' Yaakov Moshe received people 24 hours a day. People came at 3 a.m., 4 a.m., all the time.*

All those visitors had to be fed — and copiously, as far as the Kramers were concerned. There was no grocery store in Kfar Gidon. While R' Yaakov Moshe's brother Shlomo, through his job, supplied the Kramers with crates of apples, all the other food and drinks served to the guests had to be bought in Afula. Chaya Sara, accompanied by Avramele, would buy food and bottles of soda in Afula, and would *shlep* the heavy baskets back on the bus to Kfar Gidon. This despite her hernia and her chronic leg ailments.

According to Halachah, the mitzvah of hospitality is fulfilled by escorting the guest the distance of four *amos*, approximately eight steps, as a token of honor. Sheindy Leiber describes how, when she ended her visit, Rebbetzin Chaya Sara walked her all the way to the entrance of Kfar Gidon, almost a hundred meters from her house. Naomi Bohbot's daughter Nachami, who grew up in Kfar Gidon, remembers that when, as a 10-year-old child, she would visit Chaya Sara, the 60-year-old Rebbetzin would escort her half of the way home.

Miriam refers to a verse in *Tehillim* in order to describe her adopted parents' mode of giving: "All day long he sympathizes and lends." She asks the obvious question: "Is the *tzaddik* so wealthy that he can lend money to others all day long? No! The meaning of the verse is: All day long he lends *his time* to others. This was the way of Rav Yaakov Moshe and the Rebbetzin. They always listened to others."

Rebbetzin Chaya Sara with Faigy Galandauer in front of the Kramer home

Once, during the period she lived in Jerusalem, Chaya Sara received a phone call from a deeply depressed woman. Chaya Sara conversed with this woman nonstop for nine hours, without a break, until she had succeeded in alleviating the woman's despair.

Rebbetzin Chaya Sara (on right) at sheva berachos in the Gabbai home, Afula

The Kramers' generosity did not stop at the walls of their home. They gave munificent gifts for every wedding, bar mitzvah, and *bris* celebrated by a Kfar Gidon family. "The Kramers gave more — much more — than anyone else in the moshav," one neighbor recalls. In the days when fifty *liras* for a *bris* gift was typical, the Kramers would give 100 or 150 *liras*.

Once when the Bohbot family made a *bris*, R' Yaakov Moshe gave them a generous sum. Knowing that the Kramers themselves lived in utter poverty, Naomi Bohbot did not want to accept so much money from them. She tried to return the envelope to R' Yaakov Moshe. "I didn't start this mitzvah," he told her. "Avraham, Yitzchak, and Yaakov did it before me." And he adamantly refused the money.

That same bountiful generosity extended itself to repairmen and even taxi drivers. Kfar Gidon resident Chaim Cohen was an electrician. One afternoon the Kramers had a short circuit. They called Chaim to come and fix it. Chaim, who greatly admired the *tzaddikim*, was happy to render them any service. He put his ladder into his car, drove over, and fixed the short circuit. It took him two minutes. The Kramers insisted on paying him a considerable sum. Chaim refused. "It took me only two minutes," he protested. But, they argued, he had taken the trouble to bring the ladder and drive over. They pleaded with him to accept the money. Chaim absolutely refused, and went home.

The matter did not end there. Chaya Sara called Chaim's wife Tamar and tried to persuade her to take the money. Tamar demurred. She quoted to Chaya Sara the Gemara, "A good wife does the will of her husband," and sealed her refusal with, "I can't take money without my husband's approval."

Much to Tamar's surprise, Chaya Sara responded, "Yes, you can. Don't tell him!"

Tamar still declined. Later that day, Chaya Sara quietly came over to the Cohens' house and gave one of the children an envelope containing the ample payment.

Years later, when Chaya Sara was living in Jerusalem, she would occasionally take taxis. Israelis don't tip and often argue vehemently with the driver regarding the price of a taxi ride. That's why Esther Ben Chaim, who once accompanied the Rebbetzin in a cab, was amazed when Chaya Sara paid the taxi driver double the sum indicated on the meter.

The Kramers' fine art of giving required much sensitivity and forethought. Miriam describes going with her Tatty (R' Yaakov Moshe) to the Central Bus Station in Afula. A row of beggars was always sitting there. Before approaching them, R' Yaakov Moshe would count the number of beggars, then stand to the side and divide his money into that number of equal portions. Little Miriam would ask, "What does it matter how much you give each one?"

Her Tatty would reply, "My dear daughter, I don't want to favor any one of them in particular. Afterwards, they compare, and I don't want any of them to be jealous."

The walk to the Central Bus Station itself was an exercise in consummate giving. According to Miriam:

> The tzaddik always looked on both sides of the road. When
> he saw a person on a bench, deep in thought, he always

*approached him, embraced him, and began a conversation
with him. When he realized that the person's monetary situation was not 100 percent, he immediately put his hand in
his pocket, being extremely careful not to insult, and always
gave this money with closed hands; I never saw the amount.
Upon leaving, he always expounded divrei Torah. Sometimes
it seemed to these people that he was Eliahu HaNavi.*

Sometimes the price of giving was more than money or
even time. Once, while riding on a bus, R' Yaakov Moshe
noticed a religious 16-year-old girl looking very distraught.
He immediately wanted to help her but, out of modesty,
he would not sit in the seat beside her. He approached the
secular man sitting in the seat across the aisle from the girl,
and asked him if he would mind switching seats with him.
"Oh," the man retorted disparagingly, "you're interested in
the girl?"

R' Yaakov Moshe was too humble to let this insult hinder
his *chesed*. He answered quietly, "If you wouldn't mind."
The man got up and, while the other passengers jeered, R'
Yaakov Moshe sat down across from the girl and inquired
into the problem.

It turned out that she came from a seriously dysfunctional
family. R' Yaakov Moshe invited her to come home with him.
It's a measure of the purity that was evident on his face that
the girl took up his offer. She moved in with the Kramers for
six months. A year later they found her a *shidduch*. Today
she's happily married with 12 children.

Another time, R' Yaakov Moshe brought home a man with
severe epilepsy. He stayed with them for several months.

The love the Kramers bestowed on everyone was truly
unconditional. Tamar Cohen knew a social worker named Iris
K., whom she sent to the Kramers to convince them to accept
health insurance from the state for Avramele and Hindele.

Iris, who was not religious, would pay weekly visits to help with Hindele. As Iris recalls, "They gave me the desire to help them. I was very impressed by them, because they were impressive people, real *tzaddikim*." One week she showed up in long sleeves as a sign of respect for the Kramers. She told Tamar afterward that the *tzaddikim* had told her that she didn't have to dress up especially for them. "They said, 'Any way you want, come!'" Iris was overwhelmed by such whole-hearted, unconditional acceptance. Thirty years later, when she was being interviewed for this book, Iris' predominant memory of the Kramers was: "They loved me very much."

The Kramers' hospitality was a fruit that grew from the branch of their generosity. They were generous with their material resources, with their time, with their respect, and with their love. Their faucet was always turned on full force.

Jews aspire to be close to G-d, but what does that mean? As Rabbi Leib Kelemen teaches: "Closeness in the physical world is measured by inches; closeness in the spiritual world is measured by similarity." If we want to be close to G-d, we must be similar to G-d. G-d's primary observable attribute is His generosity. The entire universe is the product of His giving, as the verse states, "His kindness fills the world."

To be close to G-d entails becoming a giver. Many of our life choices require choosing between being a giver or being a taker. This essential giver/taker choice pertains not only to the obvious decisions of how much charity to give, when to take time out to help a friend, and how big a gift to give for a wedding. We choose to be a giver every time we stop to listen to an elderly person's complaints about her aches and pains, every time we flash a smile at a passerby, every time we give a drink and a sincere thanks to a repairman, and every time we give a compliment. We choose to be a taker every time we steal even the smallest item (e.g., a grape in the supermarket), every time we get off a bus or taxi without thanking the driver, every time we take a huge helping at a buffet of a dish that may run out before others have had any, and every time we take offense because others did not give us due respect.

I always considered myself a generous person, until I started researching the life of Chaya Sara Kramer and discovered what true generosity is. I had always been generous with my money, but stingy with my time. I had always had room at my Shabbos table for people I liked, but not for people who rubbed me the wrong way. I had always offered drinks to visitors, but not the chocolate-chip cookies I was saving for myself. I had always showed honor to people who are smart, interesting, and well spoken, but had little patience for people I considered tiresome and boring. The more I have immersed myself in the example of Rebbetzin Chaya Sara, the more I use as the litmus test of my life's choices the question, "What would Rebbetzin Chaya Sara have done?"

This does not mean that I can duplicate the quantity of her giving, but rather that I can emulate its quality. I don't have to give a taxi driver twice the fare, but I can refrain from quibbling with him over the price of a ride. I don't have to make myself available to people 24 hours a day, but I also don't have to treat every five-minute phone call from a tzedakkah organization as an imposition on my precious time.

Writing this chapter about Rebbetzin Chaya Sara's generosity has been an especially difficult test for me. During the six days this summer that my youngest was away at overnight camp, five days were devoted to relatives with young children who were staying with us. The last day of camp was the only day that I could work on this book without interruption or disturbance. I looked forward to that single day with relish. Then, the night before, a young *woman from up north who had been grappling with becoming religious phoned and asked me if she could come to speak with me the next day, the only day she would be in Jerusalem. The morning of my "uninterrupted day to write," my cousin, who suffers from terrible back pain, and whom I had been urging to go to my doctor, managed to get an appointment for — of course — that day, and asked me to drive her. I considered both these tests to be above my choice box. It was, I felt, beyond my level of altruism to give away my one child-free day.*

To contemplate the chesed of Chaya Sara Kramer, how-ever, is to expand the vistas of one's own potential. In the end, giving away large chunks of my child-free day was not beyond my capacity, but only beyond my imagination. If a 1-year-old baby did not see other people walking, he would never pull himself upright and attempt those first wobbly steps. Learning about Rebbetzin Chaya Sara's all-encompassing generosity shows me how expandable the limits of possibility actually are.

In the end, I drove my cousin to the doctor and spent two hours talking with the young woman. And I learned that every Jew can draw close to G-d by choosing to be a giver.

In the quality of *chesed*, R' Yaakov Moshe was his wife's mentor. Sometimes guests would drop in on Friday after-noon. Chaya Sara would worry that she did not have time to sit and talk with them because she still had so many Shabbos preparations to finish. R' Yaakov Moshe would say to her, "You'll have enough time. Now is the mitzvah."

She would obligingly sit down and speak with the guests. When they left, her husband would help her scurry through the Shabbos preparations.

Only once did Chaya Sara fail the test of hospitality. She made soup one day for a large contingent of guests. No sooner

did that group eat and depart than another group arrived. R'
Yaakov Moshe asked Chaya Sara to cook another pot of soup
for them. Exhausted and not in the mood for cooking, she said
that she would make only omelets and salad for them. Her
husband did not consider that an honorable enough meal for
their guests. "I don't have *koach* to make more soup," Chaya

Sara balked. "Once a
day is enough."

R' Yaakov Moshe
did not insist. Instead,
he himself made the
soup, with chicken,
potatoes, and farfel.

Later that same
day, Chaya Sara fell
in the house and
broke her arm. When
Anni Kalfe, one of
the young neigh-
bors, dropped by and

*Rebbetzin Chaya Sara and Faigy Galandauer,
with Avramele in the background*

found Chaya Sara's arm in a cast, the Rebbetzin told her, "The
Ribbono Shel Olam punished me because I didn't want to cook
for guests." She said to Anni that she had learned her lesson
and would never again complain about cooking.

*One can learn from the failures of a tzaddekes
as much as from her successes. A verse states:
"A tzaddik falls seven times and rises" [Mishlei
24:16]. While some interpret the verse to mean that
a tzaddik makes no more than seven mistakes,
another interpretation asserts that a person who rises
every time s/he falls will eventually become a tzaddik.
Given her spiritual level, Chaya Sara felt she had made
the wrong choice. Her response to her failure comprised*

four steps: 1) She viewed her broken arm as the result of her own action; 2) she admitted her mistake; 3) she regretted her choice; and 4) she resolved to do differently in the future.

She didn't consider her broken arm a mishap unrelated to her own deeds. (The Gemara says that when one suffers, one should question one's deeds.) She didn't try to justify her action by saying, "After all, I did cook one pot of soup already." She didn't wallow in self-deprecation. She didn't let her failure paralyze her from acting better in the future.

Sometimes our test is not whether we will make the right choice in a particular situation, but rather how we will respond to the results of our own wrong choice. Judaism always offers the possibility of doing teshuvah. The Rambam's steps of teshuvah are synonymous with Chaya Sara's steps 2-4 above. Some tests are too difficult to pass, but responding to failure the way Rebbetzin Chaya Sara did may be the real choice available to us.

Miriam's reminiscences give us a glimpse into the Shabbos hospitality of the Kramers:

> *When the tzaddik returned from the synagogue, he usually brought guests who had no place to stay. To everyone present he said individually, "A gut Shabbes." And to his wife he added, "A gut Shabbes, mein tyer kind." Only then would he begin to sing "Shalom Aleichem."*
>
> *The Shabbos seudah would begin with words of Torah. When one of the guests said a devar Torah, the tzaddik acted as if he were hearing it for the first time. He would say enthusiastically, "Yasher koach, yasher koach!" If it happened that one of the guests began a mundane discussion, the*

*tzaddik would gently go into a spiritual topic. He prepared
a bed, a cup and basin for washing hands, and a towel for
every guest, and asked if they needed anything else.*

*He always said to me, "Know, my dear daughter, that
our important mother helps me in every way. Exactly as
it is written in Eishes Chayil: 'She always does him only
good and not bad.'" I can say that the Rebbetzin was full of
wisdom and chesed, and thus merited that all those whom
she helped are like her children, as it is written: "Her children rise up and call her blessed, her husband praises her."*

If the branch that produced the fruit of the Kramers' hospitality was generosity, the trunk of their *middos*-tree, that from
which all their traits grew, was humility. Only a person ani-
mated by humility could serve others with such zeal. Only a
humble person could consider another's need for succor to be
more important than his own need for sleep. Only a humble
person could accord honor to those half her age or who possessed a fraction of her piety.

The converse is also true. Ego — a feeling of superiority
toward others — keeps one from hugging strangers, from
giving the first greeting on the street, and from undertaking
menial tasks — shlepping, serving, and cleaning up — for
the benefit of those one regards as inferior in status, wealth,
or religiosity. "I deserve those chocolate-chip cookies more
than these uninvited guests" is the sentiment that undermines Kramer-level hospitality.

The Kramers' humility is reminiscent of characters out of
chassidic stories. Whenever people would call R' Yaakov
Moshe "Rav," he would correct them, saying, "I'm not a Rav.
I have no *semichah* [Rabbinic ordination]. I'm just a simple
Jew." Chaya Sara would stand beside him and nod, "Yes, he's

not a Rav. We're simply nothing. We're equal to the peel of a garlic."

The only ones who believed them were themselves. Once, toward the end of his life, R' Yaakov Moshe walked into the hall where a *bris* was being celebrated. The crowd started to sing, "*Yamim al ye'mei melech*," the song reserved for the entrance of important rabbis. R' Yaakov Moshe looked around with curiosity and asked, "Which big rabbi has arrived?"

R' Yaakov Moshe on his way to a simchah

When strangers asked them who they were, R' Yaakov Moshe would reply that he was a farmer, and Chaya Sara would say that she was a midwife for cows.

In his favorite book, the *Noam Elimelech*, R' Yaakov Moshe's favorite passage [*Parashas Bamidbar*, the third entry] is about humility. It discusses how a person must feel humble without feeling inferior or depressed. The trick is for the person to be happy that he is a Jew. Being a Jew is a distinction that should make a person proud without making him prideful.

The first day I met Chaya Sara, in the summer of 1985, she asked me to *daven* for certain people, writing a list on the back of a soda-bottle label. The first names on the list were R' Yaakov Moshe's and her own. Then there were other names, people who needed healing or children or a *shidduch*. I did what she asked, but I wondered what good the prayers of a person like me, barely two months observant, would do. Years later I asked her. She replied: "One never knows how great a soul is, or whose prayers are accepted in heaven. It's possible that a soul is important, more so than I am."

The yielding R' Yaakov Moshe was adamant in his rejection of any form of honor. Whenever Meir Shalom Tanzee would take his leave of R' Yaakov Moshe, he would try to kiss his hand, an honor accorded to eminent rabbis in the Sephardi tradition. R' Yaakov Moshe would never allow him to do so.

Yossi Shtiglitz testifies about R' Yaakov Moshe:

> He always wanted to remain hidden. Even when Rav Klein [the official rabbi of Kfar Gidon] was absent, he didn't want to give the shiur. Someone else would give the shiur and he would help him. He made out as if he didn't know anything. He would say, "I don't know." He never answered any sha'elah. He said, "There's a rabbi of the place," and he refused to answer.

Once, when Miriam was about 12 years old, she and her younger sister were visiting the Kramers for Shabbos. During the Shabbos meal, her sister whispered to Miriam, "Do you have a safety pin?" Before Miriam could answer, R' Yaakov Moshe jumped up from his place and fetched a safety pin for the child. His humility was so profound that he never considered it beneath him to wait on the needs of other people, no matter who they were.

During the 1980's, before each of R' Yaakov Moshe's frequent trips abroad, he used to phone all the young couples in the moshav to take their leave. The memory still stirs Naomi Bohbot: "This great tzaddik would call us to say goodbye. Who were we? We were nobody. But he showed us this sign of respect."

When R' Yaakov Moshe wrote letters to Avigdor Galandauer, who was several decades his junior, he would address them:

"To the honor of the *Rav*, the *Tzaddik*, the *Gaon* Galandauer," and continue with a string of Biblically referenced epitaphs of high praise. And he would sign the letters, "Your lowly student, Yaakov Moshe the son of Chaya Kramer."

Several years before her death, I asked Rebbetzin Chaya Sara for permission to write her biography. Despising fame and honor, she refused. I tried again, this time promising to write the book without using her real name. "No one will know who I'm writing about," I promised. To this she consented. Some months later, deeply immersed in interviewing people who were eager to share their recollections of the late *tzaddik* R' Yaakov Moshe Kramer, *zt"l*, and his wife, I realized an inherent problem. I went to Rebbetzin Chaya Sara and told her, "I promised to use a pseudonym instead of your real name, but what about your husband? If I don't use his real name, no one will realize that I'm writing about R' Yaakov Moshe Kramer."

The Rebbetzin shrugged her shoulders and replied: "So what? He wasn't interested in fame either."

(Although my agreement with her was that I would publish her biography, using a pseudonym for her, during her lifetime, she prophetically told Esther Ben Chaim that I was writing her biography, and that it would be published after her death. In fact, when I wrote articles about her during her lifetime, I always used a pseudonym for her.)

Once, walking home from shul on Shabbos with the Gevirtzes, R' Yaakov Moshe saw a neighbor from Telmei Gidon desecrating Shabbos. The elderly *tzaddik* told the Gevirtzes that *Hakadosh Baruch Hu* brought him to see this act of *chillul Shabbos* because there was something inside him that he needed to repair.

Ultimate humility leads to ultimate hospitality, because one has no sense of one's own domain or proprietary rights. One *erev Pesach* during the early years, as Chaya Sara and R' Yaakov Moshe were rushing around performing the final

Pesach preparations, they heard a knock at the door. They opened the door to find an odd-looking couple. The man looked at least 20 years older than his wife, and they were acting strangely.

They announced, "We want to stay here for Pesach." The Kramers welcomed the couple in, but the guests soon started to take over the small, cleaned-for-Pesach kitchen. The woman commandeered Chaya Sara's few Pesach utensils and the kosher-for-Pesach food Chaya Sara had so laboriously prepared.

It was a Jewish housewife's worse nightmare. Pesach is a time for total stringency in the kitchen, and here were complete strangers of unknown level of observance using Chaya Sara's utensils and her one-burner kerosene stove, rendering them, as far as the Kramers were concerned, unkosher. In the back room, the young Chaya Sara whispered to her husband that she couldn't accommodate such guests.

"Of course we can," R' Yaakov Moshe replied. "I'll run into Afula right now. I'll buy you another kerosene stove. I'll buy you some new utensils."

Chaya Sara conceded. Just hours before the Seder, she koshered the kitchen again and started cooking all over again.

The guests took over the whole small house. Then they announced that they would have their Seder — alone — at the kitchen table, the only table the Kramers owned. Undaunted, R' Yaakov Moshe took two boards, placed them on a large rock outside, and covered them with a white tablecloth. "This will be our Seder table," he told an abashed Chaya Sara.

Indeed, R' Yaakov Moshe and Chaya Sara celebrated their Seder outside, on the makeshift table. On Seder night, every Jew is supposed to feel like a king, elevated from the humble origins of slaves. Despite — or because of — the bare-bones setting of their Seder, one can imagine R' Yaakov Moshe and Chaya Sara as true royalty that night, ruling over their own emotions and conditioning and the voice of the ego that carps, "Mine, not theirs."

The domineering couple stayed the entire seven days of Pesach, sleeping in the Kramers' only beds, demanding all sorts of things, and commanding the Kramers to serve them. Neither R' Yaakov Moshe nor Chaya Sara ever lost patience with their overbearing guests.

After the holiday, the couple gave a simple, "Thank you, Shalom," and left. R' Yaakov Moshe raised his hands heavenward and said, "Thank you, Hashem, that You sent us such wonderful guests."

Chaya Sara was sure that the couple were Eliyahu HaNavi. But, unlike the legends of Jewish lore, no child was born to them the year after, nor the year after that. "A mitzvah leads to another mitzvah." Perhaps the reward for passing this rigorous test was that they were given a lifetime of opportunities to extend hospitality.

CHAPTER TEN

Promises, Prayers, or Piety?

*T*HE KRAMERS' "ADOPTED" DAUGHTER MIRIAM married young and gave birth to two daughters. Then, despite Miriam's yearning and the Kramers' blessings, Miriam did not conceive again. Six long years passed. One day, Miriam heard a knock on her door. She opened it to find a young woman bearing a note from Rebbetzin Chaya Sara. The note read: "I'm sending you this girl. If you help her find a *shidduch,* I promise you that you will have a viable child."

Of course, Miriam exerted herself to find the young woman a *shidduch.* She succeeded in arranging a match for her with a fine *ben Torah.* Six months after the wedding, Miriam gave birth to a healthy son.

In 1986, on the morning of *erev Pesach,* Avigdor Galandauer's baby son Yoeli broke out in blotches all over his body. The alarmed parents rushed the boy to the doctor, who informed them that the situation was very serious and they must go immediately to the hospital. The doctor phoned a specialist at the hospital and requested that he see the child urgently because of the gravity of his condition. He also told the Galandauers that they should take their matzos and wine to the hospital, because they would definitely be spending Pesach in the pediatric ward.

The Galandauers sped home to pack their things. They had no idea what they would do for Pesach. The first Seder was only hours away, and they had no idea where or how they would make the Seder in the hospital, especially since the special Pesach-food restrictions would be impossible to maintain there. With mounting panic, amid the cries of their distraught baby, they phoned R' Yaakov Moshe in Kfar Gidon.

At first the line was busy, but finally they got through. R' Yaakov Moshe blessed the baby, saying, "It will be all right." Armed with the blessing, the Galandauers rushed their child to the hospital, where they were whisked past dozens of

R' Yaakov Moshe giving a sugar cube to Yoeli

people waiting to see the specialist. The specialist, having been alerted about the urgency of Yoeli Galandauer's condition, saw them immediately. He undressed the baby. To everyone's amazement, all the blotches had disappeared.

A resident of Kfar Gidon relates this story:

> *My sister, who lived in Be'er Sheva, was married for six years with no children. Of course, this placed great stress in her marriage, and finally she and her husband decided to divorce. They had already divided all their possessions when she phoned me to tell me that they were about to divorce. I didn't know what to say. I immediately phoned R' Yaakov Moshe and told him. He instructed me to travel to Be'er Sheva and to tell my sister and brother-in-law not to divorce and that in one year, b'ezras Hashem, they would have a child.*
> *My husband and I went to Beer Sheva that very night. We delivered the message from R' Yaakov Moshe, and the couple decided to stay together. After exactly one year, they had a son.*

The year before the Kramers moved to Jerusalem was a very bad year for agriculture. Yossi Shtiglitz, who farmed both his own plot and the Kramers' plot, was talking to R' Yaakov Moshe about his dire financial plight when he started to cry. R' Yaakov Moshe encouraged him, "Don't worry. It will be good this year. Everything will be okay."

How could everything be okay? Yossi wondered. Onions, for example, were selling for a pittance. It wasn't even worth taking them to market. Yossi put his whole onion crop in storage beneath his house. Then, two weeks later, "it was unbelievable!" Yossi exclaims. "Suddenly there were no onions in the whole country. I sold my onions for five times the usual price."

The Kramers blessed people in sundry ways: to get married, to have children, to be healed from serious or minor illnesses, and to be delivered from financial straits. No Jew's concern was too trifling for the Kramers' blessing.

A woman from Migdal HaEmek came asking for a blessing that she would succeed in getting her driver's license. A family from Beit Shean sought a blessing for their daughter's hair to stop falling out. A resident of Kfar Gidon, summoned for an audit, got a blessing that he would find favor in the eyes of the tax authorities.

Even automobiles were not too mundane for the Kramers' blessing. Young Rav Yaakov Deutsch once bought an old American jalopy. R' Yaakov Moshe blessed him that the car would take him wherever he had to go. Some time later Rav Deutsch was driving toward Kfar Gidon when the car broke down outside of Balfouria, several kilometers away. Rav Deutsch got out, opened the hood, and saw that the engine was on fire. He managed to get water from a sympathetic resident of Balfouria and put out the fire. The resident offered to let Rav Deutsch use his telephone to call to have the car towed, but Rav Deutsch, remembering the blessing, sat down in the driver's seat and implausibly attempted to start the burned-out car. To the astonishment of both of them, the car worked. Rav Deutsch drove directly to the home of R' Yaakov Moshe and told him what had happened. R' Yaakov Moshe laughed.

Just as the Kramers' blessings were diverse, so were the ways in which they gave them. Sometimes they gave a blessing with no conditions attached. At other times, they recommended *segulos* or they might suggest to a female petitioner that she cover her hair. Sometimes, they gave the petitioners an addressed envelope and asked them to send *tzedakkah* to a person in need. At still other times, they recommended a spiritual *tikkun*, such as reciting *Iggeres HaRamban* or specific psalms. To women in childbirth, they advised praying in the merit of Amaslai bas Karnavo, the mother of Avraham Avinu (as mentioned in *Bava Basra* 91a). The Kramers had no stock remedies. They looked at — or into — each soul and prescribed accordingly.

The Kramers believed that a woman could make herself into a more worthy *kli* [vessel] to receive blessings by covering her hair. Several people testified that childless women they knew who came to the Kramers for a blessing conceived after they began covering their hair. One woman remembers that her aunt was gravely ill after an operation. At R' Yaakov Moshe's prompting, she undertook to cover her hair, and she recovered.

Once a *chareidi* couple came to the Kramers' door. Chaya Sara opened it, invited them in, and inquired as to what they wanted. They explained that they had suffered many miscarriages, and wanted a blessing from the Rav to have children. Evidently, R' Yaakov Moshe was not home, but Chaya Sara told the woman, "If you stop wearing a wig and wear a kerchief instead, you'll have a child." On the spot, the woman agreed. Chaya Sara left the room for a moment; when she returned, she handed the woman the kerchief that she herself had been wearing. The woman immediately donned it, and ten months later she bore a healthy baby.

Often the blessing was accompanied by an exact time frame for its fulfillment. One Pesach, when Kfar Gidon resident Anni Kalfe's daughter Dafna had been married a year without conceiving, she asked Chaya Sara for a blessing. The Rebbetzin blessed her, and added that next year at this time Dafna would visit her and tell her that she was expecting. The following Pesach, Dafna came, bearing the happy news.

Once, after Pesach during the sixth year of the *shemittah* cycle, a woman went to R' Yaakov Moshe to ask for a blessing to marry off her first son. R' Yaakov Moshe told her, "By *shemittah*, he'll be a *chassan*." Indeed, the day before Rosh Hashanah, the boy became engaged.

The Talmud asserts: "The *tzaddik* decrees, and Hashem fulfills." But a closer examination of the blessings conferred by the Kramers reveals layer upon layer of mystery. What was the difference between when they *blessed* and when they *promised*? Did the actualization of the blessing come by fiat or as a result of heartfelt, tear-soaked prayers later that night? Did they have the power to affect Heavenly decrees, or only the spiritual vision to see the decrees before they materialized in the physical realm?

Many of the stories would support the latter thesis but obviously, we can never know. For example, a chassidic woman in England was an *agunah* (a woman whose husband's whereabouts was unknown or who had declined to give her a divorce) for nine years. One day, the day before *Rosh Chodesh* Adar, the woman phoned Rebbetzin Chaya Sara and poured out her heart. The Rebbetzin told her, "Before *Rosh Chodesh* Adar, you'll have your *get.*" That afternoon, much to her own amazement, the woman received her *get.* It seems that Rebbetzin Chaya Sara had the preternatural ability to see the *get* en route, although her power did not dispatch it.

Another time, a few days before the Hebrew month of Cheshvan, a woman called Rebbetzin Chaya Sara and told her that her son, who had been involved in *shidduchim* for some time, had not yet succeeded in finding a match. The Rebbetzin replied, "He'll be engaged during the month of Cheshvan." The woman thought this was highly unlikely, because there were no new *shidduchim* even on the horizon. As it happened, her son had been involved in a *shidduch* that had terminated. In the beginning of the month of Cheshvan, that *shidduch* resumed, and by the end of the month, they were engaged.

Did the Kramers' blessing bring about the desired result or did it simply forecast what was already fated to occur? The question arises regarding story after story. One man who had lost his job called Rebbetzin Chaya Sara and begged for a blessing for *parnassah*. She told him, "Don't worry. You'll get something much better, with double pay." Two days later, the man called her with the good news that he had found a new job. Moreover, the salary was precisely double what he had been earning.

The anatomy of a blessing, of what transpires in the realms where decrees are formed and transformed, is perhaps most enigmatically glimpsed in the story of Shani Lisser. Moshe and Shani Lisser of London were married for four years with no children. In 1985, Shani decided to travel to Israel to get the blessing of the *tzaddik* R' Yaakov Moshe Kramer. Rabbi Becker of Bnei Brak took her to Kfar Gidon, where they met with R' Yaakov Moshe.

R' Yaakov Moshe gave Shani three *segulos* that, he assured her, would facilitate her having a child:

1. To make a meal in the merit of the prophet Hoshea ben Be'ari and to feed "10 important indigent people," meaning impoverished Torah scholars.
2. To wear a necklace engraved with the Hebrew letter *hei*, because Hashem created the world with the letter *hei*.
3. To start paying school tuition for a child learning Torah.

With these three recommendations, the visit appeared to be over, but Shani was not satisfied. She asked R' Yaakov Moshe for a blessing to have a child. R' Yaakov Moshe declined, protesting, "I'm not a rebbe. I don't give blessings."

"I came to Eretz Yisrael just to get a blessing from you," Shani remonstrated, "and I'm not leaving without a blessing." She sat there gazing at R' Yaakov Moshe, who was seated across the table from her.

Suddenly R' Yaakov Moshe burst into tears and said, "You will have a child this year."

Shani emerged from the Kramers' house trembling. "I'd been to other *gedolim*," she recalls, "but I'd never had a *gadol* burst into tears and tell me, 'You'll have a child.'"

Later that same day, R' Shalom Yair Schwartz phoned R' Yaakov Moshe from London. His wife was expecting and was experiencing difficulty. He begged for a blessing that his wife would not lose the child. R' Yaakov Moshe told him that by *davening* for another expectant woman, his own wife would be healed. He gave R' Shalom Yair the Hebrew name of an expectant woman for whom to *daven*. Only months later did R' Shalom Yair learn that this was the Hebrew name of Shani Lisser, whom he knew. R' Yaakov Moshe added portentously, "This young woman was here today asking for a *yeshuah*. She already has her *yeshuah*, but she doesn't know it."

All this transpired on Monday. On Thursday night, Shani flew back to England. On Friday and Shabbos, she felt sick. On Sunday, she learned that she was expectant.

At the end of a full term, Shani Lisser gave birth to her first child, a daughter. Obviously, R' Yaakov Moshe knew that Shani had already conceived when she came to see him. Why then did he decline to bless her? And why did he burst into tears?

Several years later, during a fundraising trip to England, R' Yaakov Moshe came to the Lissers' house accompanied by Avigdor Galandauer. R' Avigdor commented that it was sad for the Lissers' daughter to be growing up as an only child. "Give the child a blessing," R' Chaim Halpern encouraged R' Yaakov Moshe, "that she should have a brother or sister."

R' Yaakov Moshe responded, "Hashem should help that she should have a brother, a sister." R' Avigdor remembered the odd phraseology, "a brother, a sister."

The following year, R' Yaakov Moshe returned to England for what would be his final trip. He was by then too frail to go from house to house to collect funds, so the Lissers offered to hold a parlor meeting for him in their home. At the end of the meeting, Moshe Lisser asked R' Yaakov

Moshe for a blessing for a second child. R' Yaakov Moshe answered, *"B'ezras Hashem* [with God's help], you'll have more children."

As Moshe escorted his distinguished guest out, he bid R' Yaakov Moshe farewell. The elderly *tzaddik* rebuffed his farewell, explaining, "I'll be here in England until Wednesday, and you'll speak to me again before I leave."

On Wednesday morning, Shani Lisser found out she was expecting. Her jubilant husband called to give the good news to R' Yaakov Moshe, uncannily aware that he knew it before the Lissers themselves.

Nearly nine months later, Shani gave birth to twins, "a brother, a sister" to her little girl.

In the mid-1980's, when R' Yaakov Moshe was staying in London, a Gerer chassid named Feldman, accompanied by his 5-year-old daughter Chaya, came to him for a blessing. R' Yaakov Moshe gave the blessing, then looked at Chaya and inquired, "Does she speak Yiddish?"

"No," was Mr. Feldman's reply.

"Teach it to her," R' Yaakov Moshe said, "because she'll need it when she gets married."

Over the next 15 years, Chaya's parents occasionally made a point of speaking Yiddish to her at the Shabbos table. When the time for *shidduchim* arrived, several British boys were suggested, but those matches proved fruitless. Then one day, a respected *shadchan* (matchmaker) called with an ideal match, a Swiss boy. The first question the *shadchan* asked was: "Does she speak Yiddish?"

Mrs. Feldman falteringly replied, "A little."

Neither the boy nor his parents understood English, but Chaya managed to converse with them in a credible Yiddish. *"Baruch Hashem*, they are happily married," Ruth Feldman recalls, "but had I answered 'no' to the Yiddish question, there would have been no *shidduch*."

R' Yaakov Moshe blessing a child

The implications of this tale are mind boggling: that R' Yaakov Moshe could look at a person and know her entire destiny. And in this case, glimpsing her destiny apparently changed her destiny. Had Chaya's father not happened to bring her along to meet the visiting *tzaddik*, she ostensively would not have learned Yiddish and would not have married her Yiddish-speaking *chassan*.

A few months before R' Yaakov Moshe died, his niece Pnina came to him in an agitated state. She had had a prenatal test that revealed that the fetus had Down Syndrome. Pnina was already a grandmother, and did not know how, at her age, she could cope with raising a Down Syndrome child. R' Yaakov Moshe told her, "Don't worry. Everything will be all right." Then he added: "But know that even a Down child has the right to live."

The child, born after R' Yaakov Moshe's demise, was totally normal and healthy. He is named Yaakov Moshe.

Again the mystery: Was the test wrong, as such tests often are, and R' Yaakov Moshe could see that the child was normal? Or did his blessing heal the child in the womb?

Once Pnina's married daughter went to visit Rebbetzin Chaya Sara. The Rebbetzin asked her if she was expecting, and she replied that she wasn't. Shortly thereafter, she found out that she was.

I had a personal experience of Rebbetzin Chaya Sara's "special vision." After five years of striving for a second child, I conceived. In my second month, I went to tell the Rebbetzin the good news. At the end of our visit, as she walked me to the door, she glanced at my torso and remarked, "It looks like a boy." Looks like a boy? Even an ultrasound that early on could not distinguish the gender of the fetus. Was it possible that she was seeing the soul of my baby, which turned out, of course, to be a boy?

According to Rav Yaakov Deutsch, himself a respected kabbalist, R' Yaakov Moshe Kramer had *ruach hakodesh*. During the period that Rav Deutsch was doing the *hatzalah* work with Rav Kramer, the younger man would sometimes hesitate to visit a family. Trying to encourage him, Rav Kramer would tell him what was about to transpire during the visit, "and that's exactly what would happen," Rav Deutsch attests.

The 11-year-old daughter of Moshe Lisser's business partner disappeared. The Orthodox community in London was highly distraught and, in addition to the police efforts, they sent a "search party" out every night with the girl's picture. On Thursday night, a week after the disappearance, Moshe and Shani Lisser took their turn canvassing one area. As Shani fervently approached passersby with the girl's photo, she noticed that her husband seemed almost disinterested in the search.

On Friday morning, the police found the girl, safe and sound, and brought her home. Shani was suspicious. Was her husband privy to information that everyone else had lacked? Moshe admitted that on Thursday morning, he had phoned R' Yaakov Moshe Kramer, who had assured him, "Don't worry, she'll be home before Shabbos."

From any number of accounts, the Kramers could see the future the way the rest of us see what's happening in front of our eyes. Kfar Gidon residents Shalom and Sharona Shtiglitz had been married 11 years without children. One *erev Pesach*, as Shalom was leaving the shul, because he had no reason to stay for the *siyum* for the firstborn, R' Yaakov Moshe said to him: "Next year, you'll have a *ben bechor* [firstborn son] and you'll stay for the *siyum*."

R' Yaakov Moshe was alluding to the custom that on the day before Pesach fathers either fast for their firstborn young sons or attend the *siyum* on their behalf. Shalom, however, knew that even if his wife finally gave birth to a son, the boy would not have the halachic status of a firstborn. "I can't have a *ben bechor*," Shalom corrected R' Yaakov Moshe, "because my wife has had many miscarriages."

Undaunted, R' Yaakov Moshe replied, "You'll have a *ben bochur*, and you'll make a *pidyon haben* [ceremony of redeeming a firstborn son]."

Six weeks later, Shalom and Sharona, who had long before applied for adoption, were notified that a baby was ready for them. The baby was a *ben bechor*, the firstborn son of his mother. The happy new parents made a *pidyon haben* for their new son, and the following *erev Pesach*, Shalom attended the *siyum*.

In this story, at least, it is clear that R' Yaakov Moshe could see the future, but had no power to decree fertility on the couple, whom he had known closely throughout their 11 anguished years of childlessness. In fact, at least two other couples, whom the Kramers dearly loved and repeatedly blessed, remained childless. It would seem that some decrees can be changed and others cannot. Despite all our efforts, it is the One Above Who grants blessings.

And what about the Kramers' own infertility? Is it conceivable that if R' Yaakov Moshe had had the power to change Heavenly decrees for children, he would not have used it on his own beloved wife? The sages teach that "an inmate cannot free himself from prison." Thus the irony that the Kramers' blessings for children were fulfilled for so many others, while they themselves remained childless.[1]

A man in England suffered from recurrent brain tumors. After two operations, another tumor appeared. For the third surgery, the doctors were planning to remove not only the tumor, but also one eye and parts of the nose, because the X-rays showed that the growth had spread.

Before the operation, the sick man went to many *tzaddikim* and received blessings. When he phoned R' Yaakov Moshe Kramer in Israel, however, the Rav refused to bless him, saying instead, "It's nothing. It's nothing. You should just go to a plain doctor." Since the man had consulted with top specialists all over the world, this advice seemed ludicrous. Yet the man phoned repeatedly, crying for a blessing. "You don't need a blessing," Rav Kramer insisted. "It's just water on the brain."

The man was admitted to the hospital, and just before the surgery, the physicians took another X-ray in order to see exactly how far the growth had spread. After a long delay, his doctor came to him and declared, "I've been looking and looking at the X-ray, and I'm absolutely amazed. I think that we've made a big mistake. It seems that what's showing up on the X-ray is actually fluid that came in during our first surgery. It's not really a growth at all. We can use a syringe and drain it out in five minutes."

And yet, there were clearly occasions when the Kramers' blessings not only perceived, but also reshaped reality. Zev Shtiglitz recalls the time in 1984 when he was summoned by the local tax authorities for an audit. Such audits were the nightmare of every citizen, as one was required to bring his books from the last five years, which were scrutinized so rigor-

---

1. [The following stories are not intended to put down the accepted medical profession. And no one should choose to rely on miracles in any situation as a result of reading these vignettes. Conventional medical procedure unless contraindicated is preferred in most cases.]

ously that virtually no one escaped unscathed. The head of the tax office near Kfar Gidon had a particularly sadistic reputation. He would notify one of the religious members of the Kfar on Friday that he had to bring his books in on Sunday morning, and when the exhausted, harried citizen appeared, the tax officer would smirk and ask, "Well, how was your Shabbos?"

Zev Shtiglitz used to ask R' Yaakov Moshe for blessings for everything in his life, and this fearsome appointment with the tax authority was no exception. R' Yaakov Moshe blessed Zev that he should "find favor in the eyes of the people in the tax office." The blessing seemed impossible, because no one, especially no religious man, ever escaped censure and a costly fine from this particular tax officer.

In trepidation, Zev entered the office and put his ledgers down on the table. The officer opened one, inspected it closely, and then asked, "Who wrote this?"

"I did," Zev answered meekly.

"Do you know what graphology is?" the officer asked him.

"Yes, it's the study of a person's handwriting," Zev offered.

"Well, I'm an expert graphologist," the officer declared, "and I can see from your handwriting that you're an honest man." With that, he closed the book and dismissed the stunned Zev. The tax authorities never bothered him again.

Although it sounds facetious, no one familiar with the Israeli income tax authorities would attribute this encounter to anything less than a miraculous manipulation of normal reality. This was not a case of seeing what would happen, but rather of making it happen.

Yet, even if we grant that the Kramers could reshape reality, a deeper question lingers: Was it the *tzaddik's* blessing or the petitioner's faith in the blessing that worked the miracle?

Once a distraught woman phoned from Toronto to tell Rebbetzin Chaya Sara that the doctors had discovered a cancerous lump. "There's nothing there," insisted the Rebbetzin.

"Don't be fearful. Just ignore the whole thing."

"No," the woman protested, "they really found something. If I ignore it, it'll grow."

"I'm telling you," the Rebbetzin asserted, "that there's nothing there. But if you don't believe me, do this: Go to a different clinic in a different city and ask them to do the same test. Just don't tell them that the doctors in Toronto found a lump."

The woman followed the Rebbetzin's instructions. She went to Sloan-Kettering in New York and repeated the test, without mentioning the previous finding. Afterward, the radiologist informed her that the test came out negative; she was clean. At that point she burst out: "Are you sure? In Toronto they found a lump!"

"In Toronto they found a lump?" the radiologist queried. "Then we have to redo the test." The second test indeed revealed a lump.

The woman phoned Rebbetzin Chaya Sara and told her what had transpired. The Rebbetzin again contended that there was nothing there. "Go to a third clinic, do the test again, and this time don't mention that anyone found a lump."

The woman complied. At the third clinic, the test came out clean. The woman relaxed, went home to Toronto and, the last time I inquired, which was some four years later, she was still healthy.

A guest at our Shabbos table, a newly married American architect in his late 20's, heard me speak about Rebbetzin Chaya Sara. A few weeks later, he phoned me. He had received "a terrible diagnosis" and he needed to see the Rebbetzin right away. I gave him her phone number. When he called, the Rebbetzin told him that he didn't need to come to see her. He was perfectly healthy, she assured him, and had nothing to worry about. The next day the young man dropped by my house on his way from the *Kosel* (Western Wall). "I went to the *Kosel* to thank Hashem for my miraculous cure," he exulted.

"You're not going to follow up with any treatment?" I asked, more skeptical than he.

"No!" the man asserted. "The Rebbetzin healed me over the phone. I'm fine."

A year later, wondering if the architect was still fine, I located his phone number and called him. His wife answered the phone. In trepidation, I asked how her husband was. "He's fine, perfectly healthy," she replied.

"And he did no treatment?"

"That's right." Her voice was breezy. "No treatment."

It didn't always work. In the mid 1990's, my American friend Dina received the dread diagnosis of cancer. Frightened of death and worried about her beloved only child, then 5 years old, Dina sank into depression. I persuaded her to come to Israel to get a blessing from Rebbetzin Chaya Sara Kramer and to visit the graves of *tzaddikim*. Dina gave a generous donation to a poor family stipulated by Rebbetzin Chaya Sara, and visited with her for an hour. The Rebbetzin told Dina that she had nothing to worry about, that she would dance at the wedding of her daughter.

Dina returned to America still anxious and apprehensive. A few months later, she died.

My own trenchant experience: In 2003, two years before the Rebbetzin's passing, I took a routine mammogram. Much to my shock, it revealed a cancerous tumor. "It's not a problem," I told the *kippah*-clad radiologist. "I know a *tzaddekes* who can take care of it."

From the clinic, I went directly to Rebbetzin Chaya Sara, who told me that there was nothing there, and I should stay away from tests, doctors, and hospitals. I also went to my Rebbe, the Amshinover Rebbe, *shlita*, who told me that I was not obligated to take the test, but since I had taken it and a tumor had shown up, I was obligated to follow the doctors' advice and have it surgically removed.

For days I was in a quandary. On the one hand, I knew the story of the woman in Toronto, whose lump had miraculously disappeared. On the other hand, I knew that ever since her trauma with Dr. Mengele in Auschwitz, Rebbetzin Chaya Sara dreaded doctors and hospitals; in almost all cases she advised against surgery. Moreover, at that stage of her life, Rebbetzin Chaya Sara's physical and mental powers were on the decline; I wondered whether her spiritual powers too had lost their potency.

After days of vacillating, I phoned the radiologist. "I know this sounds crazy," I prefaced my request. "But would you be willing to do the test over again? Perhaps my lump has disappeared."

He humored me and redid the test. The lump was still there. Two weeks later I underwent surgery, wondering, even as I was being rolled into the operating room, whether, had I had more faith in the Rebbetzin's power, I could have avoided the operation.

That both Kramers could "read minds" was patently obvious to all those who associated closely with them. When R' Yaakov Moshe was in London, many people lined up to seek his advice. One day, a Sephardi girl was admitted to the *tzaddik's* presence. A few minutes later, she exited in a state of amazement. Someone asked her what had happened. She replied that she had come with several questions to ask the *tzaddik*, but when she was ushered into his presence, she was so overcome that she was speechless. As she sat there, R' Yaakov Moshe answered all of her questions, one by one, without her saying a word.

Kfar Gidon resident Anni Kalfe reports, "After they knew me well, I didn't have to speak at all. They read my heart."

Rivki Adler, who was close to Rebbetzin Chaya Sara during her later years, reported many incidents of her clairvoyance. Although the wheelchair-bound Rivki usually phoned the Rebbetzin from her own home, one day she phoned from elsewhere. The Rebbetzin asked her, "Where are you now?" Another time, Rivki planned to go to Bnei Brak, but it didn't work out. The following day, she visited Rebbetzin Chaya Sara. The Rebbetzin's first question was, "Would you like to go to Bnei Brak?" Yet another time, Rivki was concerned because she had run up a huge phone bill for her parents. Without her mentioning it to the Rebbetzin, Chaya Sara asked Rivki if she made big phone bills for her parents, and cautioned her to talk on the phone less.

What we often referred to as Rebbetzin Chaya Sara's "*ruach hakodesh*" was obvious to all of us who frequented her home. Again and again, she would "read my thoughts" and remark on exactly what I was thinking. So consistent was this sometimes irksome habit of hers that, when I didn't want her to know something, I would work at banishing it from my mind while in her presence. Usually I did not succeed.

Only on the rarest occasion did Rebbetzin Chaya Sara mention her window into the higher worlds. Shani Lisser had a friend who conceived after years of waiting. When the woman experienced complications, Shani, alarmed, called Rebbetzin Chaya Sara for a blessing. The Rebbetzin assured her, "Don't worry. Everything will be okay."

Everything was not okay. The difficulties continued, and the woman eventually lost the baby. A distraught Shani called Rebbetzin Chaya Sara and complained. The Rebbetzin replied: "It was supposed to be okay. The decree in Heaven was changed."

Another example: Naomi Bohbot was a young wife with an 11-month-old baby when she and her husband Avraham moved to Kfar Gidon in 1976. Having come from suburban

America, Naomi had no experience of rural life. She was told to empty her garbage into a large, rusted, metal container behind their cottage. One hot summer day, noticing that the container was full, Naomi decided to burn the garbage. In the arid Israeli summer, the fire quickly spread out of control to the dry grass behind her cottage.

Neighbors rushed to help. A friend of Naomi stopped her car in front of the cottage, and ran into the house to rescue the baby in case the house caught fire. A farmer driving his combine to his fields pulled up behind the friend's car and jumped out to help put out the fire. Somehow, the combine went into first gear, rolled forward, and crushed the friend's car into a tree.

Naomi felt terrible. She was embarrassed by her stupidity in starting the fire, and felt responsible for the damage to her friend's car. Naomi went to Rebbetzin Chaya Sara and related what had happened. The Rebbetzin told her that she had no need to feel sorry. On the contrary, the friend and certain other women from Kfar Gidon had been planning to travel to Haifa later that week. Had they done so, the Rebbetzin disclosed, they would have been involved in a terrible accident. The fire and the wrecking of the car with no one in it, the Rebbetzin averred, had served as an atonement.

Those who listened closely to R' Yaakov Moshe's blessings allege that it was possible to tell from the way he spoke what the outcome would be. The refusal to give a blessing meant that the decree in Heaven could not be changed, while a *promise* was always fulfilled, even against the stiffest odds.

A childless couple from Antwerp repeatedly came to R' Yaakov Moshe for a blessing. Each time he blessed them to have a child but, despite their pleas, he declined to *promise* them a child. The couple remained barren. Finally, on yet another visit, he promised them that they would have a child in nine months. Exactly nine months later, a son was born to them.

Rebbetzin Chaya Sara never refused to give a blessing. Rather, she broadcast her blessings to all and sundry. Young Miriam, watching her adopted mother grant a blessing to every barren woman who came, complained, "This is not the way the Rebbes do it."

The Rebbetzin explained her approach to Miriam: "First of all, I bless everyone that she should have a child. Then I pray continually that my blessing should be fulfilled. If she does have a child, *baruch Hashem*. If she doesn't have a child, at least she'll be happy for a whole year because I gave her a blessing. After that, I'll be an *aus-Rebbetzin* [discredited Rebbetzin], and so what? My intention is to try to make a Jew happy."

The realm of alleged supernatural powers corrupts many of those who tread its precincts. The ego is quick to usurp the credit for wonders worked, for blessings actualized, for abilities unavailable to most of us. Perhaps the most miraculous feat performed by Chaya Sara Kramer is that she retained her pure humility.

While her husband lived, Chaya Sara deflected credit from herself by ricocheting all praise toward him. When asked for a blessing, she would often say, "I'm nothing, I'm like the peel of a garlic. Go ask my husband."

R' Yaakov Moshe, in turn, sometimes told people, "Don't go to me. Go to my wife. She has the power." His niece Pnina attests: "He always said that his koach [power] came from her. He would always say, 'She's greater than I am.'"

(The esteemed Rav Avraham Yechiel Fish was also heard to say that Rebbetzin Chaya Sara's prayers were more powerful than even her husband's.)

And so they volleyed credit back and forth, each deferring to the other. Or they rebounded the honor back to the petitioner. When people returned to R' Yaakov

Moshe and reported that his blessing for a cure or children or financial success had come to be "in the merit of the tzaddik," he would reply, "In your own merit. You are precious Jews."

As one Kfar Gidon resident testified:

> They didn't say, "I'll bless you and it'll be all right." They worked through the supplicant's reciting psalms or giving tzedakkah, as if that would bring the requested result. Chaya Sara never claimed to be great. If anyone said to her, "You're a tzaddekes," she would laugh and laugh. She would say, "Yankel Moshe is the tzaddik. I'm nothing. I'm nothing."

After Yaakov Moshe's passing, the Rebbetzin still deflected praise by passing all credit to HaKadosh Baruch Hu. When wheelchair-bound Rivki Adler found it difficult to come to the Rebbetzin, Chaya Sara told her: "You can call on the phone. You don't have to come to me in person. The blessing comes from Hashem, not from me."

Yet humility is not simply a verbal disavowal of credit. Chaya Sara's humility pervaded all her interactions with people. Her total accessibility, her down-to-earth humor, her respect for every visitor, young and old — all her interactions exuded the humility of one who genuinely did not consider herself superior to anyone.

From where did her humility issue? Certainly she was aware that not everyone could dispense blessings and see them fulfilled. A clear look at herself would have registered that she wielded powers that others lacked.

The secret of her humility is that she did not look at herself at all. She looked at HaKadosh Baruch Hu. Compared to His infinite vastness, she and all other human beings were indeed minuscule. Just as people differ in height, with some being considerably taller than others, but all people are small compared to a skyscraper, so her spiritual prowess over others faded into insignifi-

cance compared to the vastness of HaKadosh Baruch Hu, the constant object of her focus.

To focus on the greatness of G-d is a choice available to all of us. True humility does not result from discounting or ignoring our strengths, but from acknowledging their Divine Source. Talents, intelligence, personality, and business acumen are — like the Kramers' powers — a Divine gift. To convince ourselves (never mind about others) that our gifts come through ourselves but not from ourselves is a disposition of mind that we can choose. The more we focus on G-d as the Source of our strengths, the more humble we will become.

One wondrous aspect of the Kramers' blessings is the sheer variety of means through which they were conveyed. Although so many people came to them asking for the same blessings, especially for a *shidduch* or children, the Kramers prescribed a unique formula for each supplicant. There were no generic cures in their "pharmacy."

An example: Rebbetzin Baila Berger brought a young woman, an American *ba'alas teshuvah*, to R' Yaakov Moshe in Kfar Gidon for a blessing to get married. Lois had given up a lucrative job in America in order to come to Jerusalem and learn about Judaism. Her secular parents, irate at her decision to become religious, had cut her off entirely. Lois felt financially insecure. She wanted to marry someone who was learning Torah, but how would they afford to live, or even pay for the wedding? She knew that her parents wouldn't help her, and her own savings were gradually being used up.

Sitting across the table from R' Yaakov Moshe, Lois mentioned none of this. She simply asked for a blessing to get married. Inexplicably, R' Yaakov Moshe reached into his pocket, pulled out a fistful of bills, and placed them before her. Lois was horrified. Here she was sitting in this hovel, and its obviously indigent owner was giving *her* money. "I can't take this money," she protested. R' Yaakov Moshe continued to pull money out of his pockets and toss the bills at her. "What should I do?" Lois, horrified, asked Rebbetzin Berger.

"He knows what he's doing," Rebbetzin Berger declared. "Accept whatever he gives you."

Lois returned to Jerusalem and used the money to open a *gemach* [free loan society]. Two years later, she married a Torah scholar who had inherited a fortune from his grandfather. He paid for the wedding and all their living expenses and was able to sit and learn.

Once a man was visiting the Kramers when the telephone rang. An anxious-sounding Torah scholar from Jerusalem was calling for help. He said that his wife, who was in labor, had suffered a complication that required surgery. When R' Yaakov Moshe hung up the phone, he seemed gravely concerned. He urgently begged his visitor to drive him to the home of a certain poor widow who lived in Kfar Gidon. Once there, R' Yaakov Moshe begged the widow to pray for the woman in labor. They returned to the Kramers' home 15 minutes after they had left. As they entered, the phone rang. It was the same Torah scholar, happily reporting that his wife had just given birth, without surgery.

The Kramers in their Kfar Gidon home

Was the surgery averted by the widow's prayers? Or was the visit to the widow merely a smoke screen for R' Yaakov Moshe's own wonder-working?

Another time Rebbetzin Baila Berger came to Kfar Gidon seeking a blessing to have children after many years of marriage. She brought along a friend who needed a *shidduch*. R' Yaakov Moshe spent 45 minutes in deep conversation with the friend. Then Rebbetzin Berger was admitted to his study. "Here, take this," he told her, handing her a Xeroxed copy of the *Iggeres HaRamban*. He told her to recite it every day. With that the interview was over.

"I felt I had been brushed off," Rebbetzin Berger recollects. "But I went home and did it. And it really changed my life. It was exactly what I needed."

The Kramers frequently recommended to those seeking blessings that they should read Iggeres HaRamban. When someone would phone Rebbetzin Chaya Sara with an emergency, her standard response was to fervently recite Iggeres HaRamban rather than the customary practice of reciting Tehillim [Psalms].

Iggeres HaRamban is a letter written by the 12th-century sage Nachmanides to his son. The letter offers practical advice in how to overcome anger and pride and to achieve the quality of humility, which the letter calls, "the finest of all admirable traits."

Why did Rebbetzin Chaya Sara consider Iggeres HaRamban more powerful for bringing down Divine mercy than the age-old custom of reciting Tehillim? Since time immemorial, the words, syllables, and letters of psalms have been known to have supernatural powers to effect Heavenly decrees. What is the power of Iggeres HaRamban? The epistle itself ends with the words, "Every day that you read this letter, you will be answered from Heaven according to all your heart's requests." But why?

Unlike psalms, it is not the words, syllables, and letters of *Iggeres HaRamban* that work miracles. Rather, the epistle is a short manual on how to overcome anger and pride. The Ramban writes to his son: "Read this letter once a week and neglect none of it. Fulfill it, and walk always in the ways of Hashem Yisbarach." The power of *Iggeres HaRamban* lies in implementing its advice. The point of reading it is to remind and inspire oneself to practice what it counsels. "Fulfill it" and Hashem will answer your requests.

Reciting *Iggeres HaRamban* to bring down Divine mercy is vintage Chaya Sara Kramer. No magic formulas, no kabbalistic talismans, just hands-on working on her character traits was her method of working miracles. She believed — and lived — the idea that to change Heavenly decrees one must change oneself. As the Rabbis have taught, a harsh decree is like a lightning bolt aimed at a particular person. If the person changes, the lightning bolt cannot find its target, for the person has transformed into someone new.

When Rebbetzin Chaya Sara would get a telephone call about a critically ill person, she would pull out *Iggeres HaRamban* and fervently recite it. In such emergencies, there was no time to work on herself. Rather, Chaya Sara was reminding HaKadosh Baruch Hu of the inner transformation she had already effected in overcoming anger and achieving humility. She was saying: Just as I changed my nature, please change the forces of nature for the sake of this person.

This is a powerful lesson for all of us who long to change Heavenly decrees. The lesson of *Iggeres HaRamban*: Change ourselves.

Whenever a person came to the Kramers for a blessing, R' Yaakov Moshe and Chaya Sara would write down the person's name in their prayer books. Later that night they would ardently beseech Heaven for that person. Naomi Bohbot showed up unexpectedly one night and found both Kramers crying over their *siddurim*.

Kfar Gidon resident Esther Schutz recalls:

> *My son was 4 years old, and he suddenly got croup and had difficulty breathing. I ran to R' Yaakov Moshe and told him, "We have to go to the hospital." He said, "Estherke, don't be afraid. Hashem is great. Everything will be all right. Pray in the merit of the mother of Avraham Avinu, Amaslai bas Karnavo." Then he added, "I'll sit here and pray for him."*
>
> *All that night he stayed awake and prayed for my son.*

"The *tzaddik* decrees, and Hashem fulfills." Were so many of the blessings conferred by the Kramers fulfilled because they decreed it would be so, or because they poured out their hearts in prayer that it should be so? Yes, their words worked wonders. But was it their words of prophecy or their words of prayer that worked the wonders?

Once, on the night after Yom Kippur, Anni Kalfe's husband took sick and had to go to the hospital. The next day, he was completely recovered and was able to return home. Rebbetzin Chaya Sara told Anni that R' Yaakov Moshe had stayed up all night praying for him. "What she herself did," Anni adds, "she didn't say."

One night Sheindy Leiber phoned Rebbetzin Chaya Sara from London. "She was crying her eyes out for a woman who was having a painful childbirth, whom she had met only a couple times."

Was it in fact their words or their tears that brought the salvation?

People came to the Kramers not only for blessings, but also for practical advice on issues such as marital problems, child-rearing, and finances. To everyone they lent a listening ear. As Kfar Gidon resident Simcha Heizler remembers, "They really listened to people. They simply opened their ears and listened to people's troubles."

Who came to them? People from all across the religious and ethnic spectrum: chassidim, Lithuanian *chareidim*, religious Zionists, traditional Sephardim, and even completely secular people. Miriam remembers one secular policeman who came to R' Yaakov Moshe and told him that he had committed all the sins in the world. He wanted to know if there was any *tikkun* [rectification] for him. (Miriam didn't hear the Rav's answer.)

While supplicants came seeking the advice of R' Yaakov Moshe, he often asked his wife to sit down with them, especially if there was a woman among them. Rebbetzin Chaya Sara calmed the oft-distraught women, gave them emotional support, and frequently offered her advice. Her husband never contradicted her.

Meir Shalom Tanzee, the young yeshivah student who sought R' Yaakov Moshe's advice on every issue, recalls, "I must stress that the Rabbanit would also give me the correct advice. The Rav would agree with her and say, 'This is what you must do.'"

In fact, often their hearts beat in unison. An expectant woman on her way to the Kramers encountered R' Yaakov Moshe on the road. He told her, "You're going to give birth to a *tzaddik*." When she got to the house, Rebbetzin Chaya Sara told her the exact same words, "You're going to give birth to a *tzaddik*."

In 1978, Aliza was staying with Rebbetzin Chaya Sara while R' Yaakov Moshe was in America. The Rebbetzin suggested a *shidduch* for her, a God-fearing yeshivah student from Be'er Yaakov. The Rebbetzin, busy with all the work of taking care of Hindele while her husband was away, did not have time to write to him about her *shidduch* idea for Aliza. One day a letter arrived from R' Yaakov Moshe. In it he wrote to his wife that she should follow up on the *shidduch* between Aliza and the boy from Be'er Yaakov. "I was so amazed when we read the letter," Aliza recalls. "How did he know about this *shidduch*? After all, no one had told him about it!"

Frequently R' Yaakov Moshe consulted the chassidic book *Noam Elimelech* by the chassidic master Reb Elimelech of Lizhensk. Called by the initiated the *sifran shel tzaddikim*, or instruction manual for *tzaddikim*, the book hints at secrets for every soul who knows how to read between its lines. R' Yaakov Moshe would sit and contemplate the problem the petitioners had presented. Then he would open the *Noam Elimelech* at random. On the page where he had opened, he would find the solution to the problem.

In fact, R' Yaakov Moshe's copy of the *Noam Elimelech* was undoubtedly his most precious possession. During World War II, he lost all of his material possessions except his copy of the *Noam Elimelech* which, at great risk, he managed to save and bring with him to Palestine. Many years later, a distressed Israeli soldier came to R' Yaakov Moshe and confessed that he was afraid to go into battle. As if it meant nothing to him, R' Yaakov Moshe gave the soldier his precious copy of the *Naom Elimelech* as a talisman for protection.

When people who were not particularly religious came to ask for advice, blessings, or material help, R' Yaakov Moshe would gently encourage them to enroll their children in *chareidi* schools. Miriam once asked her adopted father why he would suggest this rather than ask the people to take on a mitzvah, such as Shabbos observance. R' Yaakov Moshe answered succinctly, "The cow always follows the calf."

Not everyone who sought the Kramers' help left with a miracle, but everyone left with the encouragement and fortitude to face their challenges. A case in point: Rav Asher Gabbai's wife Miriam suffered many miscarriages. Finally, the esteemed Rav Greineman of Bnei Brak advised her to go to England for a treatment then unavailable in Israel. Rabbanit Miriam, however, was afraid to fly. Although they had already purchased their tickets, she told her husband that she didn't want to go.

Rav Gabbai suggested that they go to R' Yaakov Moshe Kramer. Rabbanit Miriam agreed that whatever R' Yaakov Moshe told her, she would do. They went, and R' Yaakov Moshe encouraged her to overcome her fear. He told her to go to England, and Hashem would help her. "He gave me the strength to go," Rabbanit Miriam attests.

No miracle here, but transforming a frightened heart into a courageous one can sometimes be miracle enough.

Rebbetzin Chaya Sara also wrought miracles with the wand of encouragement. After suffering three successive miscarriages, Shani Lisser almost despaired of having any more children. Rebbetzin Chaya Sara encouraged her. Shani decided that a change of clinic may bring a change of *mazal*. At the new clinic, however, the doctor emphatically informed her that it was impossible for her to bear another child. Left without any hope, Shani phoned Rebbetzin Chaya Sara. The Rebbetzin told her to ignore the doctor's words and to go back to her former clinic. Eventually Shani conceived and gave birth to a healthy child. When she took a photo of her baby to the doctor who had told her she couldn't have another child, the doctor retorted, "G-d usually has the last word."

Even after R' Yaakov Moshe's passing, his power to work wonders did not cease. Rebbetzin Baila Berger was childless for seven years when she first sought and received R' Yaakov Moshe's blessing. Although he blessed her several times during the last three years before his death, it was to no avail. Then, when Rebbetzin Berger paid a *shivah* call to Rebbetzin Chaya Sara, the grieving widow said to her: "He can do more from where he is now." One month later, Rebbetzin Berger conceived.

Shortly before his passing, R' Yaakov Moshe gave several of his shirts to Avigdor Galandauer. R' Avigdor asked Rebbetzin Chaya Sara what to do with the shirts. She replied, "They're a *segulah*. If you put one on someone who is not well, he'll be healed."

"And that's how it was," R' Avigdor testifies. "I gave them to many ill people over the years, and they always got better."

Kfar Gidon resident Anni Kalfe relates this story: There was a young rebbetzin in Afula who was childless. One day the young rebbetzin's mother phoned Anni and asked her if she knew a *tzaddik* who could bless her daughter. Anni told her about R' Yaakov Moshe Kramer, and suggested that both mother and daughter come to Kfar Gidon for a blessing.

As it happened, they were not able to come, but they sent a *shaliach* [emissary]. Anni and the *shaliach* went to the Kramers to requisition a blessing for the childless rebbetzin. R' Yaakov Moshe wrote her a letter with instructions as to exactly what to do. He included the addresses of families of impoverished Torah scholars, to whom he directed her to send *tzedakkah*, with the request that they pray for her. The young rebbetzin followed the instructions, and one year later she gave birth to a son.

Ten years passed. By this time, R' Yaakov Moshe was no longer in this world. The rebbetzin's mother again turned to Anni for help. Anni asked if her daughter had kept R' Yaakov Moshe's letter. Hearing that she had, Anni told her to do exactly what R' Yaakov Moshe had instructed 10 years before. She did so, and bore a second child.

During the last years of R' Yaakov Moshe's life, his devoted follower Avigdor Galandauer had a problem. The office of taxation in Great Britain notified him that he owed several thousand pounds in back taxes. The distraught R' Avigdor called R' Yaakov Moshe, who intoned into the phone the words from the *Kol Nidrei* service: "*Betelin, betelin* [nullified, nullified]." With that, R' Avigdor never heard from the tax office again.

Many years went by. R' Yaakov Moshe passed away, and the devoted R' Avigdor kept a candle burning continuously in his memory. Thirteen years after R' Yaakov Moshe's death, R' Avigdor decided that perhaps it was time to stop renewing the nine-day candle. Suddenly he received a letter from the tax office asking why he hadn't paid this outstanding debt and threatening to charge him interest on all the intervening years. If he didn't pay the entire sum immediately, the letter warned, they would send the bailiff after him.

The abashed R' Avigdor immediately thought of R' Yaakov Moshe, who had taken care of the predicament so many years earlier. He inferred that the problem had resurfaced because he had been about to stop burning the candle for the deceased *tzaddik*. Then and there, he resolved to keep the candle burning perpetually. With trembling fingers, he dialed the tax office. A petulant woman clerk scolded him, "How dare you not pay this bill?"

"But it was so many years ago," R' Avigdor pleaded.

"What year was it?" she demanded.

As soon as he told her, her demeanor switched. "You know what?" she said cordially. "I'm just going to wipe the whole debt off the records."

Was it R' Yaakov Moshe winking from the next world?

CHAPTER ELEVEN

A New Era

THE MID-1970'S USHERED IN A NEW ERA FOR the Kramers.

Sometime between 1974 and 1978, R' Yaakov Moshe began traveling abroad for several months every year in order to raise funds for his *hatzalah* work. At first he went only to the *chareidi* enclaves in New York, but eventually his annual trips included three weeks in London and a few days in Antwerp. In all these places, he made such a profound impression on everyone he met that his circle of acquaintances became his coterie of admirers. Devoted followers would phone him frequently, visit him in Israel, and maintain a steady relationship with their newfound *tzaddik*.

The period of 1974 to 1980 also witnessed a radical change in the population of Kfar Gidon. The enclave of aging Hungarian Holocaust survivors was suddenly joined by an influx of young couples. Some Kfar Gidon boys married wives ethnically and culturally different from their parents: Simcha

Heizler was Sephardi; Sharona Shtiglitz was American. An even greater change was wrought by the arrival of young couples — some of them *ba'alei teshuvah* — from a rainbow of different backgrounds. In 1976, four couples moved into Kfar Gidon: Avraham Bohbot was Moroccan and his wife Naomi was American; Anni and Eli Kalfe were Algerian; Bezalel Schutz was American and his wife Esther was Persian; Gidon and Michal Ben Tzvi were French. Later other couples joined them: Chaim and Tamar Cohen were Tunisian; Eliezer and Naomi Gevirtz were Ashkenazi Lubavitch chassidim.

The influx of young couples changed not only the makeup but also the spiritual character of the moshav and the Kramers' role within it. The young couples were ardent spiritual seekers who quickly latched onto the Kramers as their mentors. Whereas the older residents had respected R' Yaakov Moshe, the new residents venerated him. Whereas the older residents were often critical of Chaya Sara, the new residents adored her. As Anni Kalfe exulted about the Kramers, "They were like my parents, my guides, my teachers, my doctors."

Chaya Sara (left background) and R' Yaakov Moshe with Kfar Gidon residents

The new couples were so religiously enthusiastic that all the young men devoutly attended the class given by the moshav rabbi. This would have been unremarkable except that Rav Klein taught the class in Yiddish, and the young men, most of them Sephardim, understood not a word. Nevertheless, they would sit there in rapt attention, causing one elderly Hungarian father to scold his truant son: "Look at the new young men! They don't understand a word, but still they come to the class!"

The Kramers embraced the young Sephardim with open arms. Once R' Yaakov Moshe, accompanied by Avraham Bohbot, went to see Rav Schach regarding an urgent matter. Rav Schach began to address them in Yiddish. R' Yaakov Moshe asked him to please speak Hebrew, since Avraham didn't understand Yiddish.

As for Rebbetzin Chaya Sara, the young wives flocked to her, for advice, for blessings, and most of all just to *shmooze*. Full-time mothers, they would push their baby strollers down the dirt road to the Kramers' shack and sit there with the Rebbetzin, reveling in the spiritual atmosphere. As Naomi Bohbot describes it: "Within the walls of their very modest home, a very strange thing occurred. I think even the walls and floors of their home absorbed their spirituality. I felt like I was entering another dimension, a dimension of love, warmth, and light."

Naomi Gevirtz reminisces:

> On the one hand, Rebbetzin Chaya Sara looked as if she belonged to a bygone era of several hundred years ago in Poland. On the other hand, she was so young in spirit. By the way she looked, she belonged to another world. On the other hand, she was very enlightened, very practical, and in tune to what was happening in the world.

Why did Chaya Sara resonate more with these young women, so unlike her in background, age, and even language, than she did with the older women with whom she had so much in common? A Hebrew expression *"bnei aliyah"* describes people who are always striving upward, who never stagnate in the same place. Chaya Sara rejoiced in these young women, who shared her most essential characteristic: They were *bnei aliyah*.

She won them over with her love. Naomi Bohbot was a 26-year-old American *ba'alas teshuvah* when she moved to Kfar Gidon. Far from family, surrounded by strangers, grappling with her new role as a wife and mother, she found in Chaya Sara a second mother. "Chaya Sara inevitably made me feel loved, accepted, a person of worth," Naomi remembers.

"She was very, very modest," Simcha Heizler recalls, "very simply dressed, no jewelry, very inexpensive clothes. But she was always happy and cheerful. She always had time to listen to whomever approached her with a problem. She always made those around her feel relaxed and secure. She was a source of unconditional love. She hugged us and kissed us."

Surrounded by these appreciative young women, Chaya Sara came into her own as a spiritual mentor. They asked her advice about problems large and small, and she guided them. As Esther Schutz summed up Chaya Sara's teachings:

> When something bad happened, she would say, "Everything comes from HaKadosh Baruch Hu. We have to accept it with love." She accepted everything with simchah. She would say, "Everything is a test." And she'd smile all the time. And she'd always end every conversation with heaps of blessings: "Esther, you should have nachas from your children, you should have parnassah, it should be easy for you."

The Schutzes had brought Bezalel's parents to live in Kfar Gidon. After his mother was widowed, she was always in Esther's house. Rebbetzin Chaya Sara helped Esther navigate the potentially tense situation of living so closely with a mother-in-law. She would constantly remind Esther that taking care of her mother-in-law was a big mitzvah. She would assure her that in the merit of that mitzvah, she would merit to have good children and heavenly assistance. She would tell Esther, "You have such a wonderful mother-in-law." And to the mother-in-law, she would say in Hungarian, "You have such a wonderful daughter-in-law." Esther sums up Rebbetzin Chaya Sara's approach: "She was like Aharon HaKohen."

So spiritually accomplished were the young residents of Kfar Gidon that R' Yaakov Moshe used to give a novel twist to the Gemara in *Sotah* that states, "And the faces of the elderly will become white." Whereas this is usually understood to mean that the younger generation will be so *chutzpadik* that they will embarrass their elders, R' Yaakov Moshe would explain it: "The older generation is embarrassed because the new, younger generation is on a higher spiritual level."

One spring a veteran Kfar Gidon farmer plowed and sowed for himself a section of the Kramers' field. This was a clear violation of the Torah prohibition against "moving the border marker." The young resident who first noticed the blatant encroachment ran to the Kramers and reported it.

R' Yaakov Moshe's reaction was to let the farmer have the land upon which he had encroached. The righteously indignant younger man, however, couldn't accept such capitulation to a Torah transgression. He argued with the *tzaddik*. R' Yaakov Moshe refused to fight with his neighbor. He tenderly told the younger man, "When my time comes, I'll have all the land I need" [meaning his grave].

The young man was not satisfied. On his own, he confronted the veteran farmer and demanded that he leave the Kramers' property. The farmer complied — for that season. The next season, however, he again plowed and planted into the Kramers' field. This time, R' Yaakov Moshe insisted that his young champion leave matters alone.

R' Yaakov Moshe Kramer

Many years later, I asked Zev Shtiglitz, "Tell me about the argument over the land." Zev replied: "There was no argument. They took the land and he let them."

In fact, the next morning, R' Yaakov Moshe was heard to greet his trespassing neighbor with a warm, *"Guten morgen."*

It was virtually impossible to pull R' Yaakov Moshe into a conflict with another Jew. As R' Yaakov Moshe's niece Pnina testifies: "I learned from my uncle *darchei shalom* [the ways of peace]."

What was Rebbetzin Chaya Sara's reaction to the theft of the land? She was irate. But when her husband told her, "Let it go," she abided by his will.

It's tempting to say of Chaya Sara's marriage: "It was easy for her, because she was married to a tzaddik." True, she was married to a tzaddik, but a tzaddik also has a personality and proclivities, and in this case her husband's were very different from her own. He loved peace; she loved justice. In all matters except religious matters, his way was to give in; her way was to stand up for what was right.

Yet she, who balked at giving in, gave in to him. Whether it was the theft of their land or giving tzedakkah to people she deemed unworthy or protecting his failing health from an incessant stream of visitors, she conceded to his will, even against her own nature and her better judgment.

This was a choice she made. She used to tell young wives: "Treat your husband like a king, and he'll treat you like a queen."

Chaya Sara managed to surrender without becoming obsequious. As Rav Asher Gabbai testified about her: "Chaya Sara was very strong, but not in a negative way. She got involved in issues, such as problems in the village. She had her opinion about what to do. Sometimes R' Yaakov Moshe would do what she said, and sometimes vice versa. I was in their home five or six times a week, and I never heard them argue about anything."

Esther Schutz's comparison of Rebbetzin Chaya Sara to Aharon HaKohen, the archetypal peace lover, is a tribute to how far the feisty young Chaya Sara had come in overcoming her own temperament. By nature, she was inclined to take sides and to fight for whomever was right. Over and over, however, she chose to emulate her husband's approach of seeking peace by affirming both sides.

Giving in for the sake of peace is a choice open to all of us. "Taking three steps back," as R' Yaakov Moshe taught young Miriam, is a difficult maneuver. It requires a relinquishment of self, of one's own rights, opinions, and preferences. For those who truly value harmony, in one's community or in one's home, it is a proven means of achieving that harmony. Even for the most obdurate of us, the choice is no more difficult than it was for Chaya Sara Kramer.

The young couples in the kfar became like the Kramers' children. R' Yaakov Moshe used to ask Eliezer Gevirtz, "How is my grandchild?" referring to Eliezer's son.

And even as his fame as a *tzaddik* spread, involving him with hundreds of admirers, R' Yaakov Moshe did not abandon his solicitude for these young men and women. Every time he left for a trip abroad, he phoned each couple to take leave of them.

Simcha Heizler, whose *shidduch* the Kramers made, remembers how R' Yaakov Moshe attended to her prior to her *chupah*. The young bride was fasting and trembling. When R' Yaakov Moshe saw her, he brought her a glass of juice to drink.

For a short period in the 1980's, the Kramers hosted a huge *melaveh malkah* in their tiny house every Saturday night. The esteemed Rav Avraham Yechiel Fish from Tel Aviv usually attended, as well as literally hundreds of people from all over the area. The Kramers' abode had only two rooms. For the *melaveh malkah* one was designated for the men, and the other for the women.

One Saturday night, Esther Schutz came with her mother and her sisters. Esther was expecting and was suffering from problems with her legs. Her doctor had told her to rest, but her overwhelming desire to partake of the Kramers' inspiring *melaveh malkah* drew her to the cramped house. Cars continued to arrive until both rooms were packed with people. Suddenly she heard R' Yaakov Moshe calling, "Esther, Esther." She looked up and saw him standing at the door of the room where the women were. She assumed that he was calling a different Esther, because why should the *tzaddik* be calling her amidst this throng? She didn't reply.

R' Yaakov Moshe returned to the room housing the men, located Esther's husband Bezalel, and asked him, "Is Esther here?" When Bezalel replied that she was, R' Yaakov Moshe again made his way to the women's side and called out, "Estherke! Estherke!" Again, Esther was mute. Finally he called through the crowd: "Is Esther Schutz here?"

An abashed Esther called out, "Yes, I'm here."

The *tzaddik*, knowing how few chairs were available, called, "Are you sitting down?"

When Esther replied, "Yes!" the 75-year-old *tzaddik* returned to his guests on the men's side.

Another expression of R' Yaakov Moshe's awesome humility: Whenever Anni Kalfe drove R' Yaakov Moshe to *simchahs*, he always asked her to pick him up early so that he could arrive an hour before the designated time. Once Anni asked him, "Yankel Moshe, why do you have to arrive an hour early? There won't be anything for you to do there."

R' Yaakov Moshe replied: "It's preferable that I wait for the *simchah* than that the *simchah* and the *ba'al simchah* should wait for me."

Like her husband, Chaya Sara always cordially greeted every resident of both Kfar Gidon and its secular counterpart Telmei Gidon but, unlike her husband, she was often treated harshly and critically by certain elderly neighbors. Every morning at 8 a.m., all the older women, both *chareidi* and secular, would gather at "the mail" to await the arrival of the mail truck. They would sit and converse in Hungarian. One young wife who understood a little Hungarian was dismayed when she heard a veteran neighbor snap at Chaya Sara, "Chaya Sara, you don't know anything." She noticed tears spring to Chaya Sara's eyes.

One elderly woman in particular was Chaya Sara's nemesis. A fellow Holocaust survivor, she would pick arguments with Chaya Sara, who was a master of the sharp retort. One day in 1978, while waiting for the mail, the two women became involved in a shouting match. Both were red in the face with anger. One of the young wives who witnessed the argument was so upset by it that she went to Chaya Sara that evening to talk to her about it.

She found Chaya Sara full of remorse. The Rebbetzin felt that she shouldn't have let herself be drawn into the argument. She was terribly upset by her own reaction. Without going into the subject of the argument, Chaya Sara explained to the younger woman that sometimes people who go through the hell that she went through in Auschwitz are vulnerable to losing control of themselves. "There's no excuse for losing my temper," Chaya Sara contended. "I have to work on my *mid-*

dos [character traits]." She maintained that a person should always be calm and peaceful, and should ward off anger by reasoning with herself. She was, she said, disappointed with herself for becoming angry. Mentioning her childlessness, she told the young woman: "I have logical reasons to be depressed, but *HaKadosh Baruch Hu* has been so good to me in other ways, that losing my temper amounts to being ungrateful to G-d."

This rare glimpse into the workings of Chaya Sara's internal battles is like a concise manual for spiritual growth. The conversation reveals several remarkable points. The first and most noteworthy is that she never mentioned her adversary. The young woman was predisposed to blame the other party, whom she considered to be petty and jealous of Chaya Sara's saintliness. Chaya Sara, however, pointed a finger only at herself. The other woman's limitations were irrelevant; only her own reaction was worth scrutinizing and rectifying.

The first step in the Jewish process of teshuvah, or self-change, is to admit one's wrongdoing. While many of us fixate on blaming the other person, the choice to shine the spotlight on ourselves and our own reaction is the beginning of spiritual growth.

Secondly, Chaya Sara desisted from making excuses for her behavior. Although she mentioned her vulnerability that resulted from her Holocaust experiences, she clearly asserted that there was no excuse for losing her temper.

In an age when psychotherapy ferrets out reasons and excuses for the most reprehensible behavior ("It was my parents!" "It was my second-grade teacher!"), Rebbetzin Chaya Sara's example counters this "It's not my fault" tendency. She took responsibility for her lapse, which is a prerequisite for change. Since few of us have a past as nightmarish as Auschwitz, we too should be able to stop making excuses and start growing.

Third, Chaya Sara's statement that she has to work on her middos is an astounding declaration for a 54-year-old woman who had already established a reputation as a tzaddekes by taking in multiple-handicapped children, living totally without material amenities, and devoting every waking moment to others. In fact, Chaya Sara never rested on her laurels, but strove to grow in good middos throughout her long life.

The lesson for all of us is clear: No matter what our age, our accomplishments, or our spiritual level, our goal must always be continued growth, as befits bnei aliyah.

Fourth, Chaya Sara always brought G-d into the picture. By saying, "I have logical reasons to be depressed, but HaKadosh Baruch Hu has been so good to me in other ways, that losing my temper amounts to being ungrateful to G-d," she was painting her emotions against the background of her relationship with G-d. In her perception of reality, G-d was the exclusive Source of everything. She saw her life as a cornucopia whose immeasurable bounty flowed from the upper point, which was HaKadosh Baruch Hu. Any negative reaction, such as anger or depression, was a repudiation of G-d's largesse. And in Chaya Sara's worldview, the worst sin was ingratitude to G-d.

I have spent years studying the life of Chaya Sara Kramer. Despite her claim, "HaKadosh Baruch Hu has been so good to me in other ways," the only manifest blessing, the only truly bright spot, I have found in her life is her marriage to the tzaddik Yaakov Moshe Kramer. Everything else — her family's murder, her Holocaust experience, her poverty, her childlessness, her difficult life taking care of disabled children — are like blotches of black on the canvas of her life. I look at her life and see one bright spot amid all the black. She looked at her life and saw only brightness. Were we looking at the same life?

No, we weren't. I was looking at the external realities of her life. What was she herself looking at? A hint to the answer is found in the foreword R' Yaakov Moshe wrote to his book, Yam Shel Shmuel. Sounding like his wife, he begins the book:

> How can I thank Hashem Yisbarach for all the good that He has bestowed on me until now, and how can I give praise and thanks to the Master of all the worlds Who had compassion on me and guarded me in this path, not to walk in the counsel of the wicked nor to sit among scoffers, Heaven forbid, and in His abundant mercy and great loving kindness rescued me from them and from the majority, and led me on the straight paths of the Holy Torah ...

The goodness for which both Kramers constantly thanked G-d was not the external circumstances of their lives, but the spiritual gifts that kept them on the true and holy path of Torah. The above words reveal how keenly R' Yaakov Moshe was aware that, being born in the early 20th century in Europe, a time and place of mass defection from Torah Judaism, not succumbing to "the majority" was in itself a blessing. The Kramers regarded their faithfulness to Hashem Yisbarach and His Torah as the paramount blessing that defined their existence. This spiritual reality was the prominent color on the canvas of their lives.

The greatness of Rebbetzin Chaya Sara Kramer is that she chose to adjust her "figure ground" perception, like a person looking at a Rubin Vase and choosing to see the white profiled faces rather than the black vase. What to a lesser soul would have been the background became to her the foreground. G-d's beneficence in blessing her with spiritual propensities and love for Him was the shining foreground of her life. The black blotches of her traumas and disappointments faded into the background.

This period witnessed the arrival of yet another new group into the Kramers' life. A community of young American and British *chareidi* families was founded by Rabbi Nachman Bulman in nearby Migdal HaEmek in the early 1980's. Different from the Kramers in every external way, this young English-speaking group felt a spiritual affinity with the "*tzaddikim*" that drew many of them into the Kramers' orbit. As a Migdal HaEmek wife remembers, "Our community merited to take in the perfume and the *ruach* of the *tzaddikim*."

In 1984, one young Migdal HaEmek mother, whom I will call Adina, was undergoing an emotional and psychological crisis. Rabbi Borenstein suggested that she visit the Kramers. That very day, she took the 15-minute bus ride to Kfar Gidon. When Adina got off the bus, someone directed her to the Kramers'

R' Yaakov Moshe with Nissin Michaely at bris of Yehudah

house. "I saw what looked like a barn," Adina remembers. "I thought, 'How can people live in there?'"

Nevertheless, as soon as she entered the house, she felt an otherworldly calmness, "because they were living without any connection to *gashmius* [materialism]. All my life I had yearned to live a happy life not burdened by *gashmius*." There, for the first time, Adina entered a realm of pure spirit unencumbered by materialism.

The Kramers received Adina warmly, but they were involved with visitors who had arrived earlier. They handed her the *Iggeres HaRamban* to read while she waited. When she read it, she felt so far from the ideal it presents that she broke down crying. Both R' Yaakov Moshe and Chaya Sara immediately went to her. They sat with her and asked her what was bothering her. "They told me that human beings go through difficult periods and they come out of them. They assured me that it was a passing stage."

Adina began frequenting the Kramers' home, sometimes on a daily basis. The Kramers would generously give of themselves in an effort to encourage her. "They would tell me chassidic stories or stories of their own lives, trying to take my mind off my pain. I felt that they were giving me as much as they could."

Rebbetzin Chaya Sara offered Adina concrete guidance in combating her depression:

> She said that all my ailments were due to my letting the yetzer hara come in. She told me, "You have to recognize that the yetzer is a thief. If you know that a thief is coming, you're going to run to the door and lock it. But not just lock it; you're going to put all kinds of barricades in front of the door so that the thief can't get in. In the same way, you have to lock your mind against the thoughts you are letting in." Those thoughts, she said, were breaking me. I had to not let them come in. For

example, worries about the future. She told me to live in the here and now and not worry about the future.

Rebbetzin Chaya Sara taught Adina a specific technique for dealing with unwanted emotions. Mussar books tell us that it is not enough to aspire for a good trait, but one must work out specific techniques for acquiring that good trait. Chaya Sara was like a general warring against the yetzer hara; she was always developing a battle plan.

Lofty aspirations usually fail not from a lack of will but from a lack of method. Just as a building cannot be built from a vision, but only from a carefully drawn architect's plan, so real self-change requires a specific plan. When we declare, "I'll never again get depressed," we doom ourselves to failure. When, however, we say, "When I feel depression overtaking me, I'll do X, Y, or Z," we are likely to succeed.

Even with all of the Kramers' instruction and encouragement, Adina's healing took a long time. They would counsel her to be patient. "Within three years," R' Yaakov Moshe told her, "I guarantee you that you're going to come out of this."

"I lived on those words," Adina testifies.

Every word the Kramers uttered was intended to be encouraging. When Adina's husband visited, Rebbetzin Chaya Sara would say to him, "Look at your wife; she's such a wonderful person." To both of them she would say, "You are like Sara Imeinu and Avraham Avinu." Adina adds: "At that point, we weren't. But later we received a lot of guests in our home. My husband started working with *ba'alei teshuvah,* and our Shabbos table would be full every week. We became what she saw."

Rebbetzin Chaya Sara would say to Adina, "You will see. You were put into this world to help other people, and you're going to see that because of your ordeal, you will be better equipped to help others."

"And that's exactly what happened," Adina declares. "After three years I began to come out of it. Now when I deal with people who are broken, I see the Rebbetzin in front of my eyes, and I say to them what she said to me."

Adina told R' Yaakov Moshe that her great-great-grandfather had served as the *shammas* of the Chasam Sofer. After that, the 72-year-old R' Yaakov Moshe would stand up for the 28-year-old Adina every time she entered the house. "I'm standing up for the Chasam Sofer," he explained. Perhaps. But perhaps he was standing up to reveal to her that just as her past was great, so her future would also be great.

R' Yaakov Moshe had two mottos that embodied his zeal to encourage everyone. He would quote the Hungarian saying, "It's good and it's going to be even better." The Yiddish motto that summed up the purpose of his life was: "To lift up the honor of Heaven and to do a favor for a *Yid*."

The Kramers' house was surrounded by dirt. They never planted a lawn or even put in a gravel path until their last years in Kfar Gidon. On rainy days, Adina waded through mud to their door, then stood there, reluctant to enter with her muddy shoes. Chaya Sara would greet her joyfully, draw her inside, and tell her "the story of the mud": A man died and went to the Heavenly tribunal. There his sins far outweighed his few good deeds. But once, he had passed a carriage that had turned over in the mud. He had waded into the mud and helped rescue an entire family, despite getting his own clothes dirty. In the Heavenly tribunal, the angels began hauling in mud — buckets and buckets of mud — and heaping them onto the good side of the scale. When Rebbetzin Chaya Sara finished relating the story to Adina, she would always assert: "The more mud, the more reward!"

Adina remembers not only the story, but also the way the Rebbetzin repeated the moral: the more mud, the more reward. "She would say it laughing, with her few teeth showing. Clearly, this was her *simchah*, to receive guests, even muddy guests like me."

"The more mud, the more reward," could have been Chaya Sara's motto. The Mishnah in Avos asserts: "Lefum tzara agra [According to the difficulty, so is the reward]." Although it is human nature to prefer ease and pleasure, spiritual growth comes from effort and hardship. Just as Chaya Sara never let the mud dissuade her from receiving a visitor, so she never shied away from anything worth doing because of its difficulty or unpleasantness. She understood on a deep level that the actions of this world can be assessed only by their ultimate effect on the soul in the world of eternity.

This choice — to accept and even relish what is immediately unpleasant when it is ultimately good — is a choice open to all of us. It requires the spiritual vision to look at the mud on the floor and to see the mud on the scales.

Adina felt so close to the Kramers that she was, in her own words, "*chutzpadik.*" A member of the Migdal HaEmek community was bedridden with a serious back problem. In addition to the physical ailment, the man was deeply depressed because his incapacity prevented him from helping people as he usually did. Rabbi Bulman was in America at that time, so Adina asked R' Yaakov Moshe to come to Migdal HaEmek to visit the sick man. On the one hand, Adina knew that it was brazen to ask a *tzaddik* to journey to someone he didn't even know, especially since R' Yaakov Moshe suffered from problems with his legs and the sick man lived two flights up in a building without an elevator. On the other hand, says Adina, "I knew that the *tzaddik* would be able to bring him a *yeshuah* [salvation]." Later that very day, both R'

Yaakov Moshe and Rebbetzin Chaya Sara showed up at the sick man's apartment in Midgal HaEmek.

Adina told the Kramers all her problems, but when it came to listening to *lashon hara*, they were "very, very careful to avoid it." At one point, Adina was troubled by a dilemma. The children of one family in their Migdal HaEmek community "were not going in the right path," and one of Adina's children was a close friend of one of those children. Adina did not know how to handle the situation, so she decided to consult R' Yaakov Moshe. "As soon as I started talking about the other family, he closed his eyes and literally fell asleep. He had a way of pushing out what he didn't want to hear."

R' Yaakov Moshe, c. 1984

Another member of the Migdal HaEmek community, Sara Dina Packer, remembers the "lack of pressure" in the Kramer house.

No one was ever in a hurry. No one had to get on with anything. Maybe they did have something to do, but they never made me feel like I was keeping them from anything, or that I was in the way. It was as if they had all the time in the world for their visitors.

Sara Dina Packer was there after dark one evening. Rebbetzin Chaya Sara went out to their kitchen garden to pick fresh squash for supper. When R' Yaakov Moshe realized this, "he was furious with her, because last time she went out to pick squash in the dark, she mistakenly picked up a snake."

During the last decade of R' Yaakov Moshe's life, his diet consisted mainly of garlic which, according to his wife, was therapeutic for his heart. Rebbetzin Chaya Sara devotedly peeled garlic cloves and put them in lemon juice. Her husband would drink down the mixture. Apparently it paid off. When R' Yaakov Moshe went to the hospital toward the end of his life, the doctors said he had "the heart of a baby, with no blocked arteries at all."

Sara Dina remembers how scrupulous the Kramers were to eat *melaveh malkah* on *Motza'ei Shabbos*. "They would eat chicken. Not leftover chicken from Shabbos, but Rebbetzin Chaya Sara would cook a whole new chicken in honor of *melaveh malkah*."

The arrival of the young couples in Kfar Gidon meant a new generation of children. R' Yaakov Moshe was determined to start a new school for them. The Yiddish-speaking *cheder* he had founded in the 1950's had closed long before, when the Kfar's children grew up. In 1982, with 10 children of kindergarten and first-grade age, R' Yaakov Moshe got the official authorization and funding to inaugurate a new Hebrew-speaking, *chareidi* school in Kfar Gidon.

The school was under the auspices of *Chinuch Atzma'i*, the *chareidi* school system "independent" of Israeli government supervision. The first teacher and principal of the school was Rivka Rochel Hess. She remembers that, due to the paucity of students, Rav Shach gave a special dispensation for boys and girls to learn together until the third grade.

R' Yaakov Moshe was the school's unofficial patron and adviser. He counseled the teachers and blessed the students. Every Friday, even after the school had grown in size, all of the children came to the Kramers' home for refreshments and to receive a blessing from the *tzaddik*.

One day an official from *Chinuch Atzma'i* came to visit the school. Appalled that there were only 10 students, he notified Rivka Rochel Hess that he intended to close down the school. Horrified, she ran to R' Yaakov Moshe who, that very day, journeyed to Bnei Brak to appeal to Rav Shach, the ultimate authority over *Chinuch Atzma'i*, to keep the school open. Rav Shach concurred.

Soon a solution for expanding the number of students appeared. Rabbi Bulman agreed to send the children from his Migdal HaEmek community to the kindergarten and first grade of the Kfar Gidon school.

The arrangement lasted only two years. The *kollel* families of Migdal HaEmek, financially strapped as they were, found it difficult to pay for the transportation back and forth to Kfar Gidon.

The departure of the Migdal HaEmek students brought the incipient Kfar Gidon school to a crossroads. R' Yaakov Moshe favored enlisting new students from throughout the Jezreel Valley by convincing less-observant Sephardi parents to send their children to the valley's sole *chareidi* school. For those parents who could not afford the tuition, R' Yaakov Moshe offered to grant financial assistance.

Most of the young parents of Kfar Gidon opposed this idea. They believed that the school should be only for the genuinely *chareidi* children of the village. They worried that their children would be adversely influenced by classmates from less religious families, children who watched television and went to the movies. As Naomi Bohbot recollects: "R' Yaakov Moshe's idea was to admit any child who wanted to come into the school because 'you can't judge a child by his family or his surroundings.' He believed that the school would influence the child, not vice versa."

In fact, this controversy pitted R' Yaakov Moshe's cherished vision of the pure soul within every child against the more superficial but nonetheless valid concern about negative externals. As he explained to Rivka Rochel Hess, an educator must see and address the higher soul of the child, which is not immediately visible. This is what will lead the child to become a *tzaddik*. He believed that the externals of family background and present pastimes could be overlooked, or rather, looked *through*, to see the luminous soul within. He told Rivka Rochel Hess to treat the students with *kavod* [honor and respect] and eventually they would grow to become what she saw in them.

In the end, R' Yaakov Moshe won, due to the sheer impossibility of maintaining a school with too few students. He paid a small crew to knock on doors in the nearby towns of Afula, Afula Ilit, Nazareth, and Beit Shean to register new students. He paid the tuition of every child whose parents couldn't afford it, as well as their transportation. "We had a lot of help from Heaven," Rivka Rochel Hess recalls, "because R' Yaakov Moshe blessed the school." When the school in the Moroccan settlement of Adirim closed, all those children enrolled in the Kfar Gidon school. Soon, busloads of children were pouring into Kfar Gidon every morning.

It was not the first time that R' Yaakov Moshe's vision of the ideal conflicted with other Kfar Gidon residents' perception of the immediate reality. A few years before, a yeshivah comprised of *ba'alei teshuvah* decided to move to Kfar Gidon. R' Yaakov Moshe welcomed them, feeling that the more Torah learning in the moshav, the better. The yeshivah moved into temporary quarters in the kfar. They applied for and got an official building permit to construct apartments for their *avreichim* [married students], but the residents of Kfar Gidon vetoed the proposition. They were concerned about the backgrounds of the students, some of whom had served time in prison prior to becoming religious. Despite R' Yaakov Moshe's most prodigious efforts, he didn't succeed in convincing the residents of Kfar Gidon to let the yeshivah remain.

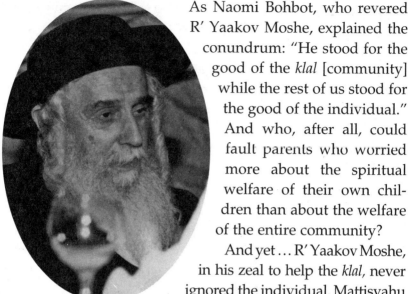

R' Yaakov Moshe, c. 1985

As Naomi Bohbot, who revered R' Yaakov Moshe, explained the conundrum: "He stood for the good of the *klal* [community] while the rest of us stood for the good of the individual." And who, after all, could fault parents who worried more about the spiritual welfare of their own children than about the welfare of the entire community?

And yet … R' Yaakov Moshe, in his zeal to help the *klal*, never ignored the individual. Mattisyahu Bohbot, a Kfar Gidon child who was in the first class of the new school and whose parents took him out by third grade, lovingly attests to the *tzaddik's* personal impact on his life:

> *He loved all the children of the kfar. Every time we came to the synagogue, he kissed us on the head and honored us for coming. This made us like to come to the synagogue and made us honor the synagogue. I once saw someone reading the newspaper in the synagogue and I was horrified.*
>
> *I was 14 years old when R' Yaakov Moshe left the kfar, but his influence is part of what made me who I am.*

Today the educational institutions in Kfar Gidon bear the name of R' Yaakov Moshe Kramer. They comprise a preschool, a kindergarten for boys, a kindergarten for girls, a *cheder*, a girls' elementary school, and a recently established Beis Yaakov high school for girls. Six hundred children from throughout the Jezreel Valley attend these schools.

Ironically, the children of Kfar Gidon are not among the students. The gap between the *tzaddik's* idealized vision and the moshav parents' realistic perception was never bridged.

Over the years, the Kramers made 405 *shidduchim*. While young Tzviki Shtiglitz considered it noteworthy that R' Yaakov Moshe acted as a *shadchan*, it seems natural that the Kramers, who cared so much about other people's welfare, should want to see them happily married.

They worked hard at it. When people came to them for a *shidduch*, they wouldn't rest until they found them a match. Esther Schutz recalls, "R' Yaakov Moshe phoned abroad trying to make a *shidduch* for my sister. He called London, Germany, and Belgium, but he refused to take money to cover the cost of the long-distance calls. He would say, 'It's my mitzvah.'"

A teaching cautions that a couple who doesn't pay their *shadchan* won't have *shalom bayis*. Therefore, when the Kramers did succeed in making a *shidduch*, they accepted one half-shekel from each side as payment.

The memoirs of R' Meir Shalom Tanzee reveal a glimpse of the lengths to which the Kramers were willing to go to make a *shidduch*:

> *When I approached the age of marrying, I insisted that my bride come from a family of strict observers of Torah. In those years, it was difficult to find a family who were all Torah observers and learned in Torah. Once I met a girl from a good family, and I had the feeling that she was my zivug [intended spouse]. For various touchy reasons, the matter didn't work out.*
> *The Rav HaTzaddik heard about this. He didn't hesitate. Upon advice from the Rabbanit [Rebbetzin Chaya Sara], he*

traveled to the family of the girl. When the family opened
the door, they were sure, from his glowing face that appeared
like the Shechinah, that Eliyahu HaNavi had entered their
house. The Rav sat and spoke with them for several hours,
and convinced the family to continue with our shidduch.
That day I was in the yeshivah. I received a telegram from the
tzaddik asking me to come to him immediately in Kfar Gidon.
When I arrived, he told me what was going on, and told me
to meet with the young woman again. Baruch Hashem, today
I'm married to her, and the father of 10 children, kein yirbu.

Once, R' Yaakov Moshe met a chassid who had learned with him in Satu Mere many years earlier. He told the chassid, "I have a girl who needs a *shidduch*." The chassid thought R' Yaakov Moshe was speaking about his own daughter. Remembering how highly the Satmar Rebbe had esteemed R' Yaakov Moshe, the chassid eagerly offered his own son for the match. Only much later in the *shidduch* process was it revealed that the girl was not the Kramers' daughter.

A young yeshivah student from Beit Shean came to see R' Yaakov Moshe. He was troubled and explained why: "I found a *shidduch*, but the girl is an orphan. She doesn't have a father."

R' Yaakov Moshe rejoined enthusiastically: "You merited the best father-in-law, *HaKadosh Baruch Hu!* As it says, 'He is the Father of orphans.'" The yeshivah student married the orphan girl and today is a Rav in Beit Shean.

In the matter of *shidduchim*, as in so much else, R' Yaakov Moshe's approach differed greatly from his wife's. As one Kfar Gidon resident remarked, "He saw in everybody the good, and he didn't see what was wrong in anybody." Or as Shimon Dankowitz of London observed: "He had a very simplistic approach to *shidduchim*. A nice boy, a nice girl. He couldn't see any reason why it wouldn't work."

Rebbetzin Chaya Sara, on the other hand, was more discriminating. She had the quality of *binah* [discriminating insight], for which Jewish women are noted. Yet, she went along with her husband's often naive *shidduch* suggestions, sometimes with comic results.

Zev Shtiglitz recollects two matches that R' Yaakov Moshe set up for him. After the first, Zev went to R' Yaakov Moshe and complained, "She stutters."

Unperturbed, R' Yaakov Moshe replied, "Moshe Rabbeinu also stuttered, and he was the leader of *Am Yisrael.*"

After a different *shidduch*, a disgruntled Zev reported to R' Yaakov Moshe, "She's older than I am."

To this the *tzaddik* answered, "I don't know how old she is. I wasn't at her *bris.*"

Zev concludes his account: "After I became engaged to my wife, and Chaya Sara met my fiancée, she said, 'Now I understand why you didn't want our *shidduchim.*'"

R' Yaakov Moshe also tried to make a *shidduch* for me. The man he chose was a head shorter than I and spoke only Hebrew, a language I barely knew at that time. In fact, the only thing we had in common was that we were both in our late 30's and we were both Jews.

When this didn't work, R' Yaakov Moshe tried again. He spoke to Rav Kreiswirth, the Chief Rabbi of Antwerp, about me. Rav Kreiswirth telephoned me, and we met in the lobby of a Jerusalem hotel to discuss a *shidduch* possibility, an eminent member of an American *kehillah*, who was close to Rav Kreiswirth. Only looking back on it afterward did I realize how implausible was the scene: the distinguished Chief Rabbi of Antwerp interviewing a woman who had been religious scarcely a year for a match with an important man. Only R' Yaakov Moshe could have concocted such an improbable amalgam.

However, I experienced that R' Yaakov Moshe's blessings were more effective than his shot-in-the-dark *shidduch* suggestions. When I asked him for a blessing to get married, he asked me what I was looking for in a husband. Although I had many requirements, I knew that my Hebrew was not good enough to communicate them, so I decided to condense them into one simple Hebrew sentence: *"Ani rotzah lev tov."* "I want a good heart." The *tzaddik* blessed me, and two months later I met my *"Leib tov,"* my good-hearted husband named Leib, a literal fulfillment of the *tzaddik's* blessing.

As the Kramers' neighbor Leah Landau recalls:

> *He made shidduchim that others wouldn't venture. He set up Hungarian boys with Sephardi girls. Once he made a shidduch for a nice girl from a good family. Her parents were very upset because, although the boy was a good yeshivah student, he had two brothers who were not. But R' Yaakov Moshe's idea was vindicated. The girl married that boy and they recently married off their fifth child!*

In the mid-1970's, Yaakov Moshe began traveling abroad every year in order to raise funds for his *hatzalah* work. This was a watershed in the Kramers' life. From that point on they did not engage in agriculture nor take in any additional handicapped children. Although Hindele would live until 1982, and became progressively more difficult to take care of as her health deteriorated, the era of the handicapped children effectively ended.

The trips abroad entailed three months in New York and, later, a three-week stopover in London plus a few days in Antwerp. These trips were hard. R' Yaakov Moshe didn't speak English. He was in his mid-60's when he started and, despite his failing health, he continued the arduous annual circuit until he was 79. While Rebbetzin Chaya Sara carefully cooked for his diet at home, R' Yaakov Moshe would not trouble his hosts abroad for his special requirements. On the airplane from Israel, he ate only what his wife had packed for him. On the airplane home, he ate nothing. In New York, London, and Antwerp, he stayed at the homes of kind Jews who offered him a place. One hostess recalls that he ate only yogurt and drank only water. Another hostess, Rebbetzin Breish, remembers: "He ate very little, but whatever he ate, he was so complimentary."

Mrs. Sheindy Leiber of London was once visiting in Boro Park. As she walked down the street, she was surprised to see R' Yaakov Moshe Kramer sitting on the ground, waiting for a bus. "He couldn't stand," she explains, "because he had trouble with his legs. And he didn't want to take any of the money he had collected to use for a taxi for himself."

Wherever he went, he impressed people with his holiness and humility. Mrs. Reizl Hus of Brooklyn was told by her husband that "a charity collector from Eretz Yisrael is coming." When she opened the door for him, "I thought an angel was standing there, so much light was coming from his face. Before he stepped into the house, he stood there and heaped blessings upon us."

R' Shaya Gross and R' Kramer

Sheindy Leiber remembers the first time R' Yaakov Moshe came to their house to collect money. "He had a shine on his face. You could tell he was different. He sat down by the table and blessed all the children. He would always sit at the end of the table unless you put him at the head of the table."

For a period, he stayed with the Breish family in London. "The first time I saw him," recalls Rebbetzin Breish, "he had a *heilige tsireh*. As he was coming into our house, there were some little children. He gave each child a kiss and spoke to them. He radiated a warmth and a caring that was unbelievable."

Two incidents that transpired while R' Yaakov Moshe and his companion R' Nachman Landau were guests in their home made a deep impression on Rebbetzin Breish:

The Breishes employed a non-Jewish cleaning woman, who came to work wearing short sleeves and overalls. Her lack of modesty bothered R' Nachman Landau. When R' Nachman complained about it, R' Yaakov Moshe retorted in Yiddish, "*Kikt men nisht,*" meaning, "So don't look." Rebbetzin Breish remarks, "That summed up his whole attitude. If you don't like something, then don't look. Instead of being critical, just don't pay attention to what's wrong."

Another time, someone noticed a spider on the kitchen floor. One of the children said, "Kill it!" R' Yaakov Moshe objected. "Don't kill it. Somewhere her children are waiting for her." With that, he took a piece of paper, got the spider to jump on it, and threw the spider out the window.

(R' Yaakov Moshe often quoted from *Tehillim* [Psalms], "His mercy is on all His creatures," which refers to kindness to animals. He and Rebbetzin Chaya Sara used to feed the stray cats in Kfar Gidon. In the early days when he worked the fields, other farmers noticed that he never whipped his donkey.)

Rabbi Chaim Breish described R' Yaakov Moshe's extraordinary humility: "He was a person who didn't take up any space."

In the beginning, R' Yaakov Moshe's method was not to go around collecting, but rather to sit in the *beis midrash*. People would come to him, asking advice and donating money.

Every year, more people came. Rav Yaakov Deutsch was once in America and noticed R' Yaakov Moshe sitting in the *beis midrash* after *Shacharis*. "I saw it with my own eyes. R' Yaakov Moshe was sitting at a table. He never said a word to anyone, and people brought him money, huge quantities of money."

In 1985, while in London, R' Yaakov Moshe stayed with Avigdor Galandauer for the first time. Although R' Avigdor's rented house was quite small, its proximity to the shul was vital for R' Yaakov Moshe, who suffered from circulation problems in his legs.

Before R' Yaakov Moshe left, R' Avigdor asked him for a blessing that next year he should also stay with them and that by then the Galandauers should be in their own house. At that time, R' Avigdor had no idea of how he could purchase his own house since he had no money at all for a down payment. The *tzaddik* blessed him. During that year a friend came up with a plan for how to buy a house without any money for the down payment, and the *tzaddik's* blessing was fulfilled.

R' Avigdor Galandauer lighting a Havdalah candle for R' Yaakov Moshe

The following year, shortly after the Galandauers moved into their own house, R' Yaakov Moshe arrived and stayed with them. The new house had only one bedroom. R' Yaakov Moshe and R' Nachman Landau, who always accompanied him from New York, slept in the bedroom, while R' Avigdor and his wife slept in the den. Before R' Yaakov Moshe left,

R' Avigdor asked him for a blessing that he should stay with them the next year and that they should be able to build another room for his next visit. The *tzaddik* blessed them.

This blessing, too, came true. The Galandauers built an extension. Although the neighbors could have disputed their right to extend, none of the neighbors ever said a word. The new room was finished just in time for Rav Kramer's visit.

Before he left, R' Avigdor again asked him for a blessing that he should stay with them the next year, and that they should be able to add another room, because they still didn't have enough room for all their children. R' Yaakov Moshe obliged and blessed him. During the course of the following year, the Galandauers added another room. "The surprising thing," recalls R' Avigdor, "is that none of the neighbors ever complained, though they could have claimed that it blocked their light. Had the neighbors complained to the Council, we'd have had to stop the work and take it down. But they never said a word."

When in New York, R' Yaakov Moshe usually stayed with R' Nachman Landau, who was the official treasurer of R' Yaakov Moshe's organization, "Tomchei Dalim, Institution for Refugee Children of Sephardic and Oriental Communities." All the money R' Yaakov Moshe collected for Tomchei Dalim, he turned over to R' Nachman.

But R' Yaakov Moshe had a private fund as well. With the end of their small dairy farm and agricultural enterprise, the Kramers' income was now limited to the rent for their land paid by Yossi Shtiglitz. This was not enough to live on, even at the bare-bones level on which the Kramers subsisted. And, as word spread with the years and more visitors needed to be fed, their need for private income grew. R' Yaakov Moshe took very seriously his *kesubah* obligation to support his wife. Therefore, he sometimes appealed for money for the Rebbetzin. This money he did not turn over to R' Nachman.

Alas, it rarely reached the Rebbetzin. With Chaya Sara's permission and urging, R' Yaakov Moshe distributed money from this fund to indigent Jews he met in New York or London. R' Shimon Dankowitz recalls: "I met R' Yaakov Moshe and Rav Landau at the airport, coming from the United States. He quietly handed me money from the Rebbetzin's fund and told me to distribute it to poor Jews in London."

R' Shimon would take the *tzaddik* around to people's homes to collect money. In one home, the apparently well-to-do owner donated 100 British pounds. Then he asked to speak to R' Kramer privately. He disclosed to R' Kramer that he was undergoing financial difficulties. R' Kramer gave him $100, saying, "I'm giving you this money in dollars, from my private fund, so Rav Nachman Landau won't know." Although the man protested, and later phoned Shimon Dankowitz to ask him what to do, R' Yaakov Moshe refused to take back the $100.

Shimon Dankowitz observes, "For himself R' Yaakov Moshe needed nothing, but for everyone else he would give in the most lavish way."

Another time, R' Shimon took R' Kramer to a family with four children of marriageable age. R' Shimon didn't realize that the father of the family was struggling with *parnassah* [livelihood], but apparently R' Kramer did. He sat down at the table and told the father a story: The Ksav Sofer had a student who didn't have enough money to make a *shidduch* for his daughter. The Ksav Sofer told him, "You make the *shidduch*, and then the gates of *parnassah* will open for you." This story became actualized in the life of this London family. A short time later, the father of the family became very affluent and married off all four of his children; afterward, he again lapsed into financial difficulties.

Her husband's lengthy absences of four months, one-third of every year, were nothing short of agonizing for Rebbetzin Chaya Sara. When he left, she cried as though her heart would break. Once Anni Kalfe asked her why she was crying so hard. Between her sobs, the Rebbetzin replied: "It's as if I'm holding my baby, and someone takes the baby from my hands."

Her reply is particularly poignant since she had no babies of her own. R' Yaakov Moshe was like her father, husband, friend, and child, all rolled into one. For the long months that he was away, her loss was total.

Rebbetzin Chaya was afraid to be left alone. She described herself to me as a "pachdanit," — a scaredy-cat. I live in the Jewish Quarter of Jerusalem's Old City, in close proximity to a large Arab population. The Rebbetzin often asked me, "Aren't you afraid to live there?" When I would reply that I wasn't, she would declare, "I would be afraid to live there. I'm afraid of Arabs." When I invited her to the bris of my only son, to be held in a hall in the Jewish Quarter, she declined to come, explaining that she was afraid.

Even in the supremely safe precincts of Meah Shearim during her later years, the Rebbetzin had three locks on the door of her apartment, and kept them all bolted even during the day.

The Kramers' shack was the last dwelling in the moshav, bordered on the north by open fields. When her husband was absent, Rebbetzin Chaya Sara was intensely afraid of "thieves" coming at night. Since the Kramers owned nothing worth stealing, what she really feared was not the loss of her belongings, but the danger of malevolent intruders. Every year before leaving, R' Yaakov Moshe arranged for someone to stay with the Rebbetzin at night. For many years, Anni Kalfe's young daughters fulfilled this role. Nevertheless, even their presence did not assuage Rebbetzin Chaya Sara's fears. She showed them a 20-centimeter crowbar that she kept under her pillow to fight off intruders.

Yet, when R' Yaakov Moshe came home, the Rebbetzin felt so secure that she didn't even bother to lock the door at night. Her husband asked her, "What? You're so brave?" She replied, "When you're home, there's light and holiness in the house. I don't have to lock the door."

Given the intense fear that her husband's absence engendered, it is all the more amazing that she agreed to his going for so long and so often. She chose to let him work for the good of others despite the enormous emotional toll it cost her.

Many of us are generous when it comes to our time, our money, or even our preferences, but when the price is our emotional well-being, we falter. To choose to help others when it causes us anxiety, repugnance, or fear is a very high level. For example, some people will give generously to a facility for severely handicapped children, but seeing such hideously handicapped children repels them so much that they will never visit the facility.

When faced with such choices, we can ask ourselves, as Rebbetzin Chaya Sara must have consciously or unconsciously asked herself: "What's more important, this person's need or my emotional comfort?"

If we could pick one vignette that epitomizes the Kramers' life in Kfar Gidon during this era it would be the *melaveh malkah* that they held every Saturday night for half a year during the early 1980's. Hundreds of people would pour into their small shack and sing and dance until 2 o'clock in the morning, long after the rest of the agricultural collectives in the Jezreel Valley were sound asleep. Rav Asher Gabbai describes these sublime events:

What simchah! The dancing! The jumping! In that house, without a floor or any real furniture, we rejoiced. We didn't worry about anything. There was complete unity

*and love. You don't see anything like it today. All kinds of
people came: chassidim from Haifa and Bnei Brak, yeshivah bachurim from all over, Sephardim, Ashkenazim,
chilonim, everyone. What true ahavas Yisrael! There were
hundreds of people in that tiny house, and everyone danced
in ecstasy.*

In the vast darkness of the valley, the tiny shack would
glow and throb with the rhythmic dancing of true unity and
love. A taste of Paradise glimmering like a solitary star in the
immense night sky.

CHAPTER TWELVE

G-d's Esrog

*T*HE SECOND MOST TRAUMATIC EVENT OF Chaya Sara's post-Holocaust life (after the abduction of Miriam) occurred in 1984. Many years earlier, she had developed a hernia, a result of either her arduous labor on the farm or from her strenuous work with the handicapped children. The only cure for a hernia is surgery, but her ordeal with Dr. Mengele in Auschwitz had permanently poisoned Chaya Sara against doctors and hospitals. Therefore, rather than undergo surgery, for years she chose to suffer the pain of the hernia, which made it impossible for her to lie down in a bed to sleep. She would sleep sitting in a chair. By the 1980's, the hernia had grown so large that the disfigurement was visible through her layers of clothing. While she never complained about the pain, she did discuss it with some of the younger women.

Suddenly, in the summer of 1984 [Tammuz, 5745], the hernia became strangulated. It was a life-threatening situation that required immediate surgery. Powerless to resist any longer, the agonized Holocaust survivor agreed to the surgery, but not without the presence of her beloved husband. R' Yaakov Moshe was in the United States at the time. Notified by telephone, he dropped everything and caught the next available flight back to Israel.

A Yiddish expression asserts: "With a big doctor goes a big angel." Rather than entering the nearby hospital in Afula or even Haifa, Rebbetzin Chaya Sara chose to endure the three-hour journey to Hadassah Hospital in Jerusalem, where she hired the top surgeon, Prof. Arye Durst, to do the surgery. (The Kramers, as Satmar chassidim, never availed themselves of the government health insurance; they paid privately for all their medical care.)

Despite her grave condition, Chaya Sara refused to enter the operating room without her husband in attendance. As soon as R' Yaakov Moshe landed at Lod Airport, he sped directly to Hadassah Hospital to join her. Only when he reached Chaya Sara's side did she consent to be wheeled into the operating room.

After the surgery, the battle began. Although she had a private surgeon, Hadassah Hospital is still a teaching hospital. During rounds every morning and evening the interns and residents would stop by her bed. Ignoring her preference for privacy and modesty, they would start to pull back her covers in order to press her abdomen. She refused to let them. "Press your own stomachs!" she would scold.

They would come every morning and evening to take her blood. "Are you bees?" she would ask, and would refuse to submit to them unless Prof. Durst specifically ordered a blood test. At one point, she developed an infection and needed an antibiotic. She was told that the efficacy of the antibiotic could be determined only after 24 hours, but 12 hours after she took it, the interns were back to take her blood. She refused to allow it.

The interns complained to Prof. Durst, who sided with Rebbetzin Chaya Sara. "Leave her alone," he would tell them. When the interns angrily reported, "She's making trouble again," the senior surgeon would say to them, "Be patient with her. She lived through the Holocaust."

Meanwhile, R' Yaakov Moshe paid Prof. Durst to give her extra personal care. He used to say, "Doctors are the only ones with a license to kill people, but when we need them, we need them." When his wife fought with the interns, he would say, "Dear Chaya Sara, now you're in their hands."

She would object, "No, I'm not in their hands. I'm in the hands of *HaKadosh Baruch Hu.*"

It is impossible for anyone who did not go through the hell of the Holocaust to understand the scope of its horror or the depth of its scars. For the last nine chapters of this biography, the Holocaust has barely been mentioned, as if it were a malevolent character vanquished in Scene Two of the play. In truth, the Holocaust hovered in the wings of Chaya Sara's life story, never quite on stage, but never absent either.

Anni Kalfe recalls that not a week went by that the Rebbetzin didn't talk of her family's murder. Both Kramers' antipathy to the Germans was so strong that they refused to accept reparations from Germany, the only survivors in Kfar Gidon who did not receive a reparations check on the 20th of every month. When Yaakov Moshe was asked why he didn't take the money and use it for his hatzalah work, he replied, "I won't take money for Jewish blood." Chaya Sara's caretaker during the final years of her life reported that she often had nightmares, a telltale remnant of her Holocaust trauma.

The "road map" approach of this book has focused on the choices Chaya Sara made, but not everything is a choice. Some experiences are so traumatic that those who suffer them cannot choose to liberate themselves from their memory or their effect on their lives. Chaya Sara's fear of doctors and hospitals, which would dominate the last five years of her life, was as indelible as the tattooed number on her arm.

And yet, it is remarkable how, in other regards, she did not allow her heart and mind to be defined by the Holocaust. For example, distrustfulness is a typical mindset of Holocaust survivors, but it did not characterize Chaya Sara. Hoarding — of food or material objects — is another survivor proclivity in which Chaya Sara never engaged. While she feared Nazis (and projected that fear onto Arabs), when she spoke of them, her voice was devoid of hatred or anger; she had clearly chosen not to waste her emotional energy on them.

Her almost pathological resistance to doctors and hospitals reminds us that Chaya Sara Kramer was a Holocaust survivor and at the same time startles us because, while examining the succeeding four decades of her life, we had almost forgotten.

There are areas in each of us — the effects of heredity or childhood traumas — that are not subject to conscious choice. And yet, within those parameters, there are still choices we can make: to choose love and trust, to eschew anger and hatred. The trauma hovers in the wings, but we do not have to give it a speaking part.

While Chaya Sara was recuperating from her surgery, R' Yaakov Moshe never left her side. A firm believer that no patient in the hospital should ever be left alone even for an hour, because the companion provides spiritual protection against the Angel of Death, he sat by her bed all day and all night. On the fast day of the 17th of Tammuz, his niece Pnina begged him to go and rest. She assured him that she would sit with her aunt. At first he refused, but finally, weak from fasting, he gave in to her importuning. Before leaving the room, he said to Pnina, "If Eliyahu HaNavi comes, wake me up."

"I will," she perfunctorily gave her promise.

But R' Yaakov Moshe was serious. "How will you recognize him?" he queried.

Pnina was stumped. She had no idea.

Her uncle peered at her and declared portentously, "He could come in any form."

R' Yaakov Moshe's own health deteriorated considerably during the course of the 1980's. He suffered from chronic circulation problems in his legs. Although the Kramers' shack was barely a 10-minute walk from the moshav synagogue, for the last decade of his life R' Yaakov Moshe could not walk that short distance.

Eli Kalfe would pick him up in his car every morning before dawn and again at *Minchah* time to bring him to shul and take him home afterward. On Shabbos, R' Yaakov Moshe trudged slowly, leaning on Eli's arm with one hand and on his cane with the other, speaking *divrei Torah* throughout the long and painful trek.

During the one month each year that Eli spent in the army reserves, his wife Anni had the honor of driving the *tzaddik*. "I would drive him with one of my children," Anni recalls, "so there wouldn't be a problem with *yichud* [the prohibition against a woman being secluded with a man]. The *tzaddik* was worried that perhaps I wouldn't wake up on time, and he wanted so much to arrive at the shul for the sunrise service. For several days, he phoned each morning. Then he saw that I arrived on time. He would be waiting for me outdoors in the cold in the wintertime. He couldn't stop thanking me and blessing me."

Like most aging individuals, R' Yaakov Moshe picked and chose the areas in which he would give in to his disability and the areas in which he wouldn't. On his last Yom Kippur in Kfar Gidon, for instance, his legs were so badly crippled that his wife asked him not to bow down on the floor at the specified places during the *Avodah* service. As the *Avodah* service approached, Chaya Sara whispered to the woman sitting next to her in the women's balcony, "You'll see yet that the Rav will bow down." And so he did.

During the final months in Kfar Gidon, R' Avigdor Galandauer visited the *tzaddik* at *Minchah* time. By that period R' Yaakov Moshe's legs were black and he couldn't stand at all. He *davened Minchah* at home, sitting down for *Shemoneh Esrei*. Then, suddenly, there was a knock at the door — a visitor! R' Yaakov Moshe jumped to his feet, greeted the man, and gave him something to eat.

In 1988 [5748], R' Yaakov Moshe published his first and only book, *Yam Shel Shmuel*. The title "Yam" is an acronym for the name "Yaakov Moshe," while "Shmuel" is his father's name. The book is a commentary on the weekly Torah portion, quoting generously from explanations he heard from his Rebbe, the Satmar Rebbe, as well as written sources, such as the *Ohr HaChaim*, the *Noam Elimelech*, and the *Me'or VaShamesh*. Where the author ventures his own novel interpretations, he sometimes prefaces them with, "And I, the small one, want to comment ... ." The commentaries are generally simple and brief, most of them only a few lines and the longest of them a single page. The second half of the book is a potpourri of R' Yaakov Moshe's favorite writings, including *Perek Shirah*, *Iggeres HaRamban*, *Iggeres HaGra*, and *Iggeres Teiman* of the Rambam. The publication expenses were covered by a Belgian couple, Dovid and Mirel Tzvia Goldberg, who dedicated the book in memory of their son Shlomo, who had been killed in Antwerp in Kislev of that year.

Publishing a book is an act of revelation that runs counter to R' Yaakov Moshe's lifelong hiddenness. Why did he do it? R' Avigdor Galandauer speculates that because the *tzaddik* had no children, he wanted to leave the book as a memorial.

Yes, a memorial, but not to himself. After acknowledging the donors, R' Yaakov Moshe devotes three pages to memorializing those of his relatives and his wife's relatives who were murdured in the Holocaust: his father, mother, two brothers, nephew, two sisters, two brothers-in-law, uncles and aunts, plus his wife Chaya Sara's parents, and his first wife Leah and her parents and their first son-in-law, as well as his uncle's wife and two unrelated men. The name of each one appears in bold print. He then writes that the book is intended for their *illui neshamos* [the elevation of their souls], and he appeals to his readers: "I request very, very much to recite at least one mishnah for the benefit of all these souls who appear in this book."

In the Foreword, he makes clear that he wrote the book in order to honor his father. He quotes the Arizal: "When a son brings forth Torah novellae, he crowns his father ..." R' Yaakov Moshe goes on to write, "Therefore, I did this in order to provide *nachas ruach* [spiritual pleasure] for my father."

Curiously enough, the book includes a 23-page biography of the Gra, to whom R' Yaakov Moshe was apparently related. (The section begins by listing the Gra's ancestry, going back four generations to a Rav Moshe Kramer, the *Av Beis Din* of Vilna.) This section begins with a quote from *Mishlei:* "The crown of the fathers are their descendants, and the splendor of the children are their ancestors."

R' Yaakov Moshe was leaving this world without any descendants to bring glory to all the generations who had preceded him. His line ended with him. The book *Yam Shel Shmuel* was apparently a substitute for the children he never had.

The pain of the Holocaust and the pain of childlessness converged in this volume. The generation above him had been murdered; the generation below him had never been born. For both Kramers, these twin sorrows were masked by their relentless good cheer. Yet, at the end of his life, R' Yaakov Moshe felt the need to address both searing lacks. He left for posterity a book; his branch of the family tree would end with the fruit of Torah.

Rebbetzin Chaya Sara could not leave even that. And her pain at her truncated family tree must have been even more acute, for while R' Yaakov Moshe had brothers who survived and produced children, Chaya Sara's only two sisters, as well as her only nieces and nephews, had been murdered. She was her parents' sole surviving descendant. Their branch ended with an exquisite flower, her life, but when it withered and fell, what trace would it leave?

Yam Shel Shmuel both revealed and hid its author's identity. As a simple commentary on the *Chumash,* it sustained R' Yaakov Moshe's insisted-upon reputation as a simple Jew who didn't know Gemara, the province of real Torah scholars.

Young Tzviki Shtiglitz, who spent all his free time in the Kramers' house, insists that R' Yaakov Moshe was not only a hidden scholar, but a hidden kabbalist as well: "He pretended he didn't know Gemara, but he knew the whole Torah. He had these old books of kabbalah, but he hid them behind other books. He didn't want others to see them. How did I see them? Because I was in the house so often. I peeked."

Was R' Yaakov Moshe a kabbalist? There is anecdotal evidence that points to that conclusion. For example, R' Naim

Benino recalls the time he was sitting with R' Yaakov Moshe in his succah, eating grapes. R' Naim dropped his grape stems onto the ground by his chair, but R' Yaakov Moshe got up, walked a couple of steps, and threw his grape stems well outside the suc-

R' Yaakov Moshe on Chol HaMoed, c. 1989

cah. When R' Naim questioned his behavior, R' Yaakov Moshe answered: "If you could see the angels surrounding us, you could not stand it for a moment."

Kfar Gidon resident Chaim Cohen relates: "Yaakov Moshe never used the word '*chashmal*' [electricity] because it's the name ascribed to a bad angel. He never ate two things of the same kind, such as two olives, but rather ate odd numbers of each item. I know he was a kabbalist."

The mitzvah of *netilas yadayim* [washing hands] was particularly important to R' Yaakov Moshe. "He used to spend a long, long time washing," R' Avigdor testifies. "It was a very important mitzvah for him." When R' Avigdor added a room onto his house where the *tzaddik* would stay while in London, R' Yaakov Moshe asked him to install a sink in the new room that R' Yaakov Moshe would pay for from his own money.

Just how important *netilas yadayim* was for R' Yaakov Moshe is revealed in a strange tale reported by Moshe Bunim Kraus. Once R' Yaakov Moshe went to Switzerland

and stayed with R' Kraus for a week. R' Kraus wanted to know what the *tzaddik* did at night, so, as in many chassidic tales, he stayed up all night and peeked through a crack in the *tzaddik's* door. This is what he saw: Until 2 a.m., R' Yaakov Moshe sat and learned Torah. Then he prepared *negel vasser* and went to sleep. After 25 minutes, he woke up, washed *negel vasser*, threw out the water, prepared new *negel vasser*, then went back to bed. He slept for another 25 minutes, woke up, washed *negel vasser*, threw out the water, prepared new *negel vasser*, and went back to bed. He repeated this routine six times, until about 5 a.m., when he got up and went to shul.

We can only speculate about this strange procedure. Since *ruach ra* [an unclean force] attaches itself to a person only after a half-hour of sleep, was R' Yaakov Moshe trying to stave off *ruach ra* by sleeping less than half an hour? If so, why did he have to wash *negel vasser*, which implies that there is an unclean spiritual force from which to purify oneself? Is this a secret kabbalistic ritual known only to the initiated?

R' Avigdor once wrote to R' Yaakov Moshe asking certain question related to kabbalah. In his reply, the *tzaddik* disavows all knowledge of mysticism:

> *I received your important letter, which speaks about higher matters of kabbalah. Now I'm going to answer immediately so that you don't have to wait for an answer.*
>
> *I am absolutely unacquainted with kabbalah and I'm not a Rebbe and I'm a simple Yid. I once asked a great Rav about a shidduch. He showed me a pasuk from Parashas Shoftim: "Tamim teheye—You should be tamim with Hashem your G-d." One should study Rashi on this pasuk. Then one will understand that one should rejoice and be satisfied with Hashem's ways, and should always hope to Hashem and ask Hashem that He should help, and then*

one is with Him and in his own portion. I can't help you in any way in this matter. Hashem should help you and should fulfill all your requests. Amen v'amen.

Yaakov Moshe Kramer ben Chaya

Was R' Yaakov Moshe a kabbalist? Judaism allows Torah scholars to hide their knowledge even to the point of feigning ignorance. Yes, he was a man of truth, so we believe his disavowal. Yet, he was a master of hiddenness, so we are left wondering.

In the end, he gave away even his hiddenness. By 1985, the *"Tzaddik* of Kfar Gidon" had become so well known that visitors eager to receive his blessing descended on his abode day and night. Neighbors testified that a taxi or two was always parked outside the Kramers' shack, and even at 2 or 3 a.m., the sound of cars could be heard on the gravel road leading to the Kramers. On *Chol HaMoed,* busloads of visitors swarmed into Kfar Gidon looking for the *tzaddik.*

Chaya Sara escorting visitors on their way, Kfar Gidon, c. 1985

R' Yaakov Moshe used to say, "'*Mesirus nefesh'* doesn't mean giving away one's body; it means giving away one's *nefesh,* one's soul. One has to give away even one's own *Yiddishkeit* for somebody else." An illustration of his own *mesirus nefesh:* Although he always spent a long, long time washing *netilas yadayim,* if someone was waiting in line behind him, he washed very quickly, lest his own spiritual practice inconvenience another Jew.

R' Yaakov Moshe's ultimate *mesirus nefesh* was in giving away his hiddenness. He once told someone, "Don't talk about Mr. Green to people. He might be a *nistar* [hidden *tzaddik*]." The person he related this to added: "He himself left this world when he became well known."

Yet his drive to help people superseded his desire to remain hidden. Shia Ehrenreich and his wife were Satmar chassidim living in Williamsburg. By 1985, they had been married for six years without children. They came to Eretz Yisrael to pray at the graves of *tzaddikim.* Late one stormy night, they got a ride with a friend from Meiron back to Jerusalem. On the way, the friend turned off the road and announced that he had to stop there and drop off something by R' Yaakov Moshe Kramer. Since the Ehrenreichs had never heard of R' Kramer and it was the middle of the night, they remained in the car while the friend got out.

Suddenly they saw a figure running through the rain toward the car. "He looked like Eliyahu HaNavi," Mrs. Ehrenreich recalls. "The *Shechinah* was on his face." When R' Yaakov Moshe reached the car, he said to R' Shia, "I heard that Rav K.'s son-in-law is in the car." He coaxed them to come inside, and then prevailed on the driver to wait while he spoke with the couple privately. Although they had no intention of mentioning their childlessness, "he started pulling out of us that we had no children." At the end of the interview, he cut off a piece of cardboard from a tissue box and on it wrote out a *"Yehi ratzon"* for the couple to say before and after they recited *Tehillim.* "My husband got more attached to him than a chassid for his Rebbe," Mrs. Ehrenreich concludes her account. Three years after the *tzaddik* left this world, the Ehrenreichs had a child, the first of several.

Had hiddenness been his priority, R' Yaakov Moshe would have stayed inside his house on that dark, rainy night. But, instead, helping people was his priority. The price he paid was his hiddenness — and perhaps his life, as hidden *tzaddikim* do not stay in this world long after their identity becomes known.

Even on the physical level, the onslaught of visitors cost him greatly. Leah Landau recalls: "Many, many guests came to see Yaakov Moshe. Buses full of yeshivah *bachurim* came. They exhausted him. Chaya Sara was somewhat against the constant stream of visitors. She complained to her husband about it. She was afraid for his health. But in the end, everyone came."

Rebbetzin Chaya Sara tried her best to protect him from the constant exertion of receiving people. When visitors arrived while the *tzaddik* was resting, she asked them to wait. When he woke up, he would gently reprimand her: "Why did you make these Jews wait? You should have woken me up."

"Even when he didn't feel well, he worried for everyone," relates R' Avigdor. "Sometimes he would fall asleep from exhaustion while he was talking, and, almost immediately, he would wake up. He made his nights like days for other people."

R' Yaakov Moshe made his final fund-raising trip abroad in 1989, at the age of 79. As usual, he traveled to America after Pesach for about three months, and

R' Avigdor Galandauer helping
R' Yaakov Moshe on his last trip to London

arrived in England at the end of Tammuz. His followers there could see how his energy and stamina had declined. Every time he sat down in a car to go somewhere, he fell asleep. And it was hard for him to climb stairs. "It was a big *mesirus nefesh* that he came," observes R' Avigdor.

At the end of every previous visit, R' Yaakov Moshe would say, "Next year, *b'ezras Hashem*, I'll be back." But that year he never referred to a forthcoming visit. R' Nachman Landau had, several years before, bought him a new *shtriemel* to wear while he was abroad, insisting that he must look presentable when he went around collecting money. While R' Yaakov Moshe always took this *shtriemel* with him, two days before the end of that final

R' Yaakov Moshe with Avigdor Galandauer

visit, he brought the *shtriemel* to R' Shimon Dankowitz and said, "I want to leave this with you." Apparently he knew he would no longer need it.

On the *tzaddik's* last day in Golder's Green, many people lined up outside his door to receive his blessing. One man entered and did not leave for a very long time. The others in the line became impatient and sent R' Avigdor in to remind the *tzaddik* that many people were waiting. Despite R' Avigdor's periodic nudging, R' Yaakov Moshe continued speaking with this one man. Again and again the other people sent R' Avigdor in to terminate the conversation, but the *tzaddik* continued his conversation and ignored R' Avigdor.

Eventually, this person exited, and the other people filed in and received their blessings.

In the car afterward, R' Avigdor asked R' Yaakov Moshe about his strange behavior: "All those people were waiting in line, and you just kept on and on with this one person."

R' Yaakov Moshe answered, "You never know why I came all the way to England. Maybe I came all the way to England just to help this one person."

"And that was his whole attitude with every *Yid*," observes R' Avigdor. "He looked at every *Yid* as if he came to this world just to help that person. Every *Yid* was to him like his *ben yachid*, his only child."

In Antwerp that year, a portentous incident occurred. While R' Yaakov Moshe used to travel to Antwerp every Elul, that year he pushed off his fund-raising trip until later, arriving in Antwerp in Kislev (December 1989). He went to the shul of the famous *tzaddik* Reb Yankele in order to pay his respects. According to all accounts, Reb Yankele loved R' Yaakov Moshe very much. That day, Reb Yankele entered the shul, walked directly over to R' Yaakov Moshe, and said to him: "I think that you and I should go into retirement."

R' Yaakov Moshe turned white. He understood that Reb Yankele meant that both of them should "retire" from this world. Shocked, he objected, "No, no, I still have lots of work to do in this world." But Reb Yankele had already walked away.

That very week in Antwerp, R' Yaakov Moshe became ill with pneumonia. He returned immediately to Eretz Yisrael, but he never regained his health.

As for Reb Yankele, he likewise became very ill that year. Although he lived for another nine years, he rarely spoke or emerged from his room, as if he had indeed retired from this world.

When R' Yaakov Moshe, weak and ill, returned home just before Chanukah 5750 (1989), it was clear that his years in Kfar Gidon were over. He needed to be in a metropolitan area, close to good medical care. One of his admirers abroad had offered him an apartment in Bnei Brak, but Chaya Sara favored Jerusalem.

On *erev Shabbos Chanukah* (Friday, December 29, 1989), R' Yaakov Moshe summoned his beloved young friend, Yossi Shtiglitz, who had been renting the Kramers' land for two decades. He offered to sell Yossi his farm for $15,000, although it was worth $50,000. Yossi, reluctant to overextend himself, sadly declined the offer. (The farm would not be sold until after R' Yaakov Moshe's death, and Chaya Sara would not receive the proceeds.) Immediately after Chanukah, the Kramers left Kfar Gidon for Jerusalem, never to return.

Their departure left a void in Kfar Gidon that would never be filled. As resident Esther Schutz recounts:

> *Their leaving was very difficult for all of us. All of us felt like a part of us had left. As is written in the commentary to Parashas Vayeitzei: When a tzaddik is in the city, the tzaddik is the light and beauty of the city. When he leaves, the spiritual light and honor leaves with him. So we felt, like a flock without a shepherd.*

The Kramers, including Avramele, took up temporary residence in the home of R' Nissan Taktuk, R' Yaakov Moshe's assistant in the *hatzalah* work. The Taktuks lived in the chassidic enclave of Meah Shearim. This neighborhood, where everyone at all hours was involved in learning, praying, or otherwise serving *HaKadosh Baruch Hu*, was paradise to Rebbetzin Chaya Sara.

I once asked her, "Do you miss Kfar Gidon?"

Shaking her head, she replied emphatically, "No. I don't. I prefer living in a Torah'dig neighborhood."

In the 1950's, the Chazon Ish had told the Kramers to stay in Kfar Gidon, and stay they did, for another 35 years. From her comment, "I prefer living in a Torah'dig neighborhood," it is evident that living in Kfar Gidon was a trial for Chaya Sara. It was not that she wanted a homogeneous support group. She loved Jews of all kinds — as long as they were "bnei aliyah," individuals striving for spiritual advancement. This is what she loved about Meah Shearim — the zest of its residents to serve HaKadosh Baruch Hu.

Nevertheless, she persevered in what were to her alien surroundings for four decades, while she and her husband brought the light of Torah to many thousands of Jews in the Jezreel Valley and its environs. Rav Shach called R' Yaakov Moshe, "the mezuzah of the Valley." It is forbidden to remove a mezuzah from a Jewish house unless the new residents are sure to replace it. In the Kramers' case, it was impossible to replace "the mezuzah," that is, themselves. In that sense, they were prohibited from leaving, whatever their preferences.

In the mid-1980's, with both of them suffering health problems that required medical attention, the Kramers had a "heter" to leave. At that time, Shlomo Kramer actually brought them a prospective buyer. Rebbetzin Chaya Sara wanted to sell and move, but her husband wanted to stay on in Kfar Gidon. She submitted to his will, and they stayed until the last year of R' Yaakov Moshe's life, when remaining was no longer feasible.

Living in close proximity to incompatible neighbors is a trial that faces many people. The question most of us ask is: "Where would I be most comfortable?" The question the Kramers asked was: "Where could I do the most good?"

❧

R' Yaakov Moshe knew that his end was near. In April 1985, he had written a spiritual will, calling on, "my friends and my loved ones and my acquaintances from far and near," to continue to support his *hatzalah* work through Chaya Sara:

> *Behold, I turn to them to support my dear and esteemed wife*
> *in material support in order that she may be able to continue*
> *to help to elevate the honor of Hashem Yisbarach and to*
> *save children, boys in yeshivah and girls in holy institutions,*
> *as she has helped me throughout all the years with great*
> *mesirus nefesh and great resolve to save these children whose*
> *parents beg us to save their sons and daughters. In this way*
> *you will merit to be partners in the mitzvos of saving souls ...*

On March 8, 1990 (5750), he wrote a second spiritual will. At this time, a scant half-year before his death, his penultimate concern was providing for his beloved wife:

> *Behold, I turn to all Jews, in every place, with my request*
> *that they should make an effort to send my wife assistance*
> *with her livelihood, because she is a God-fearing woman,*
> *and I can say absolutely that the woman Chaya Sara bas*
> *Malka has helped me throughout all these years in all the*
> *matters of saving children, and in the matters of tzedakkah*
> *and chesed she tries in all ways to help in order to uplift*
> *the honor of Hashem Yisbarach.*
>
> *Fortunate is the lot of one who helps her with her*
> *livelihood.*

His *Kesubah* stipulated responsibility to support his wife, both in this world and the next world, weighed heavily on him during those final months. In February 1990, he wrote an appeal in Yiddish:

> *To our brethren bnei Yisrael in every place,*
>
> *Hashem Yisbarach should bless you and guard you from*
> *obstacles. Only good and chesed and mercy and life and*
> *peace should surround you also in this world and also in*

*the next world. You should always merit to uplift the honor
of Hashem until Mashiach comes and forever.*

*I would like to ask that you should please make an effort
to send money for Chaya Sara bas Malka, t'hiyeh, that
she should have from what to live. And in this merit one
may hope that Hashem Yisbarach will help all those precious Jews who will send and will donate for Chaya Sara
bas Malka with livelihood and with favor and loving kindness and mercy to be saved from all trouble and all illness.
And they should see descendants and have a long life and
succeed in uplifting the honor of Hashem until Mashiach
comes and forever.*

Among his admirers in England the word went out that
helping support Rebbetzin Chaya Sara would assure the
donor R' Yaakov Moshe's intercession in heaven. As Chanah
Simmi Beer told me years later: "Everyone knows that R'
Yaakov Moshe promised anyone who helped his Rebbetzin
that he would intercede for them in the Next World." Or, as
Sheindy Leiber quoted him: "Whoever goes and helps her
now, I'll pay them back."

It was all he could do for her. Even in the Next World, he
would provide for her.

*If Rebbetzin Chaya Sara was apprehensive about
her financial security during her impending widowhood, she did not show it. This was the period
(mentioned in Chapter Eight above) when I asked
her for her recipe for happiness, and she answered,
"You have eyes and they see. You have ears and they
hear. You have feet and they take you wherever you
want to go. How can you not be happy?!"*

*Her financial situation was exceedingly perilous, since
she had no savings, no assets (except the farm, whose
proceeds she would never see), no pension, no govern-*

ment social security, and no children to provide for her. R' Yaakov Moshe was keenly aware of this, and he was concerned about it.

She, on the other hand, worried only about him. Her future financial status was of trivial concern compared to her beloved husband's rapidly deteriorating health.

In times of crisis, when many troubles converge, it's easy to feel overwhelmed. While Rebbetzin Chaya Sara was practical about her finances, she chose to prioritize, to worry about what was most worthy of her concern — her husband's health. In her later years, when her finances indeed became strained, she likewise chose to worry about Avramele's future rather than her inability to pay her bills. She was not oblivious to financial exigencies, but she never allowed them to blind her to the more important human needs.

This is a form of spiritual triage. Just as at a disaster site, the medics must classify the wounded according to the urgency of their needs, so spiritual maturity requires classifying problems according to their urgency and importance. From Rebbetzin Chaya Sara's example, we learn that priority should always be given to human dilemmas over financial predicaments.

A steady stream of visitors came to the Taktuk apartment seeking the blessing of R' Yaakov Moshe. The neighbors, aware that a *tzaddik* was in their midst, rallied to supply the Kramers' needs. Menachem Glick and his family invited the Kramers to stay in their more spacious apartment nearby. For Pesach, the Glicks moved out of their apartment entirely so that the Kramers would have the full use of it.

On *Chol HaMo'ed Pesach*, R' Yaakov Moshe phoned R' Shulem Yoel Schwartz in London and requested that he come to Jerusalem with R' Avigdor Galandauer for one day. The *tzaddik* wanted to explain to the two younger men how his *hatzalah* work operated. Too weak to continue his life's work, he begged the two younger men to take over. It was a difficult time for R' Avigdor to get away. He phoned his mentor and asked if they could make arrangements over the telephone. R' Yaakov Moshe insisted that he needed to hand the work over to them in person. He pleaded with R' Avigdor to come. The day after Pesach, they made the trip.

R' Avigdor was to see that, although the *tzaddik's* physical powers had waned, his spiritual powers had not. On his way to the London airport, R' Avigdor stopped at his bank to deposit 2,000 British pounds. Heavily involved in helping London's poor, he had borrowed this sum for his *tzedakkah* work. The bank, unfortunately, was busy. A long line stood before each teller.

With a plane to catch, R' Avigdor did not have time to stand in line. He noticed one empty window, so, figuring that the bank knew him well, he put the 2,000 pounds cash, together with his bank deposit book, under the glass, telling the clerk at the next window, "I'm putting in this money. I need it in my account today. Please take it in. I'm going away today and tomorrow I'll be back, and I'll pick up the bank book." With that, he continued on his way to the airport.

A short while later his car phone rang. The bank manager himself was calling. He informed R' Avigdor, "The money has been stolen."

Alarmed, R' Avigdor exclaimed, "How could it be stolen? I put it through the window!"

The bank manager rejoined, "Just like you could put it in, someone else put their hand in and stole it while the clerk went inside for a minute. I'm terribly sorry, but somebody stole the money."

R' Avigdor was, of course, terribly perturbed, because it was a large sum of money that was not even his. Knowing there was nothing he could do about it, however, he continued on his way to the airport, where he and R' Shulem Yoel flew to Eretz Yisrael.

They arrived in Jerusalem late that night, and the next morning went directly to R' Yaakov Moshe. He was overjoyed to see them. "I didn't want to dampen his spirits by telling him about the stolen 2,000 pounds," remembers R' Avigdor. "So we talked and talked, and he explained to us about the *hatzalah*. He was in a very good mood."

When they had finished their business, R' Avigdor disclosed the story about the stolen 2,000 pounds. R' Yaakov Moshe was very disturbed, especially because his young friend had been rushing to the airport to fulfill his request. R' Avigdor asked him, "Will I get the money back?"

R' Yaakov Moshe was silent for a long minute, then his face lit up. He lifted up his hand, and said "Yes, yes!"

Less than an hour later, the phone rang. It was a flabbergasted Mrs. Galandauer reporting that the bank manager had just called to say that someone had thrown the 2,000 pounds into the bank postbox with a note saying, "I stole this money yesterday, and I regret it. Here is the money back."

A British admirer had offered R' Yaakov Moshe money to buy an apartment in Meah Shearim, but good apartments were rarely for sale. Over a period of months, several of the Taktuks' neighbors sought a dwelling in the area, but their search was in vain.

Because R' Yaakov Moshe could hardly walk, daily *minyanim* were held in the Glicks' apartment. A *sefer Torah* had been brought to the apartment for the *minyanim*. One day when she was alone, a desperate Chaya Sara went up to the *sefer Torah* and prayed intensely for a suitable apartment.

The very next day Rebbetzin Miriam Stern, a neighbor of the Taktuks, found the perfect apartment for the Kramers to buy. Located at 11 Slonim Street in Meah Shearim, it was just a few steps up from street level, making it easy for R' Yaakov Moshe to access. It had excellent neighbors, and had been recently renovated. The apartment had three rooms, a kitchen, and a closed balcony overlooking the street. The balcony was of crucial importance for Avramele. Since he would not be able to roam freely in the city as he had in Kfar Gidon, the balcony afforded him a place to sit all day and view the passing parade of people and vehicles.

Right before Shavuos, the Kramers moved in. R' Yaakov Moshe registered the apartment in his wife's name alone. He bought an olivewood doorplate and had written on it: "Rabbanit Chaya Sara Kramer." Clearly, the apartment was to be her home. For him, it was merely the final relay point on his life's journey.

At the beginning of Av, R' Avigdor visited again, this time to bring the Kramers 30,000 pounds from the British donor for the Rebbetzin's apartment. He planned to come to Eretz Yisrael

R' Yaakov Moshe in the Meah Shearim apartment, June, 1990

*R' Yaakov Moshe shortly
before his passing*

again with his wife in two weeks' time in order to visit the *tzaddik*. Alas, it was not to be. "The way he said goodbye the last time I was there, it was clear that he knew he was saying goodbye for the last time. He was bedridden and couldn't stand at that point, but when I left, he wanted to bring a chair to the front door. He sat at the front door and waved and waved for five minutes until my taxi departed."

On *erev Shabbos*, the fifth of Av (July 27, 1990), R' Yaakov Moshe, leaning on his cane, limped around the new apartment, surveying each room. Finally, he turned to his wife and said to her, "I've provided well for you. You have good neighbors. You're not alone."

Rebbetzin Chaya Sara understood that her husband felt free to take leave of her. She became filled with fright. That night he suffered a massive stroke, from which he never recovered.

The Hatzalah ambulance was called. R' Yaakov Moshe, still conscious, did not want to go to the hospital. He fought not to go, holding on to the doorpost as they carried him out on a stretcher. By the time the ambulance reached Shaarei Tzedek Hospital, he had lost consciousness.

He remained in that state for 70 days, as his anguished wife stood by, powerless. In a letter she wrote after his death, she compares those days to the torture of Rebbe Akiva:

> *In the Torah it says that you should serve Hashem with all your heart, soul, and possessions, and he [R' Yaakov*

Moshe] fulfilled this exactly as it says. Rebbe Akiva, when they combed him with iron combs, said, "Now I'm fulfilling b'chol nafshecha [loving Hashem with my whole soul]." This was the 70 days in the hospital, very unfortunately accepting Hashem's decree.

The doctors wanted to do electroshock on his heart. The Rebbetzin refused. In later years she would say that if they hadn't taken him to the hospital, he would have lived.

Occasionally, there were flickers of response. During that first month, Anni Kalfe was in Shaarei Tzedek Hospital where she had given birth. When she and her husband Eli went upstairs to visit R' Yaakov Moshe, they saw Rebbetzin Chaya Sara walking in the hospital corridor, looking depressed. The Rebbetzin shook her head and told them, "He's not going to respond to you. He did not respond to me." Nevertheless, the Kalfes entered the room, and Eli approached the *tzaddik's* bed. R' Yaakov Moshe looked at Eli, picked up his hand, and waved.

Another time, on a Friday afternoon, the staff put R' Yaakov Moshe in a chair. Just as the sun was setting to usher in Shabbos, R' Yaakov Moshe lifted up his hand and straightened his *peyos* and his beard.

On the first night of Succos, Dovid Kubitchek and Menachem Glick attended to the *tzaddik*. Early the next morning (October 4, 1990), with only Menachem Glick present, R' Yaakov Moshe Kramer went to his eternal reward.

R' Machloof Tanzee, who had known R' Yaakov Moshe 45 years earlier, not as a famous *tzaddik*, but as a carpenter who refused to talk during working hours lest he be stealing from his employer, said when he heard the news: "What angel in heaven can stand together with him?"

The massive funeral was held at Shamgar Funeral Home. The *tzaddik* was buried on Har HaMenuchos, next to the tomb of the great Kabbalist Rav Ashlag. At the point during the

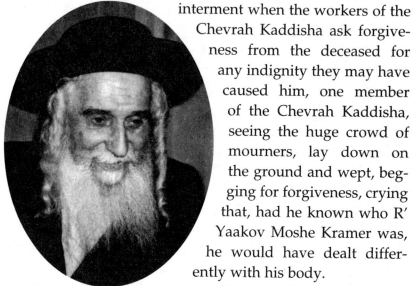

R' Yaakov Moshe Kramer

interment when the workers of the Chevrah Kaddisha ask forgiveness from the deceased for any indignity they may have caused him, one member of the Chevrah Kaddisha, seeing the huge crowd of mourners, lay down on the ground and wept, begging for forgiveness, crying that, had he known who R' Yaakov Moshe Kramer was, he would have dealt differently with his body.

Had he known who R' Yaakov Moshe Kramer really was, he would have understood that he did not have to beg for his forgiveness.

During the holiday of Succos, no eulogies are delivered. On the *sheloshim* [the 30th day after the death], a large gathering was held at the Zupnick synagogue. Eulogies were given by leading rabbis, such as Rav Moshe Arye Freund, Rav Shimon Lamberger, Rav Moshe Zaks, Rav Yaakov Hillel, and the *maggid*, Rav Shabsai Yudelevich.

Rav Moshe Arye Freund, the *Av Beis Din* and Chief Rabbi of Jerusalem, captured the essence of R' Yaakov Moshe Kramer with a metaphor. He said that, of the four species taken on Succos, the esrog represents both the human heart and the type of Jew who has both Torah learning and good deeds. The sages say that Hashem Himself fulfills the *mitzvos*. Thus, on the first day of Succos, *Hashem Yisbarach* also is obligated to take the four species. On that day, said Rav Freund, G-d took a beautiful *esrog* — the soul of Yaakov Moshe ben Shmuel Zanvill.

CHAPTER THIRTEEN

Who Will Light a Candle for Me?

*I*N THE WAKE OF HER HUSBAND'S PASSING, Rebbetzin Chaya Sara became, in the words of one American devotee, "like a Rebbe in Jerusalem." People, especially women, from all over the world came to her Meah Shearim apartment, and her telephone rang throughout the day and night. They came seeking blessings, advice, and encouragement. "Everyone who came in upset," observed Chaya Rochel Benedikt, "walked out feeling happy."

Esther Ben Chaim had been a frequent visitor at the Kramers' Kfar Gidon home when she lived in Migdal HaEmek. Upon moving to Jerusalem with her large family, she sought an administrative job in the Bais Yaakov school system. It was already midsummer, when few jobs are available, but she succeeded in finding a plum position as the principal of a Bais Yaakov school in Beit Shemesh, an hour's bus ride from Jerusalem.

Esther consulted Rebbetzin Chaya Sara before accepting the position. The Rebbetzin disapproved of her working so far away from home while she still had small children. She advised Esther not to take the job, and blessed her that she would find just as good a position within the precincts of Jerusalem.

Esther spent the rest of the summer searching, to no avail. When the school year began, she was still without employment. Five days into the term, she heard about a new Bais Yaakov school for Russian immigrant girls that was opening in the center of Jerusalem. Applications for the job of principal were being accepted. Esther phoned the advertised number all day and evening, but it was constantly busy. At midnight, just before giving up and going to sleep, she dialed one last time. Someone answered and told her to come for an interview the following morning, Friday, at 10 a.m.

When she arrived, she found the waiting room crowded with applicants. Esther sat down to wait her turn. As she listened to the conversations around her, she realized that the other women, who had previously worked as principals, were far more qualified than she, whose only previous educational experience was as a house mother. One woman had been a principal for eight years, another for ten. At noon, Esther decided that it was a waste of time to wait any longer.

Esther Ben Chaim with Rebbetzin Chaya Sara, 2002

As she prepared to leave, the door to the inner office opened, and a man asked her why she was leaving. She explained that she had to go home and cook for Shabbos. The man urged her to wait just a few more minutes. Soon she was called in and interviewed. At the conclusion of the interview, the man told her, "I feel that you will work for us with great dedication. The job is yours. You begin on Sunday morning."

Thrilled, she raced to Rebbetzin Chaya Sara to tell her the good news. "I prayed very hard for you," commented the Rebbetzin with a broad smile.

Blessings — for *shidduchim*, children, healing, *parnassah*, and success in every area — poured from Rebbetzin Chaya Sara like water gushing from a spring after the winter rains. A letter she wrote to the Galandauers during the first year of her widowhood illustrates her zeal to bestow blessings. The purpose of the letter was to communicate that she received the money R' Avigdor had sent, yet only one sentence out of this whole letter is devoted to that point.

Sunday, Parashas Nitzavim, Elul, 5751 [September, 1991]

To HaRav HaTzaddik Rabbi Avigdor Akiva ben Chaya Leah, Shlita, Perfect Tzaddikim and the important Tzidkanus, a woman of valor, the crown of her husband, blessed like the women of the tent, the eminent spouse, Rebbetzin Feigel Rochel bas Chana, t'lita, and their children, Yoel Moshe Shmuel, Sara Baila, Nechama Mindel, Yehuda Eliezer, and Baruch Menachem. Hashem Yisbarach should bless you and all Israel with a good inscription and sealing, a healthy and blessed year, with nachas from the household. And Hashem Yisbarach should inscribe you all in the book of the completely righteous, l'alter l'chaim tovim v'shalom, with health and with good long years. And Hashem should guard you from all trouble, and Hashem should deal with you with graciousness and kindness and mercy, and sur-round you and all of Israel, in soul and body, and you should be very successful. I received from you $1400, and a great yasher koach to you, and Hashem should pay you back *only good. He should watch over you and all Yisrael. "On one stone seven eyes."*

Warmest regards to your important Rebbetzin,

The widow of the tzaddik of the generation, Yaakov Moshe a"h ben Shmuel Zanvill, Chaya Sara bas Malka

When I first read the English translation (from Yiddish) of this letter, I thought, "She wasn't very businesslike." Then I realized: giving blessings *was* her business.

(left) Rebbetzin Chaya Sara with visitors

(below) Rebbetzin Chaya Sara and Avramele at an upsherin in her apartment, c. 1999

People — all kinds of people — came to her for advice. A religious officer in the Israeli Air Force would visit her once a month, seeking advice about the education of his children. Rebbetzin Chaya Sara derived *nachas* from counting the stripes and stars on his epaulets and watching how his rank advanced over the years. Although she herself was staunchly opposed to the State, she enjoyed seeing this Jewish officer's success.

Although most of those who consulted with her had known her illustrious husband, often total strangers phoned her for help. Miriam, the Rebbetzin's adopted daughter, was visiting from Bnei Brak one day when the phone rang. A woman from America was calling because her child was very sick. Although the Rebbetzin did not know this family, she stopped what she was doing, took out her copy of *Iggeres HaRamban*, and started to recite it with intense feeling and tears.

Much of her advice was counterintuitive, obviously drawn from a source beyond human calculation. For example, when Chavi, a young, divorced woman, came for a blessing to get married, Rebbetzin Chaya Sara advised her to *daven* for her ex-husband to get married. Finally, four years after their divorce, the ex-husband became engaged. Just two months later, Chavi became a *kallah*.

Esther Ben Chaim was visiting one day when the Rebbetzin's phone rang. A man was calling from America to ask whether he should invest $500,000 in a certain business venture. The Rebbetzin asked many intricate questions, as Esther sat there, witnessing her awesome display of business acumen. "She was amazingly intelligent," Esther observes.

R' Yaakov Moshe's brother Peretz used to call Chaya Sara "half a doctor," because of her common sense and knowledge of natural cures. Chaya Rochel Benedikt, at home in Boro Park, once developed terrible stomach cramps. She phoned Rebbetzin Chaya Sara, who advised her to rest in bed and drink chamomile tea. Thus she recovered.

Esther Ben Chaim holding her baby, Yaakov Moshe, January 1996.
Rebbetzin Chaya Sara is on right.

"She always used to know everything," Mrs. Benedikt remarks, relating this story: Mrs. Benedikt visited Jerusalem and was invited for the third meal of Shabbos to a family in Ezras Torah, a neighborhood she didn't know well. She arranged with her niece, who lived in Meah Shearim, to meet her at 6 p.m. at the apartment she was renting, to guide her to Ezras Torah. Mrs. Benedikt spent Shabbos afternoon with Rebbetzin Chaya Sara. At some point she glanced at her watch and realized that it was well past 6 p.m. Discomfited,

Rebbetzin Chaya Sara and a visitor
in her Meah Shearim apartment

she exclaimed, "I've missed my appointment! How will I find my niece now? How will I find my way to Ezras Torah?"

Rebbetzin Chaya Sara calmed her and said, "Go to your niece's house. She's probably still napping in bed."

Mrs. Benedikt followed the Rebbetzin's instructions, and sure enough, her niece was still in bed.

Once a British woman came to Rebbetzin Kramer for the first time.

She was shy to discuss the three questions she had been deliberating over: which kind of head covering to wear; how to do *chesed*; and how to relate to her husband. One by one, Rebbetzin Chaya Sara raised and answered each question.

Another time, a chassidic woman complained to the Rebbetzin that her son was already 19½ years old and not married, which was considered late in their particular circle. Rebbetzin Chaya Sara replied, "His *kallah* has to grow up." Sure enough, when he got engaged a while later, his *kallah* was only 16½ years old.

The Rebbetzin's uncanny ability to read minds sometimes made visits to her turn out very differently than expected. Once a young woman, whom I'll call Avigail, asked me to take her to the *tzaddekes* for a blessing. Avigail had been married several years without children. She had suffered many miscarriages and had lost an infant that had been born very prematurely. Now the doctors were telling her that she needed surgery to remove a polyp. Avigail was frightened and wanted a blessing from the *tzaddekes*.

I cautioned Avigail just to ask for a blessing and not to mention any specifics, especially about her upcoming surgery, since Rebbetzin Chaya Sara was so opposed to all operations, she would surely tell her not to do it. We were a group of five women sitting in the Rebbetzin's receiving room, but the Rebbetzin focused only on Avigail. She kept asking Avigail searching questions about her medical history. Avigail, fidgeting in her seat, kept glancing at me. It was getting increasingly difficult to keep the secret of her upcoming surgery. Finally the Rebbetzin asked her outright: "And what do the doctors say you should do now?"

Avigail, caught in the Rebbetzin's piercing gaze, had no choice but to confess the whole story. I was sure Rebbetzin Chaya Sara would say, "Don't do the surgery," but instead, much to my surprise, she said, "You should consult Rebbetzin Finkel before you do anything." Rebbetzin Finkel, the wife of

Rav Beinish Finkel, *Rosh Yeshivah* of Mir, was renowned for her medical advice.

"Rebbetzin Finkel?!" Avigail exclaimed. "I've been trying to find her for weeks! Do you know how to reach her?"

As my eyes widened, Rebbetzin Chaya Sara replied, "She lives upstairs, in the apartment above mine. Just go knock on her door."

Rebbetzin Chaya Sara sent me along to translate, although it turned out that Rebbetzin Finkel spoke perfect English. (I think the *tzaddekes* just wanted me to hear the answer.) Sitting at Rebbetzin Finkel's dining-room table, Avigail related her entire medical history and what the doctors proposed to do in the operation scheduled for the following Tuesday. Rebbetzin Finkel did not mince words. "You should do this surgery," she stated flatly, "if you want to end your reproductive career."

Obviously, Avigail canceled the operation. A year later, she gave birth to a baby boy. When I last bumped into her, she had three children.

Rebbetzin Chaya Sara with the author in 2000

One woman asked her, "What kind of *shidduch* should I seek for my daughters?" The Rebbetzin laid out just three criteria: "He shouldn't be prone to anger. He shouldn't be stingy. And he should be normal."

Since most of her supplicants were women, most of Rebbetzin Chaya Sara's advice was aimed at women. Her wisdom ranged from the most mundane ("Never give a baby a cold bottle. Never hold a baby upside down. Don't save money on your children's food.") to the most sublime. ("Women need to guard their souls by resting.")

Distinguished educator Rivka Rochel Hess would regularly consult with Rebbetzin Chaya Sara. "She told me to conserve my energy for my home, not to devote it all to my school. She disapproved of women working too hard and not taking care of themselves. She used to say that just as Hashem created the world in six days, not one day, so women shouldn't attempt to clean the whole house in one day. Women should learn the proper balance between working and resting."

In dealing with issues of *shalom bayis* [marital harmony], Rebbetzin Chaya Sara expected both the wife and the husband to give 100 percent. She would tell women to keep quiet during arguments. "A wooden house burns easily, but if the wife keeps quiet, even the wood won't be able to burn. If the wife keeps quiet, the *Shechinah* will not flee."

To husbands, she quoted R' Yaakov Moshe, who always emphasized the importance of honoring one's wife. She would refer them to the book, *Sefer Avodas HaKodesh* by the Chida: "And more than anything, he should have *shalom* with his wife. He should be careful to honor her, and he should have in mind in every detail the honor of the *Shechinah* …"

She would quote her husband that *parnassah* comes in the merit of the wife, and she would cite the Gemara that states that Rava merited wealth because he honored his wife. She would relate R' Yaakov Moshe's teaching that if someone has a *parnassah* problem, he should show more honor to his wife.

Chaya Rochel Benedikt, a sought-after public speaker for women's gatherings in New York, would often be asked about *shalom bayis* problems, and she would in turn consult Rebbetzin Chaya Sara. Once she asked her about a particular couple. "These two people are good people, and I don't understand what could have gone wrong."

The Rebbetzin replied: "Every family is like a separate country. Just as Russia would not tell America what's going on inside its borders, so no one really knows what's going on in a different family. The real truth nobody knows."

For the most part, the Rebbetzin was not interested in theoretical teaching. She brought her wisdom down to the most practical level. Yes, she taught Mrs. Benedikt the principles of *shalom bayis*, but she also inquired, whenever Mrs. Benedikt came to Jerusalem and visited her, whether she had first visited her mother-in-law, who lived nearby, and whether she had brought her mother-in-law a gift. This constituted *shalom bayis* in action.

Despite the limitations of her health and finances during those later years, Rebbetzin Chaya Sara continued to do much *chesed* from her dining-room chair. When Esther Ben Chaim's son was denied admission to a particular *cheder*, Rebbetzin Chaya Sara took it upon herself to intervene. She phoned the *cheder* and introduced herself as the widow of R' Yaakov Moshe Kramer. The administrator who answered the phone exclaimed, "Why, I was a chassid of R' Yaakov Moshe! Don't worry, I'll take care of everything."

When Esther went abroad to collect money for the school of which she was the principal, Rebbetzin Chaya Sara wrote her reference letters to give to R' Yaakov Moshe's supporters. When supplicants came to Rebbetzin Chaya Sara for financial help, and she didn't have it, she would borrow money to give them.

Pirkei Avos advises: "Say little and do much." This could have been Rebbetzin Chaya Sara's credo. Although she had learned a great deal of Torah from her husband, she taught by example rather than preaching. While I often tried to engage her in philosophical discussions, she always brought matters down to the practical level. Whatever the question, she answered with a relevant story, out of chassidic lore or her own life. Whatever the question, the answer was always real people doing real things.

Kreindy Dankowitz of London attests: "No class I have ever been to has taught me as much as watching R' Yaakov Moshe and the Rebbetzin. I've been to many classes and have met many great people, but nothing has affected me like they have. They made me feel that every human being can do so much. They gave me an expanded concept of chesed, like I've never seen in this world. Now, when I'm asked to stay in the hospital overnight with an elderly person and it's hard, I think of them. Their example inspires me to undertake chesed."

It's easier for all of us to escape into the world of the mind than to fling ourselves into hands-on chesed. How often, when asked to contribute to someone in a difficult situation, do we analyze the situation and give recommendations rather than taking out our checkbook? How often do we choose to anguish over someone's distress rather than alleviate it?

Rebbetzin Chaya Sara was highly intelligent, but she used her mind exclusively to help people. In this final chapter of her biography, I had intended to write about "her life and teachings." I discovered that her life <u>was</u> her teachings.

She spent the 15 years of her widowhood giving blessings, advice, and encouragement. Not all the blessings were fulfilled. Not all the advice was heeded. But all the encouragement worked — for the simple reason that she didn't stop encouraging until she succeeded.

According to Miriam Stern, "She received telephone calls all day and all night, from all over Israel and the world. Brokenhearted people called her. She wouldn't stop talking to them until their mood had lifted. She spent hours giving them *chizuk* [strength]. Once she spoke to a woman for nine hours straight, until her depression dissipated."

Rebbetzin Stern sums up the essence of Rebbetzin Chaya Sara's final years: "Her mitzvah was to speak to people and make them happy."

While other people might ask someone, "Why do you look so pale?" the Rebbetzin would say, "You look good." The former, even if true, brings a person down, while the Rebbetzin's comment would give the person courage and encouragement. The Rebbetzin used to say that a compliment makes a person feel better; it's an actual gift. She would say, "Give a person a good word. It doesn't cost money."

When Toibe Blender, the Rebbetzin's attendant for the last five years of her life, was asked, "What did you learn from Rebbetzin Chaya Sara?" she replied, "To help a *Yid*."

Rebbetzin Chaya Sara was a master at lifting people's moods. She could do it in person, by phone, and even by mail. Chaya Rochel Benedikt testifies: "On a day when I would get a letter from her, it would change my whole day."

I can likewise attest to this special power of Rebbetzin Chaya Sara. Inevitably, whenever I went to her apartment, I walked in, but I flew out. She did not so much solve my problems as dissolve my problems, like rock salt plunged into a vat of warm water. Indeed, her ambiance was like a warm bath. It surrounded me, suffused every pore of my soul, and buoyed me up. When I left, couldn't every pedestrian on Slonim Street see the glow that I carried with me as a souvenir from her?

It wasn't what she said. It was the Rebbetzin herself. Her light, her inner joy, her G-d-consciousness were contagious. She never had to convince me of deeper truths. In her presence, Hashem's all-pervading reality was simply self-evident.

Yet, it was also what she said. She always called me a "*tzaddekes*," both when she spoke to me and when she spoke to others in the room about me. I would be embarrassed and think, "She doesn't really know me. I'm no *tzaddekes*." But a voice within me would whisper, "The Rebbetzin's not a liar. If she says it, she must be seeing something, however minuscule, some tiny seed that needs to be nurtured." And in my life I would strive to become what she saw in me.

She called many a visitor, "*tzaddekes*." When I brought my mother to meet her, the Rebbetzin gazed at my mother, who was very virtuous but not totally observant, and pronounced, "Your mother is a *tzaddekes*." She also called each of the young Israeli and Russian *ba'alas teshuvah* women who frequented her home, "*tzaddekes*." Like me, they didn't feel they were, but they wondered if they could become.

"She always knew what to say to make a person feel like a million dollars," recalls Mrs. Benedikt. Mrs. Benedikt's counseling work posed a problem to her. A highly sensitive person, she found it intolerable to be privy to people's bad behavior. Rather than define this as a weakness, Rebbetzin Chaya Sara would tell her that she was like a piece of silk. "Just like silk can't take dirt, so you can't take it if people act badly."

The Rebbetzin would also tell Mrs. Benedikt, "You're greater than I am. If I would be as great as you are, *Mashiach* would arrive."

Rebbetzin Chanah Simmi Beer describes her first meeting with Rebbetzin Chaya Sara:

> The first time I went to see Rebbetzin Chaya Sara, I went with my husband, who is a very chashuv [important] person. But the Rebbetzin kept looking at me, and every other minute she would say to me, "You're a very chashuvah neshamah, you're a great neshamah."

Later, I went back to her and asked, "What do you see? If I'm an important neshamah, what am I supposed to do with my life?"

Rebbetzin Chaya Sara sidestepped the question. Perhaps she didn't want to reveal that she saw neshamos. I kept insisting, until she told me to give kavod to my husband and to serve him.

I asked, "That's all there is to my avodah [Divine service]?" She replied, "That's a very big avodah."

Rebbetzin Chaya Sara would shower her verbal encouragement on all who came to her, even children. When Toibe Blender's young daughters visited, the Rebbetzin would tell them, "If I had children like you, I'd be the happiest person in the world."

The Rebbetzin was not peddling vain compliments. She was convinced that reality could be redefined by people's beliefs about themselves, and beliefs could be redefined by positive, encouraging words.

I witnessed an astounding display of this conviction when I brought my friend Leiba to get a blessing. Leiba, aged 41, was in an advanced stage of cancer. Her body was racked by pain, which barely responded to a constant flow of morphine administered through a tube connected between her back and a gadget in her purse. Weakened by repeated bouts of chemotherapy, depressed, and despairing, Leiba entered the Rebbetzin's receiving room. She sat down across the dining-room table and feebly asked for a blessing.

Rebbetzin Chaya Sara looked clueless. "For what?"

"I'm very sick," Leiba responded.

"You are?" the Rebbetzin asked, surprised. "But you look so well!"

"No," Leiba insisted. "I'm very, very ill."

"Who told you that you're ill?" the Rebbetzin challenged.

"Why, the doctors. But even without their telling me, I'd know. I'm in terrible pain."

"You're in pain?" the Rebbetzin asked. "Have you tried Acamol [Israeli version of Tylenol]?"

I sat there appalled. Had the Rebbetzin lost her mind? I had told her that Leiba had cancer, and she was prescribing Acamol?

"Acamol?" Leiba asked, incredulously. "I'm on morphine. High doses of morphine."

"Well, you might have pain, but that doesn't mean you're sick," the Rebbetzin insisted. "There's nothing wrong with you. You're entirely well."

Leiba and her husband looked at me, confused. I had said I was bringing them to a great *tzaddekes*, but instead I had brought them to someone totally out of touch with reality. I sat there, mortified. The conversation continued for a few more minutes, with Leiba insisting that she was sick and the Rebbetzin insisting that she was well. I felt like I had entered a reality warp. What was going on here?

After I escorted Leiba and her husband out, I returned to the Rebbetzin's receiving room. She sat there sadly shaking her head. "She's a very sick woman," is all she said.

I realized in a flash that Rebbetzin Chaya Sara had been trying to pull off a desperate ploy. The Rebbetzin always used to say, "No one dies of cancer. They die of fear." If she could convince Leiba that she wasn't really dying, if she could thus banish her

Rebbetzin Chaya Sara at a simchah, c. 1998

depression and fear, perhaps there was a chance — however remote — that she could live.

It was not to be. Leiba passed away one month later. But if she had jumped into the picture that Rebbetzin Chaya Sara painted for her, could she have survived?

We'll never know.

Two extraordinary women played major roles in Rebbetzin Chaya Sara's final years.

Rebbetzin Miriam Stern, a Breslover chasidah, the mother of

over a dozen children, gradually took on the complete responsibility for Rebbetzin Chaya

(left) Rebbetzin Chaya Sara at a wedding

(below) At the Bar Mitzvah of Nissim Ben Chaim. Front row (l-r): Rebbetzin Chaya Sara, Yaakov Moshe Ben Chaim, Miriam Stern, August 2000

Sara's welfare. She and her husband, a grandson of R' Yaakov Yosef Herman (*All for the Boss*), lived next door to the Taktuks, where the Kramers first stayed upon coming to Meah Shearim. Rebbetzin Stern quickly discerned that a *tzaddekes* was living next door, and she did everything she could to help her.

As the Rebbetzin grew older and found it increasingly more difficult to walk, Rebbetzin Stern would volunteer to do the shopping for her, accompany her to the synagogue on holidays, help her get to the bank, and escort her to *simchahs*.

Steadily they became closer and closer. Rebbetzin Chaya Sara would tell her young friend, "If you take a friend, she must be similar to you. Otherwise, there's no connection." In fact, their fondness was mutual. Rebbetzin Stern chose to serve the *tzaddekes*, but the *tzaddekes* chose Miriam Stern as her close friend and companion.

They both smiled constantly and performed *mitzvos* with alacrity. Once I took two friends to see the Rebbetzin. The three of us sat on one side of the table, while Rebbetzin Kramer and Rebbetzin Stern, beaming broadly, sat on the other. Afterwards, I asked my friends, "Did you notice that their team was all lit up?"

When the Rebbetzin's deteriorating health made it impossible for her to continue to take care of herself and Avramele, Miriam Stern took over. Despite having to manage her own household a block away, Rebbetzin Stern popped into the Rebbetzin's apartment several times a day, served her breakfast and lunch, gave her her pills, and handled her finances.

When asked, after her mentor's passing, what she had learned from the Rebbetzin, Miriam Stern replied: "To take time to talk to people. I wasn't like that. I was more reserved. I learned from her to encourage other people with words."

From the year 5760 (2000), Rebbetzin Kramer needed full-time help to care for herself and Avramele. Finding a suitable attendant was a difficult chore for Rebbetzin Stern. I remember stopping by one day as Rebbetzin Chaya Sara was finishing her lunch. She was eating a chocolate-covered ice-cream bar, and insisted I have one, too. But when she asked her attendant to bring it to me, the woman objected that there weren't enough in the freezer. "It's okay, I don't need it," I declared. But the Rebbetzin shook her head bitterly. Her expression betrayed the pain it caused her not to be able to feed her guest. The next time I visited, that attendant was no longer in the Rebbetzin's employ.

Against this background, the reader can appreciate what a blessing Toibe Blender was to the last five years of the Rebbetzin's life. A chassidah of the *Admor* of Toldos Avrohom Yitzchak, Toibe Blender looked like those denizens of Meah Shearim who wear a tight black kerchief over their shaven heads. I had always felt intimidated by these severe-looking women. This unease melted away as I got to know the gentle, kindly, loving Toibe Blender, whom those in the Rebbetzin's circle called simply, "Blender."

Blender attended to the Rebbetzin for five hours every evening. She did the Rebbetzin's bidding with perfect fidelity and consummate sensitivity.

The Rebbetzin did her best to help Blender as well. Thus, when Blender was marrying off her 11th child, a well-to-do couple from abroad visited Rebbetzin Kramer. They were facing a major court case, and asked the Rebbetzin to pray that it would be resolved in their favor. The Rebbetzin replied that she would bless them if they would do the mitzvah of *hachnassas kallah* by giving money to Blender for her child's wedding. She named a specific, large figure. The couple was reluctant. They tried to bargain, suggesting that they would contribute part now, part later, or even give a check post-dated for two months from now. Rebbetzin Chaya Sara, however, was adamant. If they wanted to come out victorious in the court case, they must give Blender the entire sum now. They did.

The 15 years of Rebbetzin Chaya Sara's widowhood were beset by financial and health problems. Although she did not worry about her finances, she did have to expend much time and energy to make ends meet.

Her husband had left her an apartment and a letter. The letter was intended to raise funds to pay for Rebbetzin Chaya Sara's and Avramele's living expenses, but it was effective only when she sent out photocopies of the letter accompanied by her own handwritten notes full of blessings. She spent hours writing these epistles. In some of them she promised to pray at the *tzaddik's* grave on behalf of those who contributed to her upkeep.

Whenever she asked for money, either by mail or phone, people sent it. When, during the last two years of her life, she became too weak to write letters or even to speak on the phone, most people did not send their contributions. At the end, when the contributions slowed to a trickle, she lived off a small sum she had saved in the bank. By Divine Providence, the money ran out at the same time as her life.

A letter she wrote to R' Avigdor two years after her husband's passing reveals both her financial and physical tribulations:

> *Parashas Ki Savo, 5752 [September 1992]*
>
> *... Kesivah v'chasimah tovah. Hashem's Name should be great and holy in the entire world.*
>
> *You told me that L., shlita, will send every month for me. And somebody called that he has money for me, and I didn't receive it. It's before Rosh Hashanah, so I forgive everyone. I don't hold a cheshbon [account] with anyone. Whoever wants, helps me. And whoever doesn't, doesn't have to. Hashem is great and He is the only one Who helps. Somebody telephoned me that he has money from you, and I never got it.*

... Hashem Yisbarach doesn't forget me, and my bita-
chon is only in Hashem. Refuah sheleimah is from Hashem
only. You and all of Beis Yisrael should be inscribed in the
book of complete tzaddikim. Hashem doesn't forget, and
He provides for the whole world, and Hashem has time to
listen to my embittered heart, and He helps me very much,
and He lives for now and always. He is from always and
for always, now and for always.

... I've been lying in bed for three weeks in my home and
the faithful Healer is taking care of me. "Hashem saves, the
King will answer us on the day that we call upon Him."
For this I rely on Hashem alone.

It seems her husband's letter was not sufficient to generate enough income, because just four years after his passing
she turned to Rav Moshe Arye Freund, the *Av Beis Din* and
Chief Rabbi of Jerusalem, for an additional letter. In an appeal
dated 5754 [1994], the distinguished rabbi wrote:

Behold I join myself to this call to the rabbis, to awaken
the hearts of our Jewish brethren, to recommend for the
widow of the Tzaddik HaRav Yaakov Moshe Kramer,
zt'l, from Kfar Gidon, who did a lot of work to bring
many Jewish children under the wings of the Shechinah.
He supported many broken hearts and widows and
orphans. His widow, the tzaddekes, stood by his side
with mesirus nefesh in all of his activities. Now when
her husband is gone, she herself remains broken and
shattered in several senses. She desperately needs healing
and medicines that cost a lot of money. And neverthe-
less, she continues in her acts of tzeddakah and chesed.
There's no way to measure the greatness of the mitzvah
of sustaining her and making her happy with a generous
hand and a generous spirit.

Whatever the ups and downs of her financial situation, Rebbetzin Chaya Sara's reliance on the generosity of *HaKadosh Baruch Hu* was total. Once Chaya Rochel Benedikt was raising money for a widow in her Boro Park neighborhood. When she mentioned to the widow that she was also raising money for Rebbetzin Kramer in Jerusalem, the widow retorted, "It's not necessary to send money to Rebbetzin Kramer. She has enough money." Dubious, Mrs. Benedikt asked Rebbetzin Chaya Sara whether she was indeed taken care of. The Rebbetzin replied, "Yes, I have a very, very rich supporter, the richest supporter in the world: the *Ribbono Shel Olam*. He's my Supporter."

Her trust in Divine care expressed itself again and again in both verbal and written statements to Mrs. Benedikt. She used to tell her that all worry about *parnassah* was in vain because Hashem provides for all living creatures, "from the horns of the wild ox to the eggs of lice." In one letter she wrote:

> *We are commanded to have trust in Hashem, and a person should remove from himself all his worries, and should throw his whole burden and all his needs on Hashem. According to this, a person is not allowed to ever worry, only to accept everything that Hashem does with love and to walk around with a very happy heart, and to trust in Hashem Yisbarach, because Hashem helps everyone.*

R' Yaakov Moshe had left his wife with a letter, but it turned Rebbetzin Chaya Sara into a beggar of sorts. Apparently, it did not hurt her pride to have to depend on charity. She knew how to give and she knew how to receive — with graciousness and gratitude.

For many people, it's harder to receive than to give. One's sense of self-worth is bolstered by giving, but potentially damaged by receiving. Rebbetzin Chaya Sara's stratagem was that she saw HaKodosh Baruch Hu as the only real giver. Whether He gave directly or through people made little difference to her.

In health matters, as in financial matters, Rebbetzin Chaya Sara trusted only in *HaKadosh Baruch Hu*. She resorted to doctors (whom she called, "the flesh-and-blood healers," as opposed to Hashem, the real Healer) only when she had no choice, and she always resisted going to the hospital, which she considered a place people go to die. (She herself, she said, preferred to die at home.) As she wrote to Chaya Rochel Benedikt: "A big professor, the flesh-and-blood doctor, told me that I need an operation and I'm very afraid, but I believe only in *Hashem Yisbarach*, Who is the faithful Healer, and He can heal, and I'm waiting for Him to heal me completely."

Throughout her widowhood, she suffered from recurrent health crises. The first occurred two years after her husband's passing, when she was diagnosed with gallstones. She wrote to R' Avigdor at that time:

Parashas Balak, 5752 [1992]

... Now, dear important Rabbi Avigdor ben Chaya Leah, shlita, I ask you to pray for me to Hashem, the precious, holy One and only Creator of the worlds, that Chaya Sara bas Malka should have a complete recovery, quickly and easily. I am a great ba'alas yesurim [one who suffers]. I don't have my husband, a"h, the tzaddik yesod olam, in this world and I have no children (no one should experience this). I have only the One and Only Hashem Yisbarach. I have small gallstones and high cholesterol 324, and one is allowed to have from 140 – 240, and triglycerides 207, and this one may have 10 – 190. These two things are high by me, and that means the fat in the blood is high. My feet swell up. ... Dr. Zilberman is afraid to give me tablets, so

that the medicine shouldn't harm me in other ways. My
blood pressure is a little bit high and the gallstones are
painful. I'm a ba'alas yesurim. I praise Hashem for every-
thing. I love Hashem very much, and I'm secure only with
Him. I have a tremendous fear of doctors and hospitals. ...
I don't believe them at all. ...

Once Rebbetzin Chaya Sara suffered from a bad cold. Miriam Stern brought a doctor to the house, who insisted that she needed to go to the hospital to undergo tests. A taxi was called, and the Rebbetzin and Miriam Stern departed. Three-quarters of an hour later, as they neared Hadassah Hospital in Ein Kerem, the Rebbetzin changed her mind. She told the cab driver to turn around and take her home. The cab driver protested that they were almost at the hospital. "I'll pay you for the round trip," the Rebbetzin assured him. "What difference does it make to you?"

Rebbetzin Chaya Sara's panacea for all problems was *sim-chah*. Throughout her own challenging life, she was a paragon of *simchah*, but her last 15 years were nothing less than a war against the *yetzer hara* of depression. She won that war, but not without many battle scars.

She fought sadness on several fronts. Her most obvious cause of depression was the loss of the *tzaddik*, her beloved husband. He had been everything to her: father, husband, friend, even child. Once, witnessing her disappointment at her barrenness, he had said to her, quoting the Biblical Elkanah, "Am I not better to you than 10 children?" A year after his death, she wrote to R' Avigdor:

Parashas Vayishlach, 5752 [Nov., 1991]
... Believe me that I would write more, but since my
dear husband Yaakov Moshe ben Shmuel Zanvill a"h is

not in this world, I am very broken. My suffering is inde-
scribable. We see that our mothers Sara, Rivkah, Rachel,
and Chanah all wanted children. Now I am a lonely
widow of a tzaddik. I have no patience for anyone. I cry
myself out to Hashem. He helps me.

Although the face she showed her visitors generally beamed with joy, during one conversation two years after the *tzaddik's* passing, she became somber and said to me, "It makes me sad to think about my husband."

Rebbetzin Chaya Sara in her Meah Shearim apartment

The *yetzer hara* of dejection also attacked her through her own temperament. By nature, Rebbetzin Chaya Sara was exceedingly sensitive. She cried whenever she listened to sad songs, such as those that evoked the lost glory of the *Beis Ha-Mikdash.* Whenever she heard a chassidic story, she empathized so much with the characters that she cried for their pain and rejoiced with their joy. She also cried when she prayed. On Rosh Hashanah in the synagogue, when she would reach the prayer, "*HaMelech hayoshev al kisei ... ,*" she would begin crying. All the women who saw her cry would cry with her. On Yom Kippur in the synagogue, when the Torah reading mentioned the deaths of the sons of Aharon HaKohen, she wept bitterly.

She also identified keenly with the pain of the Jewish people. Rebbetzin Chaya Sara had always followed current events, reading the Satmar Yiddish newspaper "*Der Yid*" whenever she had spare time. During the years of her widowhood, the

Jews of Israel suffered from waves of terrorism that left many hundreds of families grieving for their dead. Rebbetzin Chaya Kohn, the daughter-in-law of the previous *Admor* of Toldos Aharon, was a close confidante of Rebbetzin Chaya Sara during that period. She remembers her speaking often and sadly about the flood of troubles that beset the Jews of Israel.

Such sensitivity was both a plus and a minus for someone whose whole day was spent listening to the troubles of other people. On the one hand, her empathy assured her petitioners that she truly heard their plight. On the other hand, since almost everyone who called or came was beset by minor or major troubles, the Rebbetzin's life was a parade of hardship that her tender heart shared. Hers was hardly a vocation conducive to *simchah*.

And she worried about the fate of the Jews of Israel. She told Rebbetzin Chaya Kohn that she feared that the Arabs would attack. She said that because so many Jews were concentrated in one area, namely the major Israeli cities, they were easy prey for an Arab onslaught. Rebbetzin Chaya Sara prayed constantly that the Jews of Israel should be safeguarded from the Arabs. The danger weighed heavily on her heart.

Another front on which the *yetzer hara* of depression attacked her was her barrenness. More and more during the years of her widowhood, she spoke mournfully about her lack of children.

Once, during the first year after the *tzaddik's* passing, Chaya Rochel Benedikt entered the Slonim Street apartment and noticed a candle burning on the dining room table. She asked the Rebbetzin, "Why the candle?"

Rebbetzin Chaya Sara broke down and wept bitterly. "I'm lighting the candle for my husband," she cried, "but who will light a candle for me when I pass away?"

She used to tell Esther Ben Chaim's husband, who was blessed with many children but not much money, "Children are wealth. You are very rich."

In a letter to Mrs. Benedikt, she wrote: "I'm a lonely widow and I have no children. The Jewish people are my children." Others would console her by saying that she had thousands of children — all the children she had raised and helped.

Rebbetzin Chaya Sara worked tirelessly to convince herself that this was true. "There was a period when she was less happy," recalls Mrs. Benedikt, "but that was a brief period. I saw that she worked on herself. She asked me to bless her that she would be happy. But even when she wasn't happy, she made everyone else happy. She always said, '*Mitzvah gedolah l'heyos b'simchah.*—It's a great mitzvah to be happy.'"

Every tzaddik comes to heal the ills of his/her generation. One of the greatest yetzer haras of the current generation is depression. No society has ever spent more time and energy in pursuing happiness, yet, according to the statistics of clinical depression, no generation has ever been sadder. Rebbetzin Chaya Sara spoke much about simchah, but perhaps the greatest gift she bequeathed to us was the example of her own valiant and victorious battle against depression.

What were her strategies? A study of her letters and pronouncements reveals four weapons that she wielded

against sadness. The first was a simple, unyielding commit-
ment to simchah. To her, simchah was not the serendipitous
result of good fortune. On the contrary, she believed that a
person must pursue simchah with the same determination
that most people reserve for pursuing wealth.

She used to say, "If a person is sad, it's like drowning
in the sea." Just as a drowning person will flail his arms
and gasp for breath, so a sad person must fight with all
his strength to avoid drowning in depression.

"Everything goes better with simchah and with joy,"
she wrote. "It's crucial to serve Hashem Yisbarach with
song and happiness, because Hashem loves happy peo-
ple." She would say that the Shechinah never leaves a
happy person.

She told the women who came to her that serving
Hashem with simchah is so important that they must do
whatever is necessary, so long as it is halachically per-
missible, to dispel depression in their hearts. "The best
antidote for any problem," she would claim, "is to be
happy." Notice that simchah is the solution to the prob-
lem, rather than being the result of the solution.

Her most compelling aphorism was: "If a person is
happy even though they have no reason to be happy,
then Hashem will give them a reason to be happy."

Her second weapon against depression was her lilting
gratitude to Hashem. What did she have to be grateful
for? Like her husband, she focused on her spiritual, rather
than physical, gifts. When she recited the morning bless-
ing thanking G-d for not making her a gentile, she fairly
danced with joy. She used to tell people how happy she
was that she had been born a Jew. For someone who had
endured Auschwitz, this is no mean accomplishment.

Focusing on what she had to be grateful for was a
deliberate strategy she used to fight depression. In one
letter, she poignantly reveals this process, describing it
with a metaphor: "Often a person is beset, so I covered

*up my pain with white paint." The pain did not disappear,
but she deliberately covered it up. The "white paint" she
used was gratitude. That same letter, written in 5752 [1992],
reads like a litany of Hashem's kindness to her:*

> *It's better to spill my bitter heart to Hashem than to
> a person because Hashem has time to hear me. ...
> Hashem lives always; I can tell Him everything. ...
> Hashem Yisbarach understands me and Hashem
> Yisbarach always did great kindnesses for me from
> birth on. Someone wanted to kidnap me when I was 6
> years old, and Hashem saved me. Then I went through
> difficult times in Auschwitz and Hashem always helped
> me. Then He gave me the most precious husband in
> the world, and, although he wasn't a robust person, he
> lived over 80 years. He was never in the hospital and
> he truly served Hashem Yisbarach and he was a per-
> son who gave refuge to every embittered soul. He was
> a father for every embittered person. His good middos
> were endless. And I place my hope in Hashem that He
> will never abandon me.*

*In Chapter 8 above, we explored the deepest cause of
her simchah — her constant giving to others. This was
the third method she used for achieving simchah. She
told Chaya Rochel Benedikt, "When you do chesed for
someone else, you get simchah." This she referred to as
"simchah shel mitzvah," the simchah involved in doing
a mitzvah.*

*Even during her later years, when she was physically
unable to care for handicapped children or to cook
for crowds of visitors, she found a way to serve others
through her words of blessing and encouragement. The
"faucet" was still turned on full blast, day and night.*

*Unfortunately, as her energy ebbed and she became
weaker and sicker, she was not able to render even this*

service. *My last visit to her, three weeks before she died, was the only time she did not break into a smile when I entered her room. Too weak to speak, she had no more strength to pour out, and therefore her simchah diminished accordingly.*

Yet, as she aged, she fashioned a fourth weapon against depression: rugged faith in Hashem's goodness. This became a recurrent theme in her letters and utterances. "Hashem loves people who accept whatever Hashem sends them for the good," she wrote, "and they serve Hashem with simchah, and they know that nothing bad comes from Hashem."

A letter she wrote to Chaya Rochel Benedikt reads:

> *If a person is full of simchah in his heart and accepts everything with love from the lovable, dear Creator of all the worlds, he realizes that from Hashem Yisbarach nothing bad ever comes. And the person has to understand that Hashem, Who is the director of all the worlds, "Who enlightens the world and its inhabitants with mercy and with His goodness …" He directs the world, the dear, lovable, only Hashem Yisbarach, praised be His holy Name.*

Rebbetzin Chaya Sara in her Meah Shearim apartment, 1999

These four methods for fighting depression — commitment to simchah, gratitude, serving others, and faith in the *goodness of G-d — were all choices she made. In our depression-wracked generation, those of us who can wield any one of her weapons can become, as she was, a resting place for the Shechinah.*

In the last act of her life's drama, as the characters, one by one, exited from the stage and the props were gradually removed, Rebbetzin Chaya Sara's spiritual path was most starkly revealed. Freed from chores and responsibilities, she finally had time to devote to spiritual practices. Yet the basic spiritual practice she engaged in was none other than the one she had practiced throughout her life, while milking her cows, feeding her handicapped children, or serving her myriad of guests.

Her basic spiritual practice was loving and conversing with *Hashem Yisbarach.* "I love the *Eibishter* very, very much," she used to say.

Rebbetzin Chaya Sara cutting the hair of Menachem Mendel Yosef Ben Chaim (named for her father), 2001

Once I asked her what she most loves in this world. "*HaKadosh Baruch Hu*," she replied, giggling shyly like a love-struck young bride.

"The Rebbetzin had simple faith," testifies Mrs. Benedikt. "She didn't go to the graves of *tzaddikim* or anything like that. She used to say, 'I have a direct connection with *HaKadosh Baruch Hu*, right from my house.'"

In a rare disquisition on the weekly Torah portion in a letter to the Galandauers, Rebbetzin Chaya Sara explains the distinction between direct connection to G-d and indirect connection:

> *Last week in parashas Devarim, it mentions the bless-ing of Moshe Rabbeinu a"h and the blessing of Hashem. So I saw a very nice question: If Hashem blessed the Jews, why was the blessing of Moshe Rabbeinu neces-sary? ... Rashi z"l says about this that Moshe Rabbeinu a"h said to the Jews, "My blessing is that you should be a thousand times more than you are now. And Hashem should bless you as He said to you." There's a question: If Hashem's blessing to the Jews is that they should be as many as the dust of the earth and the stars of the heaven, then His blessing is sufficient. Why did Moshe Rabbeinu have to give a blessing?*
>
> *The answer is: Afterward, Moshe Rabbeinu, a"h, refers to the Hashem of your fathers and your ancestors. If you will be good and pious and you will say, "our G-d," then the blessing is infinite, because Hashem is also infinite. But if you will say, "the G-d of our ancestors and our fathers," and you want to cover yourselves with the merit of your fathers, then you're less pious ... .*
>
> *If we will recognize our Father in Heaven up close, and we will say to Hashem, "our dear Father, help us," then the blessing is from Hashem. ... If one is whole with Hashem Yisbarach, then the blessing of Hashem is sufficient. And if*

*the person knows that he is lacking in being whole, then he
has to come to the tzaddik of the generation, that the tzaddik of the generation should bless him.*

*One must know that one cannot rely on any human
being. If one would ask me if one should invest large sums
with a person because that person gives large profits, then
I would say that one should not rely on these things. Do it
yourself and be a partner with Hashem. Hashem won't fool
anyone and Hashem doesn't go bankrupt.*

Knowing that the basis of a Jewish man's spiritual life is
learning Torah and the basis of a Jewish woman's spiritual life
is prayer, I was eager to uncover the secret of Rebbetzin Chaya
Sara's way of prayer. I asked her exactly how much of the *siddur* she recited, especially during the years when she was so
busy with the farm and the handicapped children.

She told me that she used to wake up early and milk the
cows. ("They couldn't wait," she explained.) Then she would
daven: morning blessings, *Pesukei D'Zimrah,* and *Shema.* On
Shabbos mornings, she would *daven* at greater length. She
recited *Shemoneh Esrei* only on holidays, when she attended
the synagogue.

The essence of her prayer life, she admitted, was not
in the formal prayers. Rather, she made a constant habit
of conversing with *HaKadosh Baruch Hu*, asking Him for
every small thing that she needed, thanking Him for every
breath. "I did little formal prayer," she explained, "but I
requested much from Him, all the time. A person needs
Him for every breath."

"If He wants to hear from me," she declared another time,
"why shouldn't I talk to Him?"

When she was in her 70's, she revealed the lifelong secret
of her spiritual life: "I never forgot *HaKadosh Baruch Hu* for
a moment."

G-d-consciousness is a moment-by-moment choice. Many women complain that it is easier for men who spend their time learning Torah to be conscious of the Divine than for women who are occupied with "mundane" chores such as changing diapers and doing housework. Rebbetzin Chaya Sara, who spent 20 years changing diapers of even adult "children" and whose lack of labor-saving devices kept her busy from early morning to late at night, never felt that she had been relegated to the "low road" on the spiritual journey. She simply kept up a running conversation with HaKadosh Baruch Hu as she did her chores and plied through her day.

Once I asked her: "What do women today most need to know?"

She replied simply: "HaKadosh Baruch Hu."

"But how?" I persisted. Many years of spiritual questing had shown me the difficulty of replacing random thoughts, plans, and worries with thoughts directed toward G-d.

Rebbetzin Chaya Sara pondered the question for a few moments. Finally she pointed to the table at which we were sitting and replied: "A person needs to know that this table didn't get here by itself. Everything was made by an expert. Just so, HaKadosh Baruch Hu gives every breath. A person could focus on her breath. A person could focus on Hashem's mercy in every breath."

The Jewish spiritual path, pioneered by Avraham Avinu, is to recognize that there is a source. As the Midrashic parable goes, a beautiful mansion could not have assembled itself; it had to have been designed and built by someone. So, too, the world and everything in it — every flower, bird, and blood vessel — was created, and not by some cold, mechanical process, but by a loving and merciful G-d.

Rebbetzin Chaya Sara constantly practiced this two-step dance: 1) She recognized that whatever she was

*seeing/handling/interacting with came from G-d's mercy
and 2) She expressed her gratitude to Him. That is how,
against all odds, she was able to dance rather than trudge
through her exceedingly difficult life.*

In Elul of 5761 [September 2001], Rebbetzin Chaya Sara
suffered a major health crisis. Miriam Stern was in childbirth and therefore was not on hand to do the Rebbetzin's
bidding. When the 76-year-old Rebbetzin lost consciousness, those attending her called an ambulance and she was
taken to Hadassah Hospital in Ein Kerem. There the doctors
diagnosed a serious problem in her lungs and administered
intravenous antibiotics. The Rebbetzin spent two grim weeks,
including Rosh Hashanah, in the hospital.

Immediately after her baby's *bris*, Miriam Stern went to the
hospital. Rebbetzin Chaya Sara, feeling better, begged to be
rescued. She wanted to leave the hospital as soon as possible,
and she promised that she would bless with every possible
blessing whoever liberated her. I was also in the Rebbetzin's
hospital room that day. College educated, sensible, a believer
in Western medicine, I explained to the Rebbetzin why she
was not well enough to go home just yet. While I discoursed,
Miriam Stern went and ordered a private ambulance to take
the Rebbetzin home.

The scene unfolded like a jailbreak out of the Keystone Kops.
I stood on one side of the Rebbetzin's bed conversing in English
with the chief doctor, who stood on the other side. He explained
to me the details of the Rebbetzin's condition and why, despite
her wish to leave, she needed further care. Coming from a family in which my brother and all my male cousins are doctors, I
nodded my head sagely. Of course, I understood medical technicalities that neither Rebbetzin Kramer nor Rebbetzin Stern

could fathom. Meanwhile, Rebbetzin Stern, at the foot of the bed, crammed the Rebbetzin's belongings into a large plastic bag. Then she vanished. A few minutes after the doctor left, Rebbetzin Stern, walking quickly, rolled a wheelchair into the ward. "What are you doing?" I asked in consternation.

"The Rebbetzin wants to go home," she replied, stuffing the Rebbetzin's shoes into a second plastic bag. With the help of another woman present, she lifted the Rebbetzin into the wheelchair.

"You can't leave against the doctor's orders," I sputtered. Rebbetzin Stern deftly rolled up the Rebbetzin's special foam mattress (used to combat bed sores), tied it up, and then, smiling sweetly, rolled the wheelchair containing the Rebbetzin right past the nurses' station, into the elevator, and down to the waiting ambulance.

"How she blessed me!" Miriam Stern recalled years later. "All the blessings from her whole heart!"

Rebbetzin Chaya Sara, happily ensconced in her own home, proceeded to get well. Rebbetzin Stern proceeded to quit her job as a sewing teacher in a local school and from that day she devoted herself full-time to the Rebbetzin's care.

Rebbetzin Chaya Sara's next major health crisis, two years later, did not end as salubriously. One Shabbos in 5763 [2003], the Rebbetzin herself admitted that she was sick, and asked Miriam Stern to summon a doctor. On *Motza'ei Shabbos*, the Rebbetzin agreed to be admitted to the hospital. By the time the ambulance reached Hadassah Ein Kerem, she had lost consciousness. Her condition was so grave that a *minyan* of chassidim was gathered to say *"Shema Yisrael"* by her bedside.

Rebbetzin Chaya Kohn, the daughter-in-law of the *Admor* of Toldos Aharon, had had a lot of medical experience during the years that her late mother-in-law was sick. She told Miriam Stern to hire the Head of the Department to tend to Rebbetzin Kramer and to pay him privately whatever he asked. Although the doctor was on vacation, he came immediately, and ordered Rebbetzin Kramer to be moved to the Intensive Care Unit. When I asked him for his prognosis, he told me that he did not expect her to live through the night.

For many days she hovered between life and death. Miriam Stern arranged for repeated *minyanim* to pray at the grave of the *tzaddik* R' Yaakov Moshe, *zt"l*, and phone calls relayed around the world elicited prayers for her. As Avramele hovered in the corridor of the I.C.U., all of us who loved her were assigned shifts around the clock to stand by her bed and pray.

Rebbetzin Chaya Sara with a visitor, 2003

Eventually, she rallied. She regained consciousness, spoke, and even occasionally laughed. She

Rebbetzin Chaya Sara with Miriam's daughter Sarah, 1995

spent a month in Hadassah Hospital, going back and forth to the I.C.U., and then two more weeks recuperating in Herzog Hospital, where a step-down level of care was delivered.

She never fully recovered. Suffering from congestive heart failure, she was too weak to even stand up. She returned to her beloved home, but the rest of her life was spent in her room, between her bed and her armchair, with a nurse lifting her from one to the other. And she, who had submitted to so many challenges, had to submit to the final degradation of being totally dependent on other people for everything.

I came to visit one morning and found her lying in bed, waiting for the nurse to come and get her up. Seeing how it vexed her to be taken care of by strangers, I asked her why she didn't move to Miriam's apartment in Bnei Brak, where Miriam, the only one in the world who called her "Mommy," would have been more than happy to take care of her. She replied simply, "Avramele doesn't like Miriam."

So, for Avramele's sake, she stayed in Jerusalem, in her apartment, in her room. And she promised to bequeath her apartment to anyone who would undertake to care for Avramele after her passing. Occasionally she would broach the subject to Avramele, trying to explain to him what would happen after her death, how he would remain in the apartment and continue to be taken care of. Avramele, however, refused to face the inevitable. He would interrupt her and quote R' Yaakov Moshe, "Only wicked people talk about death."

As Rebbetzin Chaya Sara grew weaker and weaker, Avramele was less and less able to cope. He locked himself into the kitchen, which adjoined his beloved balcony, and came out only to open the door when the bell rang.

Eventually, he stopped even answering the door. Wild with fear that he was about to lose Chaya Sara, the gentle Avramele became aggressive and violent. He barricaded himself in the kitchen and would try to scare the Rebbetzin's visitors away by yelling and banging the kitchen door with a stick.

It worked. All but the closest circle stopped coming. Rebbetzin Stern tried to calm Avramele with tranquilizers passed off as vitamins, but his fear of losing the Rebbetzin made him intractable. Even Esther Ben Chaim, one of the closest devotees, was afraid to come after Avramele hit her with a pot, inflicting a large bruise.

(Ironically, after Rebbetzin Chaya Sara passed on, Avramele calmed down completely. Now he sits on her bed and cries. He lets people in, answers the phone, and interacts gently with the members of Miriam Stern's family who take care of him. And he phones Blender several times a day just to chat.)

The final months of Rebbetzin Chaya Sara's life were lonely. Whenever someone did visit and got up to leave, she would ask, "Why are you leaving so soon?"

After Pesach 5765 [2005], she told several people that her parents were calling her. And she told Blender that she was getting ready to go above.

Chaya Rochel Benedikt came from America to visit Rebbetzin Chaya Sara on what would turn out to be the last Shabbos of her life, *Shabbos Bamidbar* [June 4, 2005]. Sitting in her armchair, the Rebbetzin did not speak and barely opened her eyes. Once, Mrs. Benedikt asked her to smile, and she obliged, always willing to smile for the sake of someone else. When Mrs. Benedikt finally rose to leave, Rebbetzin Chaya Sara held tightly to her hand, until the visitor finally had to forcibly extricate herself.

Thursday, June 9, 2005 (2 Sivan 5765), was the last day of her life. As always, she recited *berachos* when given something to drink, but she was too weak to eat. When Miriam Stern asked her to tell Avramele how a person should act, with *derech eretz* or without, she replied softly, "With *derech eretz*."

That evening, sitting in her chair, her breathing became labored. Blender asked her, "You don't feel well?"

She moved her lips to pronounce, almost inaudibly, "*Baruch Hashem. Baruch Hashem.*" These expressions of praise and gratitude to Hashem were her last words.

Blender called a doctor and Hatzalah. They all agreed that the situation was grave, but there was nothing to do. Then Blender called for a *minyan*, who recited "*Shema Yisrael.*" As they were filing out, Miriam Stern arrived. Some 15 minutes later, around 9 p.m., Chaya Sara bas Mendel Yosef returned her pure, pure soul to her Maker. She was 81 years old.

She was buried that night, the third of Sivan, in the cemetery of *Har HaMenuchos*, some 20 meters from the grave of her beloved husband.[1]

On the final Purim of her life, less than three months before she died, she was sitting propped up in her armchair, receiving visitors. Suddenly, a troupe of young Satmar chassidim danced in. They were dressed in the elaborate costumes of royal guards of centuries past — tall burgundy hats, gold-trimmed uniforms with brass buttons and epaulets, gold breeches, white stockings, and black shoes with brass buckles. They sang and danced around her room, as the Rebbetzin looked on, smiling.

Then one of them approached her chair, stooped down, and asked her for a blessing to get married. With a full heart and voice, she blessed him. Then, another young man approached and squatted. She blessed him, too. One by one, all of them asked for and received a blessing from the *tzaddekes*.

Seventy-two years before, her father had told her, "If you have the power to curse, you have the power to bless." At the end of her life, when she no longer had the power to walk, stand, or even feed herself, she still had the power to bless.

---

1. The exact location of the grave is on Derech Talpiot, Gush Tes-Zayin (16), Chelkah beis (2). It is the eighth plot, along the fence.

Glossary

agunah a woman who is unable to remarry because her husband refuses to grant her a divorce; or, because there is no binding proof of his demise

Akeidah the sacrifice of Isaac

alef-beis Hebrew alphabet

bachur yeshivah student

Beis HaMikdash Holy Temple in Jerusalem

ben bayis member of the household

berachah (berachos) blessing(s)

binah understanding, insight

bnei aliyah those who strive to elevate themselves spiritually

bris (pl. brissos) circumcision

chalutzim pioneers

chareidi lit. "tremblers." Jews whose primary focus is the study and observance of Torah

chassan	bridegroom
cheder	elementary school for boys, where Torah study is the basic curriculum
chesed	acts of lovingkindness
Chol HaMoed	the intermediate days of the festivals of Succos and Pesach
chumrah	stringency
daven	pray
Eliyahu HaNavi	the prophet Elijah, who never died, and whose anonymous visits have provided the stuff of Jewish lore for many generations
emes	truth
gabbai	synagogue sexton; attendant of a chassidic Rebbe
gadol hador	the greatest rabbi of the generation
Gan Eden	the Paradise in which man was first created and to which the deserving will return
gashmius	materialism
gedolim	great rabbis of their respective generations
gemach	free-loan society
hachnassas kallah	financial assistance for indigent brides
HaKadosh Baruch Hu	The Holy One, Blessed is He
Hashem Yisbarach	G-d, May He be Blessed
hatzalah	rescue
hechsher	kashrus certification
illui neshamah	elevation of the soul
kadosh	holy
kallah	bride
kavod	honor, respect
Keren HaShviis	fund for helping those farmers who allow the land to lie fallow in the shemittah year
kibbutz	community settlement where everything is collectively owned

klal	community
koach	strength
kollel	academy of higher Jewish learning, whose students are usually married men
Kosel	Western Wall; last remaining wall of the Temple Courtyard in Jerusalem.
kvittel	a note given by a supplicant to a Rebbe, asking for a blessing
lashon hara	derogatory speech
lira	Israeli currency prior to the shekel
maaras ayin	the principle that something should not only *be* right, but also should *look* right, so as not to mislead observers.
mashgiach	kashrus supervisor
Mashiach	Messiah
mazal	one's specific fortune
Melaveh Malkah	Saturday night observance to "escort out" the Shabbos Queen.
melamed	elementary-school teacher of Torah subjects
mesiras nefesh	self-sacrifice for a higher purpose
middah	character trait
mitzvos	commandments
moshav	communal settlement
Mussar Movement	a movement founded by R' Yisrael of Salant which encourages the study of mussar as a means of refining one's character
nachas	pleasure
parnassah	livelihood
peyos	side curls
refuah shleimah	complete recovery
Ruach HaKodesh	holy spirit, the Divinely inspired spiritual power to see into the higher worlds
sandek	the one who holds the baby during a circumcision
seder yom	daily schedule

segulah	an auspicious sign or action that facilitates receiving a blessing
semichah	Rabbinic ordination
seudah	meal
Shabbos	the Jewish day of rest, corresponding to Saturday
Shacharis	the morning prayer
shadchan	matchmaker
shaliach	emissary
Shas	the Talmud as a whole; an acronym of "Shishah Sidrei Mishnah," the Six Orders of the Mishnah
Shechinah	Divine Presence
sheitel	wig
sheloshim	the 30-day mourning period observed for a deceased relative
shemittah year	occurs once every seven years, when the Torah commands farmers to let their fields rest
Shemoneh Esrei	prayer recited silently, while one is standing, that is the main feature of the daily prayers
shidduch	matching of a man and woman for the purpose of marriage
shochet	ritual slaughterer
shofar	ram's horn, blown on Rosh Hashanah
shtetl	village; used in reference to small towns in Eastern Europe
shtriemel	hat trimmed with fur worn by married chassidic men
siddur	prayerbook
simchah	joy
siyum (for firstborn on Erev Pesach)	a celebration marking the completion of a course of study; it is made on Erev Pesach to absolve the firstborn from fasting
succah	booth in which a Jew is commanded to dwell during Succos

talmid chacham	a scholar learned in Torah
Tehillim	The Book of Psalms
tichal	kerchief
tzaddekes or tzaddikah	holy woman
tzaddik	extremely righteous man; one who has perfected his service of G-d
tzaros	problems
tzedakkah	charity
tzenius	modesty
tzitzis	ritual fringes
Ushpizin	the "seven shepherds" who are the spiritual guests in every succah during the seven nights of Succos
vatranus	the quality of yielding, waiving one's precious ego-rights for the lofty goal of peace. A vatran (male) or vatranis (female) is one who lives by the ideals of vatranus
yasher koach	lit. may your strength be increased. It means "Thank you" or "Well done"
yeshuah	salvation, rescue, liberation from trouble
yesod olam	foundation of the world
yetzer hara	evil inclination
yichud	the prohibition of a man and a woman who are not wed to each other nor siblings being alone in a closed, private space
Yiddishe	Jewish
Yom Tov	holiday
zivug	spouse